Sinicizing Buddhism
Studies in Doctrine, Practice, Fine Arts, Performing Arts

SINICIZING BUDDHISM

Studies in Doctrine, Practice, Fine Arts, Performing Arts

A.W. Barber

Vogelstein Press
Calgary, Alberta

Published by:
VOGELSTEIN PRESS
Calgary, Alberta, Canada

Library of Congress Cataloging-in-Publication Data
Barber, A.W. 1952–
Sinicizing Buddhism Studies In Doctrine, Practice, Fine Arts, Performing Arts/
A.W. Barber
p. cm.
Includes: endnotes, bibliographical references, index
1. Sinicization—Buddhism.
2. Culture—India, China.
I. Title
ISBN 978-0-9949088-9-6.

cover: Main Shrine/ Avataṃsaka Temple. ©A.W. Barber

This book is dedicated to the memory of
Peter and Magdaline.

Contents

Acknowledgments		i
Conventions Used		iii
Abbreviations		v
Introduction		1
Chapter One:	Buddhist Historiography in China	17
Chapter Two:	What Self?	43
Chapter Three:	Dragons, Lions and Buddhas	73
Chapter Four:	Buddha Play	101
Chapter Five:	A Comparison of the Ritual Creation and Use of Chan and Pure Land Art in China	125
Chapter Six:	Early Chan Buddhist Activity	147
Chapter Seven:	Buddhist Praxis in Light of Eschatology	183
Conclusion		215
Endnotes		229
Selected Bibliography		257
Index		277

Acknowledgments

This material was first used in one of my upper division university classes in Buddhist Studies. The students in that class and other students who have read through the work have offered valuable suggestions. In particular, I would like to thank ivana[1] for reminding me to provide assumed background information. This made the volume more comprehensible for the students. I also wanted to thank Al and Reverend Mike Jones for their corrections and valuable suggestions. Having a keen interest but not being an experts in Buddhist Studies, they provided me with many questions that helped in the reworking of different parts of this text. I would also like to thank my wife and sons who have had to deal with my absence and my being overly focused during the research and writing phase of this project.

Conventions Used

This work brings together material drawn from a wide variety of sources. I have referred to the Sanskrit original of texts used in this volume. This, however, is not always the case and Chinese translations of original Indic texts have been employed. In the general identification of Buddhist texts, where possible the Sanskrit titles, whether known or recreated and accepted in the scholarly community, have been used throughout. This includes the reporting of information gained from extant Chinese or Tibetan translations. If no Sanskrit title for a particular work is known or title accepted, then the Chinese title has been retained. In cases of well-known original Chinese composition both the pinyin minus diacritics for convenience and the Wade-Giles is provided at first use. Lesser studied works only have the title in pinyin. In general, the format of most Chinese titles follows the standard library format wherein each character's Romanization appears separated. It is hoped that this format will aid other researchers. In the majority of cases, the Chinese characters are provided inline. In all cases the annotations provide the reader with the original source that was consulted for these studies. Sanskrit transliterations follow the conventions provided by A.L. Basham (Calcutta: Rupa & Co. 1991, pg. 508). These same conventions were followed in transliterations from the Pali. Pinyin was used in the Romanization of Chinese words except inside quotes where other systems of Romanization were employed by the original author. All translations are my own unless noted.

I have used Standard English spelling for any Buddhist, Indian and Chinese technical term that has become acceptable in English such as sutra for *sūtra* although all personal pronouns employ diacritics for clarity. Asian language words that are not yet part of Standard English appear in italics using one of the scholarly conventions as mentioned above except place names. Words that have an Asian language base but have been derived or treated as an English word, do not appear in italic. For example, "dharmas" from the Sanskrit *dharma* is treated as a regular English word. Although titles appear in italics, the names of classes of literature do not. For example, "abhidharma," "jātaka," and "vinaya" appear without italics. Finally, all dates are in the Current Era (CE) unless otherwise noted.

Abbreviations

Sanskrit titles:

Aṣṭasāhasrikā	(*Aṣṭasāhasrikā prajñāpāramitā Sūtra*)
Avataṃsaka	(*Buddhāvataṃsaka Sūtra*)
Diamond Sutra	(*Vajracchedikāprajñāpāramitā Sūtra*)
Heart Sutra	(*Prajñāpāramitāhṛdaya Sūtra*)
Laṅkāvatāra	(*Laṅkāvatāra Sūtra*)
Lotus Sutra	(*Saddharmapuṇḍarīka Sūtra*)
Mahāparinirvāṇa	(*Mahāparinirvāṇa Sūtra*)
Mahāprajñā Sūtra	(*Mahāprajñāpāramitā Sūtra*)
Pratyutpanna	(*Pratyutpannabuddha Saṃmukhāvasthitasamādhi Sūtra*)
Saptaśatikā	(*Saptaśatikāprajñāpāramitā Sūtra*)
Śrīmālādevī	(*Śrīmālādevī Siṃhanāda Sūtra*)
Vimalakīrtinirdeśa	(*Vimalakīrtinirdeśa Sūtra*)

Chinese titles:

Awakening of Confidence	(*Da cheng qi xin lun*)

Introduction

Sinicizing Buddhism

Pondering the cultural context wherein a particular society's spirituality grows, is nourished and matures, is indeed a difficult task. The history of the ideas, sentiments, symbols, experiences and various dynamics that take place within a particular cultural setting is often a fragmentary picture at best to the researcher. This is compounded when we understand that any great culture has within it a multitude of subcultures which mutually interface and interact fostering constant long-term change but often achieve a stable relational pattern in the short-term which may be referred to as a norm. An excellent example of this is the African-American subculture influencing mainstream American music such as jazz, blues, doo wop and more. If into this dynamic situation there are assimilated significant elements of another culture, the historic developments in areas such as philosophy, arts and sciences, social structure, *et cetera* may reach noticeably impressive heights but the breadth and the subtlety may be extremely difficult to fathom.

The region of the Asian continent we identify as "China," has constantly changed in terms of the areas actually under a central government's or group of governments' control. Yet the region often provided the culturally dominant force influencing its neighbor in different ways. It is evident at many levels how Chinese culture influenced its neighbors but the effect of other cultures on China is expansive and profoundly subtle at times as well. The difficulty of foreign ideas influencing Chinese culture was intensified by the fact that although "China" was never really isolated it was insulated by the geography of the region. As noted by Needham, "… China was, among the ancient civilizations of the Old World, the one which was most isolated from the others."[1] The great Takla Makan to the west, the eastern extent of the Tien Shan mountains to the northwest, the Kunlun Shan mountains to the southwest, the expanse of the Gobi desert to its north, the rugged mountains in the southeast (Ailoushan, Wuliangshan, *etc*.), and the seas in the east allowed China to foster a unique, solid cultural foundation with limited influences from outside. This limit of foreign influences is more apparent in the earlier centuries of China's advancement than in the latter. This is certainly in part due to the fact that the Silk Route was not established until the closing centuries before the Current Era, over a millennium after much of that foundation was well in place.

Foreign influences did come both in terms of new technologies and new ideas. Until recent times, the single greatest influence has been from Buddhism. In general, China was the equal to India in terms of cultural development in ancient times. So unlike Buddhism's movement into Thailand or Tibet, both of which were culturally less advanced than India, Buddhism's movement into China was far more complex and required multiple approaches. For example, Tibet had no writing system until its encounter with Buddhism. This allowed for the creation of a new technical literary language; clearly built upon the preclassical Tibetan but created specifically for translation and to accommodate the sophistication of Sanskrit in Buddhist text. Although attempts to do the same occurred in China (perhaps Xuanzang's 玄奘 translations may well be understood within this light) overall significant movement from the literary standards set by the literati were not looked on favorably. Thus, translated Buddhist texts had to fit within the existing linguistic parameters. The coinage of new terms was limited but accepted. New grammatical expressions in attempts to mimic Sanskrit syntax were seen as cumbersome however. It is not that these and other strategies were not employed but they were viewed as "not Chinese enough." Hence, Kumārajīva's translations which better conform to those parameters are still favored today as being better Chinese over Xuanzang's translations.

What, then, is sinicization? The simple answer of "making things Chinese" opens up more questions than it answers. "Chineseness" was never just one thing, belonging to one group of people, in one time or place. Classical Chinese culture in its totality was an aggregate of forces and was never static. The people themselves were not completely homogeneous but were of mixed origins as the dominant group intermingled with other tribes and ethnic groups. Homogeneity in culture was also lacking. For example, although we normally think of China as being patrilineal, it also has matrilineal groups. Many people often confuse making things "*Han*" (漢族; the largest ethnic group) as sinicization. However, the *Han* are only one such group and even within that group there are major differences in sub-cultures. Furthermore, the whole concept of *Han* was and is a construct. Even the languages spoken in "China" were not all from the same linguistic family and the spoken tongues that did belong to the dominant family were often highly regionalized. As one can glean from these brief statements this opens up a door to many topics.

We could also raise the question of which "Buddhism" are we discussing? Although we are comfortable in thinking in terms of some phenomena called "Buddhism," there are really many different Buddhisms. As noted by Derris and

Gummer:

> Numerous studies have demonstrated that Orientalist definitions of "Buddhism" reflected to a large degree the assumptions, preferences, and agendas of Western scholars, and have explored the ongoing legacy of these earlier definitions in recent scholarship on Buddhist traditions.[2]

As the process of sinicization involved many different Buddhist traditions, I simply use the word "Buddhism" and "Buddhist" as a collective umbrella term. For most of the details found in these studies I speak of particular individuals, traditions and texts. Understanding the process of the sinicization of Buddhism is further complicated by the fact that each scholar, myself included, really presents his or her interpretation of "Buddhism." Therefore, the dialogue regarding Buddhism or Buddhisms is an on-going process. I try to address some of the issues that arise from these considerations by making my studies focused in the above mentioned ways. This does not necessarily dismiss these concerns but it is hoped they will be somewhat mitigated.

Here I wish to be clear on my use of the word "sinicization." In part, I mean specifically making things Buddhist acceptable to the Chinese cultural elite. In classic times, although linguistically the Chinese were challenged with oral communications, they shared the written language both in terms of grammatical expression and lexicon. The Chinese characters and the Chinese *Weltanschauung* that it encapsulated proved to be an overwhelming influence on the whole project of transforming Buddhism into something Chinese.

This literary homogeneity was fostered by a group of men who had received extremely similar educations so that they could pass national level exams in the time period under consideration.[3] Thus, someone studying in the far southeast was educated to the same standards as someone from the extreme northwest in terms of required abilities and texts studied. Having achieved rank in society, these elite were the arbitrators and directors of not only literature but ethics, good government, public works, "religion," diplomacy, the military and more. In short, they set the standards that things Buddhist had to meet to be accepted in high society. Things once accepted trickled down to the other classes and were even fostered. A good example of the elite's importance in the formation of Chinese Buddhism, was the monk's or bhikṣu's position *vis-à-vis* the emperor.

In India, Buddhist bhikṣus were understood to be outside of society. Having the power to renounce social conventions and comforts even emperors would bow to them and set them on high. In China, there were debates about whether or not bhikṣus were under the emperor and should bow to him. The final outcome was that not only did bhikṣus bow to the emperor but the government controlled who became a *bhikṣu* or *bhikṣunī*. This clearly demonstrates that the Confucian norm of all being under the emperor overruled the Indian Buddhist norms.

There were less than 200 individuals that could speak authoritatively from experience about Buddhism in India and Central Asia who worked in China over a period of about 1,000 years that we know.[4] Most of these were foreign monks and a few were Chinese who traveled to India and/or Central Asia and returned. The spread of Buddhism in China was far more reliant on the translation of Buddhist texts and the propagation of the Buddha's teachings by native Chinese than on a Chinese person meeting a foreign master. The famous translators of the fifth and sixth centuries were usually government sponsored and assisted. Erik Zurcher has pointed out that the Chinese individuals who worked to make foreign Buddhist materials available to the Chinese in the Sui (隋朝 589–618) and Tang (唐朝 618–907) dynasties were of a very similar ilk and some were even government officials.[5] Many of the Chinese bhikṣus and others who helped in the translation projects were educated in the same manner as all literati.[6] With regard to Chinese exegesis he further states:

> Without going into details, it may be said that also in this sector we again find the combination of (i) a very small élite of highly educated monks; (ii) an important role played by imperial sponsorship; and (iii) a concentration of activities in a limited number of large, richly-endowed monasteries.[7]

This well demonstrates the ability that the literati had to influence how Buddhism progressed in the Middle Kingdom.

In part, by "sinicization" I also mean the process whereby some phenomena created by Chinese Buddhists answered a need in the general community at a particular time and place and eventually spread coming to be accepted by various levels of society. This process is much more difficult to trace because of the lack of documents that support research of this nature. Scholars must depend on anthropological, archaeological, art historic, architectural and other similar types of studies in an effort to create a more comprehensive picture. A good example of this may be the elaboration of several forms of the Bodhisattva Guanyin not attested to in canonical works.[8] In this volume, I provide an example in depth on two performing arts that have significant Buddhist elements.

This naturally leads one to question just how the Chinese made Buddhism into a Chinese phenomenon. Other researchers have presented information on this topic from different vantages. For example, Paul Demiéville periodizes the movement of Buddhism into China and called the third stage "*le Bouddhisme recommencera a se sinister*."[9] Zurcher provided a historic study of the beginning centuries of Buddhism in China presenting both accounts of some of the most important people and the challenges they faced in bringing Buddhism to the Middle Kingdom.[10] Another approach is the detailed study of an individual master's writings as found in Peter Gregory's work on Tsung-mi.[11] However, perhaps the best work providing focused studies on a spectrum of topics demonstrating sinicization is Kenneth Ch'en's publication wherein he takes up five major disparate areas in his investigation. This included: ethics, politics, economics, literature, education and social life.[12] Robert Sharf's study of the *Treasure Store Treatise*[13] demonstrates the appropriation of Buddhism by the Chinese. This last work was a more detailed analysis of Chinese material than the previously published *Chinese Buddhist Apocrypha* which was a collection of topical essays.[14] James Whitehead's detailed study of sinicization with regard to one text, the *Vimalakīrtinirdeśa*, presented yet another approach.[15]

The overall methodological approach I attempt in these pages is to present germane information on a particular topic from the Indian Buddhist perspective. Sometimes this may involve non-Buddhist information to properly locate the Buddhist position within the Indian cultural and philosophical context. I do this providing information both from textual and cultural sources. I look at the same topic in the Chinese setting and again investigate textual and cultural sources. The generalized goal is to show the "movement" in ideas or phenomena and how those ideas progressed once in China. I am not attempting to present here a thorough and comprehensive investigation of each of the topics under consideration. Although such would be a worthy publication, it makes presenting an array of examples of sinicization in one volume impossible. This volume is trying to demonstrate some of the strategies that were used in the sinicization process, which at times only requires a broader approach to the topic as we view two different cultures. This was the same approach use by Ch'en that acted as an overarching model for this work. In these studies, I do not posit or imply that Indian Buddhism is the standard from which Chinese Buddhism is to be measured. That is certainly not the goal of my studies. However, it is necessary to recognize that the sources of the topic under investigation originate in India and then to show the movement or maturation that transpired in China. Personally, I hold it is very difficult to have an appreciation of Chinese Buddhism in whole or part, if it is not approached on Chinese terms.

Specifically, the following work investigates a number of discrete phenomena in an attempt to understand in greater detail some of the processes that came into play in the development of Buddhism in China. Since an array of topics is presented, there has been a mixed methodological approach utilized in the production of these studies. Some aspects of the studies are based on a history of ideas—that is the tracing of particular notions from India to China through assorted primary sources in the main. Some aspects of the material presented herein are based on careful literary analysis noting sources that were influential. In one chapter there is a study of performing arts and in another chapter a study on the fine arts both using methodologies appropriate to each undertaking. The overall work attempts to show how Buddhism changed both through adaptation and in the creation of new phenomena as the culture of China embraced Buddhism. This, it is hoped, will shed needed light on the ways that Buddhist ideas, teachings, art, and more were able to move from culture to culture and how China was able to accept something so very foreign and make it its own.

The time period under consideration spans the Han (漢朝) to the Song (宋朝) dynasties (*i.e.*, 206 BCE–1279 CE) al-though at times minor information from both before and after this period is pertinent to the presentations. The focus however is primarily from the Sui to the Song dynasties (*i.e.*, 581–1279). The tracing of influences from Chinese literary sources is in general limited to a small collection of indigenous works. These are the Confucian classics, the *Dao de jing* (*Tao Te Ching* 道德 經) and the *Zhuangzi* (*Chuang Tzu* 莊 子). It is not the case that other texts had no influence in the process of making Buddhism Chinese. It is to say that the selected texts in particular had a sustained significant impact on this process. It has been repeatedly claimed that the Buddhist "borrowed" from the above texts. So my examination of textual influences is in part an attempt to argue that our notion of "borrowings" needs to be far more nuanced.

Ch'en, as well as others, noted the application of the *geyi* (*ko-yi* 格義: "matching meaning") method in the expounding of Chinese Buddhism, and specifically in the translation and explanation of the prajñāpāramitā sūtras, on Chinese soil.[16] Perhaps Zenryū Tsukamoto expressed this notion most succinctly, "…(Buddhism) then proceeded to the stage of *ko yi*, at which Buddhist doctrine was interpreted by resort to the ideas of Lao-tzu and Chuang-tzu;…"[17]

Leaving aside the question of how a particular translator undertook the job in classic times, Tsukamoto and Ch'en note the fact that it is the works of Laozi and Zhuangzi that are overwhelmingly employed in these endeavors. Ascribing the translation and exegetic endeavors (certainly not a "stage") to borrowings from the Daoist religion, perhaps reads too much into the status of these sources. It would be a very different situation if extensive borrowings from the inner chapters of the *Bao pu zi* (抱樸子)[18] and similar Daoists alchemical texts were found in the Buddhist canon, for example. It seems to be more prudent to think that the translators and commentators of Buddhist tracts in the main were using standard works that were available in their intellectual tradition. As a counter-balance, one should note that Buddhist works translated and composed in the same time period also used Confucian terminology and ideas. An excellent example would be the *Mou zi li huo lun* (牟子理惑論).[19] Almost three quarters of a century ago, Fung Yu-Lan notes that the *Yi Jing* (*I Ching* 易經), usually classified as one of the Confucian works, was also used by some monks to explain Buddhist concepts.[20] Further, Sharf in chapter two of his book provided an excellent discussion of how Chinese cosmology played a significant role in the fostering of Chinese Buddhism.[21]

The *Dao de jing* and the *Zhuangzi* are both classic works that enjoyed a wide readership among literate individuals. This is not to say that these two works were not used by Daoists and that they did not provide some of the philosophical foundation for Daoism. It is to say that just because two long-term popular works are quoted or paraphrased, does not prove that Daoism as a religion was influencing Buddhism to a degree unmatched by other influences. This would be the equivalent of saying that some playwright quoting the famous *locus communis* from Dante's *Inferno*: "Abandon every hope, all you who enter,"[22] was trying to use Christian doctrine to drive home his/her point completely disregarding the long diverse use of this quote by such authors as Cray, Longfellow, Norton, Carlyle-Wicksteed, Singleton, Mandelbaum, and Saunders to mention a few. Given that the *Dao de jing* was included in the national exams in the Tang dynasty, certainly every educated person had to memorize it. Even after it was no longer required examination material, it still enjoyed a large readership amongst the Confucians and others. Further, even Confucians were influenced by the *Dao de jing* and the *Zhuangzi.*[23]

Finally on this point, Mair's excellent chapter investigating "*geyi*" demonstrates that our way of viewing this technical device has been inappropriate. He states:

> From this investigation, it emerges clearly that *geyi* had nothing whatsoever to do with translation, but that it was instead a highly ephemeral and not-very-successful attempt on the part of a small number of Chinese teachers to cope with the flood of numbered list of categories, ideas, and so forth (of which Indian thinkers were so much enamored) that came to China in the wake of Buddhism.[24]

I have also endeavored to provide ample annotation for each chapter. One of the earliest studies undertaken for this volume was "Dragons, Lions and Buddhas." Through researching the Dragon and Lion Dances, I discovered that there was actually little previous research on some aspects and some previous research, while still relevant, was dated. In trying to be both sufficiently thorough and systematic, I have included notes that provide some useful references to historically important studies, although overwhelmingly, I have referenced sources from the later part of the twentieth century. Further, I have tried to document much of my information with adequate annotation particularly primary sources that were utilized. There is also on occasion further explanation in the notes where needed. These materials are placed here as part of the scholastic apparatus.

Finally, each chapter presents material on how the same or similar topic or phenomena were understood and utilized within Chinese Buddhist circles. This is undertaken by looking at how particular traditions (*e.g.*, Chan, Pure Land, to a lesser extent others) have employed or understood the phenomena in question. Not every chapter delves into these traditions with a compare and contrast format and the chapters do not try to present a balance between the traditions. The intent here is simply to provide examples of similarities and differences with regard to the topic under consideration. Because of this, comprehensive studies of a particular topic in a selected tradition are not presented. Further, these chapters are not designed to be studies into Chan, Pure Land or any other tradition. Although the chapters do provide sometimes considerable information with regard to a tradition, exemplifying the development is sufficient for our intended purposes of studying sinicization.

Two of these studies began as conference papers. In these cases there have been considerable advances made from the original presentation. This reflects my own thoughts on the topic as more research and reconsiderations progressed particularly in light of comments made by colleagues. The other chapters are all original studies undertaken for this volume.

Chapter one, "Buddhist Historiography in China," is an investigation into the notion of historiography that was advanced in Chinese Buddhist writings. Beginning with recent psychological research, I present materials showing that Indian Buddhist were cautious with the use of memory as a source. It continues by pointing out some interesting dynamics in the acquiring of a "sense of history" that are encountered in Indian Buddhism in its formation. Finally, an explanation of some of the key concepts that are of concern in Indian Buddhist historiography is presented. It next looks into Chinese historiography in pre-Buddhist China with regard to the use of memory as acceptable source material. Then an investigation into some of the key concepts in Chinese historiography is elaborated upon. This is followed by a general description of Chinese Buddhist historiography with a focus on how the Indian and Chinese concepts were complimentary. The chapter concludes by looking at how two Chinese Buddhist traditions used history in their sectarian literature.

Chapter two, "What self?" is an exploration of the notion of "self" and its use in China. It begins with an overview of the Indian notion of self (*ātman*) as found in the Upaniṣads. It next looks into the Buddhist idea of no-self (*anātman*) and discusses various interpretations. The chapter discusses some textual and philosophical problems that a radical interpretation of the no-self doctrine generated and how different

Indian Buddhist groups attempted to address these problems. Next, a brief view of the pre-Buddhist Chinese idea of self is presented. This is followed by a detailed investigation of parallel technical vocabulary between early Chan teachings and the *Zhuangzi* with a focus on looking at the notion of self as found in the Chan tradition based on the *Mahāparinirvāṇa*.

Chapter three, "Dragons, Lions and Buddhas," is an investigation into two different performing arts which have considerable overlapping ritual space. The Dragon Dance is a puppet show created to bring about rain by means of sympathetic magic ritual producing general good fortune. Although existing before the arrival of Buddhism it was modified with the addition of the "pearl of wisdom" based on Buddhist influences. The Lion Dance, also a sympathetic magic ritual, is a masked dance requiring two people in costume. The existence of this good luck dance is well documented in Tang sources. This chapter traces the origin of the lion to the Indian motif of Mañjuśrī's mount.

Chapter four, "Buddha Play" is an investigation into the notion that by the four means of reaching the goal, the four applications of mindfulness, the four meditational states, the four stages, the four appropriate exertions, the four marvelous signs, the four resolutions, the four ways of cultivating concentration, the four dharmas that deal with happiness, and the four measureless the buddhas play. This chapter progresses to document the use of "play" in the Pali and Sanskrit Buddhist literature and then to present the multiple attempts to translate the idea into Chinese. It is argued in this chapter that the multiple attempts at translation indicate the possibility of the Chinese having difficulties with the concept that an august being like a buddha would see his spiritual mastery as "play". The chapter ends with examples of how the concept of "buddha play" was used in the Pure Land and Chan literature.

Chapter five, "A Comparison of the Ritual Creation and Use of Chan and Pure Land Art in China," presents information on the use of ritual in the creation and viewing of Buddhist art. It initiates this presentation by looking at Indian Buddhist art and how art functioned in that cultural context. The chapter briefly looks at how Tiantai Pure Land teachings used art ritualistically and compares this with how the Pure Land teachings expounded upon by Shandao and his "lineage" used Pure Land art. This, then, is contrasted with the ritual production and viewing of art (primarily landscapes) in the Chan tradition. The conclusion is that the Tiantai uses art in a manner similar to that found in India. Shandao's line of teachings uses art for pedagogic and inspirational reasons. Finally, Chan breaks new ground by using art in a manner similar to a *gong'an* (公案).

The sixth chapter in this volume is "Buddhist Activities in early Chan." The *Er ru si xing lun* (*Erh-ju ssu-hsing* 二入四行論) and Tanlin's "Preface" form the primary source. With layman Xiang's, Huike's and other letters providing a more expanded view of early activities that are investigated. The chapter produces information on what these activities entail and identifies the sutra sources for these Buddhist activities along with explanation where needed. In conclusion, this chapter documents that the majority of activities mentioned in these beginning Chan texts are all traceable to standard Buddhist activities presented in the sutras.

Chapter seven, "Buddhist Praxis in Light of Eschatology," is an in-depth look at Buddhist eschatology and how the notions of the "End of the Dharma (teachings)" are addressed in Buddhist praxis. This chapter opens with a detailed explanation of the cosmos and exactly what is destroyed at the end of the *kalpa* (eon). Chapter seven then looks at the different ages of Dharma how this is understood and the mechanisms advanced within Indian Buddhism to address concerns generated by this theory. I next investigate the tripartite system that became popular in China and developments upon which it is based. The chapter concludes by analyzing the Pure Land and Chan response to this theory.

The whole of the work draws to a close with a conclusion illuminating the approaches, strategies, and advances in sinicizing Buddhism that were highlighted in the forgoing chapters. Approaches such as using native ideas of history, incorporating Indian motifs into preexisting Chinese forms, and others help make different aspects of Buddhism more closely identifiable and located within the parameters of the spiritual dialogue of Chinese culture and not just Indian forms grafted on to a Chinese trunk. It is hoped that these chapters have helped bring to the fore certain pertinent information that demonstrates how an originally foreign spiritual system became such an integral part of the Chinese landscape. In addition to providing information on the sinicization of Buddhism as it entered the Chinese consciousness, the conclusion also presents a summation of how different Chinese Buddhist traditions viewed and utilized the developments detailed in the preceding chapters.

Chapter One

Buddhist Historiography in China[1]

Introduction

It is indeed curious that any sense of history was acquired in Buddhism. There are unambiguous statements in the sutras declaring that expending effort on the usual materials employed in the historic project is a waste of time. Further, since it was rare that actual recordings of events took place while they were transpiring, histories often relied on memories. The use of memory in the creation of history ought to have been questioned in ancient times because the Indian Buddhists were quite aware of faulty memory.

This chapter investigates the praxis-oriented approach that Buddhism has employed in the use of history by first presenting information on faulty memory based on modern research. Second, the chapter shows that in ancient times Indian Buddhists were aware of some of the problems with memory. Further, there is a discussion on the prohibition placed on the historic project by Śākyamuni Buddha and an argument for a praxis-oriented understanding of the development of histories in Buddhism. Finally, the way historiography was understood and interpreted within the context of Chinese Buddhism with a comparative analysis between Pure Land use of history and Chan use of history is presented.

Memory

Modern research on faulty memory has been greatly enhanced by recent discoveries in various brain imaging technologies and brain chemistry. In addition, psychological studies with a focus on memory have also advanced the field. The medical profession has known for some time that the hippocampus is the central processing unit employed in recalling long term memory, memory of the location of objects or people and emotional responses. In an active memory search, the hippocampus will be assisted by the frontal cortex.

Research by W. Gardner, C. Pickett, and M. Brewer has shown that memory is highly selective. In two well-composed studies, this team of investigators discovered that just as physical hunger induces selective memory for food-relevant stimuli; social hunger (*i.e.*, belongingness) also induces selective memory for socially relevant stimuli.[2] One of the outcomes of this research is the understanding that our memories are often relationally constructed and therefore not one hundred percent accurate in the creation phase of memory.

This lack of accuracy in memory is also noted in the research of B. Woike, S. Mcleod, and M. Geggin with regard to accessing memories. Their study suggested that "implicit motives are linked to accessibility of specific and emotional experiences, whereas explicit motives are linked more strongly to accessibility of specific and general memories that relate to the self-concept."[3] In this research, "explicit motives" are conscious, easily articulated impulse and "implicit motives" are less conscious and not easily articulated.

Thus, the stories we compose with regard to the events

of our lives not only shape our memories but also can influence our current views making new memories subjective. Instead of a record of actual events, which is how we view our memories, in fact, the subjective version of events is what is recalled. Memories are one's perspective on events selectively emphasizing, de-emphasizing and altogether forgetting aspects of the actual events.

These are just a few examples of some of the research that is ongoing. They lead us to the understanding that in both the creation of memories and in the recalling of memories, our mental facilities can be less than one hundred percent accurate. Emotional, psychological, and sociological factors all play a role in the memory process making it in fact, much less than it seems. The ancient Buddhists were well aware of some of these outcomes.

The abhidharma literature mentions memory in many places and presents a few detailed discussions about memory that were quite advanced for their day. These are supplemented with post-canonical works by various Buddhist masters. The sophistication that is presented in the discussion on memory in several texts is indeed impressive. For example this is illustrated in a passage in the *Milindapañha:*

> The king said: "In how many ways,
> Nāgasena does memory spring up?"
>
> "In sixteen ways, O King. That is to say:
> by personal experience,...or by outward
> aid,...or by the impression made by the
> greatness of some occasion,...by the impres-
> sion made by joy,...or by the impression

> made by sorrow,...or by similar appearances,...or by difference of appearance,... or by the knowledge of speech,...or by a sign,...or from effort to recollect,...or by calculation,...or by arithmetic,...or by learning by heart,...or by meditation,...or by reference to a book,...or by a pledge,...or by associations."[4]

In general, the abhidharma literature presents memory as being the reoccurring of the arising of particular conglomerates of dharmas (experiential supports) that could be triggered by various circumstances. However, I think it would be incorrect to regard memory as explained in the abhidharma as being understood as positivistic. This is because neither the empirical self nor the empirical world were seen as real. The abhidharmic discussion avoids falling into the trap of Formism.[5]

Memory is mentioned in several places in Vasubandhu's *Abhidharmakośa* and *Abhidharmakośabhāṣya* and classified under *kleśamahābhūmikas.* False memory is identified as *muṣitasmṛtitā.* This term is a compound of *muṣita* meaning "obscured, clouded," and *smṛtitā* meaning "remember, recollect, call to mind, *et cetera.*"[6] Some of the various connotations regarding *smṛti* were already mentioned long before composition of the Vasubandhu's historic work. For example, one reads in the *Dhammasaṅgaṇī:*

> The mindfulness (Pali: *sati/* Skt. *smṛti*) which on that occasion is recollecting, calling back to mind; the mindfulness which is remember-

> ing, bearing in mind the opposite of superficiality and of obliviousness, mindfulness as faculty, mindfulness as power, Right mindfulness-this is the faculty of mindfulness that there then is.[7]

The longest discussion regarding memory in the *Abhidharmakośa* and *Abhidharmakośabhāṣya*, works that became authoritative, occurs in the section on Pudgalavādins:

> Pudgalavādin: If the self does not absolutely exist how can the momentary mental events (*cittas*) be capable of the remembrance or recognition of an object experienced (*anubhūta*) a long time ago?
>
> Vasubandhu: A special type of mental event connected (*anvaya*) with the conceptual identification (*saṃjña*) of the object already perceived—which is hence called object of memory"—produces memory and recognition.
>
> Pudgalavādin: What is this special condition of the mental event which is immediately followed by memory (*smṛti*)?
>
> Vasubandhu: The following conditions are required:
>
> 1. *tadābhoga*: There should be "bending"

(*ābhoga*) of the mental event, *i.e.*, a turning of attention towards that object.

2. *sadriśa-samjña*: That mental event should have a conceptual identification which resembles the (conceptual identification of the past) object, should such a resemblance exist (*e.g.*, a memory of a fire seen in the past a-roused by its resemblance to the conceptual identification of fire in the present).

3. *sambandha-samjña*: Or, that mental events should have a conceptual identification suggesting a relation (*sambandha*) to the past object (*e.g.*, a memory of a past fire aroused by the conceptual identification of smoke seen in the present).

4. *praṇidhāna*: The mental event should have a certain resolution (*praṇidhāna*), for example, "I shall remember this at a certain time."

5. *anupahata-prabhāva*: There should be no impairment of the mental even on account of bodily pain, grief, or distraction, *etc*.

These conditions are necessary but not adequate to produce a memory. If these conditions are fulfilled but the mental event is not

> connected with a previous concept of the object to be remembered then also there can be no memory. On the other hand, if the mental event is so connected but the above conditions are absent, it likewise is not able to produce the memory. Both factors, namely connection to the previous conceptual identification and a suitable state of mind, are necessary for the emergency of a memory. A mental event which is not like this is incapable of evoking memory.[8]

Here, I will not entertain the many interesting aspects of Vasubandhu's theory with regard to momentariness, the occurrence of past and present moments, dharmas and other aspects of his thought as it is not pertinent to the discussion at hand. However, it is of importance that Vasubandhu's discussion of memory began a line of thought among his disciples of later generations that matured into a full negative critique of the use of memory in reasoned thought.

In the logical/philosophical system that originates with Asaṅga-Vasubandhu (4th c.), up to Dignāga-Dharmakīrti (5th c.) we find that the use of memory is disallowed in a discussion of "authority" in logic which for the latter only included perception and inference. The reason for its nonacceptance was that it did not meet the criterion of non-deceptiveness. In their system of thought, a true memory was only possible in *samādhi*—a meditative state wherein self is no longer operational.[9]

This is an important point for our discussion of memory and history. As long as one's *modus operandi* was within the greater field of "self" then the possibility of having a nondeceptive memory could not be ultimately ruled out. This is a fairly bold statement on the possible faultiness of memory and thus *exceptis excipiendis*. Further, the above information can adequately demonstrate that in classic times the Indian Buddhists were critical about memory and understood its limits within the intellectual tradition. The above material shows they understood, like modern medical science, that memory could be faulty and that it could be influenced. Let us now turn our attention to the prohibition of using historic materials.

The Case For and Against History

The Pali canon's version of the *Brahmajāla Sūtra*, is one of the most influential texts in Buddhism because it delineated the differences between Śākyamuni's position on important topics and that of other teachers. In that text we find the following interesting quotation:

> (17) 'Or he might say: "Whereas some recluses and Brahmans, while living on food provided by the faithful, continue addicted to such low conversation as these: Tales of kings, of robbers, of ministers of state; tales of war, of terrors, of battles, talk about food and drinks, cloths, beds, garlands, perfumes, talks about relationships, equipages, villages, towns, cities, and countries, tales about women, and about heroes …
>
> Gotama the recluse holds aloof from such low conversations."[10]

In fact, tales of kings, ministers, heroes, customs, relationships, towns, countries, women, *et cetera* are the usual materials for the creation of histories as noted by others.[11] The reason why Śākyamuni stays away from such conversations is because they are not conducive to the awakening project. Tales of great events and people are about the past and distracting from the project.

Further, because Buddhist doctrine is founded on the idea of impermanence, any event would be of a fleeting nature and thus philosophically of no intrinsic historic value.[12] As is well known, Buddhism does not give the awake-state reality greater validity than the reality of the dream state. If we also include the Mahayana Buddhist notion of all things being *śūnyatā* (empty), then not only are the people and events essentially empty but even the notion of time can no longer be maintained.[13]

Given the above, it is a wonder that a sense of history arose at all in Buddhism. However, there were other currents at work as well. Perhaps the first genre of literature that helps us bridge this lacuna is the extremely popular jātakas. The jātakas are a collection of more than 547 stories with the verse portion considered canonical and the accompanying stories considered commentaries on the verses. Some of the jātakas are found in the Tripitaka and thus can be dated at least before the first century BCE. This is not the place to enter into the details of these stories but there are two points that I think are germane for our discussion about historiography. The first is that the stories about people are acceptable because they teach morality and cause and effect. Both of these points are important to the awakening project.[14] The tales teaching morality, engender Buddhist values and doctrinal understanding into the living experience of adherents.

At the same time, the teaching of cause and effect gets instilled in the audience and this is one of the major Buddhist doctrinal points. These early tales in the canon are joined with many others and by the second century we see considerable growth in the avadāna (noble deeds) literature. In fact, the collection of these stories is called Bodhisattva Avadāna. The oldest collection of these tales is the *Avadānaśataka.*[15]

The second source for the development of history in Buddhism was the spotty information on Śākyamuni's life found in the sutras and vinaya. However, these sources focused on his awakening and his *parinirvāṇa.* A complete account of his life was not expounded until centuries after his death.[16] One of the earliest Sanskrit works being the *Mahāvastu*, part of the vinaya of the Lokottaravādin branch of the Mahāsāṃghika. His full life story therefore had to come into existence between one hundred years after the *parinirvāṇa* and the first century BCE.[17] Other similar texts presenting the full account of his life are to be found. Further, short stories on the lives of the arhats (worthy ones) need to be mentioned as well.

For the purposes of this study, the salient point is that these accounts present an understanding of the awakened state and a picture of what it is like to be awakened in the world. We will return to these two points below. In addition, since one aspect of Buddhism is the cult of Śākyamuni, we find many tracts that are laudatory of past times. The "golden age" orientation that is often part of the cult of a deceased figure became a feature of Buddhist thinking with regard to time. Although ultimately time is non-existent, on the mundane level time itself was seen as cyclic in a similar fashion to most Indian systems. There are yet two more sources that become increasingly important in the maturation of Buddhist historical thought, and those are the accounts of sects and the vinaya transmission.

Sometimes in works presenting material on the different doctrines of various sects within Buddhism, one finds historic material on the formation and activities of some of these groups. The earliest of these works seems to be the *Samayabhedoparacanacakra*[18] by Vasumitra. This was probably composed in the first century. This was followed by the *Mahāvibhāṣā*[19] (2nd c.), Bhāvaviveka's account[20] (6th c.), and other sources. Although these texts fall short of the critical study of history as presently understood in the academy, they were early attempts to account for divisions and sub-divisions among the sangha (community). By the time of their composition, the accounts presented were usually long past and these accounts are as much legend as useful history. Modern studies have been critical, comparative and where finding agreement, have considered those as a possible historic elements. Overall, this body of literature is both small in number and late in production.

It is difficult to know with any degree of certainty, but at some point in a time past the *parinirvāṇa* of the Buddha Śākyamuni, keeping track of the lineage list of the vinaya transmission became an important consideration. Some of the impetus surely came from the fact that there were a number of schools that sprouted up in and around the time of Emperor Aśoka's official patronage of Buddhism, to whatever degree that extended. We find in the *Parivāra* section of the Pali canon's vinaya, an account listing the vinaya masters from Upāli (#1) to Moggaliputtatissa (#5). The *Parivāra* is considered to have been composed sometime between the first century BCE and the first century CE.[21] The list continues past Moggaliputtatissa, who some have associated with

Upagupta, with the masters in Sri Lanka. Further the *Aśoka-Avadāna* (2nd c.) mentions four teachers that form a lineage.[22]

In the fifth century, Buddhaghoṣa provides us with a lengthy list of the lineage of the abhidharma. This demonstrates that by this date the necessity of providing a lineage for the teachings was already well grounded.[23] There are other works of perhaps a more secondary nature that could be referred to but let the above examples suffice. The pulse of Indian Buddhist historical writings has been shown to be not focused on the accuracy of the facts as retold but driven by its *modus docendi.* The Buddhist had early on realized that memory was not trustworthy for supporting certain intellectual undertakings. The fact that the usual materials used in making histories were considered a waste of time and considering the doctrinal position on impermanence and *śūnyatā*, these points contributed to using "history" in a manner that would support the goal of liberation instead of attempting to be a factual accounting or critical analysis of past events.

Next in this study we examine the historic project as it was conceived in China. Following that, we will investigate Chinese Buddhist history.

Chinese Historiography

The historic tradition in China is both long and diverse. There were many different trends over the centuries showing a rich and stimulating intellectual tradition. The very fact that the succeeding dynasty usually wrote the official history of its predecessor guaranteed that Chinese approaches to history would be critical. While true that the ancient's sense of critical scholarship may well not conform to the demands of modern historical scholarship, it is highly admirable that it incorporated such elements at its foundational level.[24] This chapter is not the place to delve into Chinese historiography in either depth or breadth. However, I will point out some salient features that were important to the development of the topic at hand, Chinese Buddhist history.

From the earliest histories such as the *Spring and Autumn Annals* (春秋), supported by the *Shu jing* (書經; traditionally considered as of ancient vintage), and many other texts, we can see the advancing of an approach to history that is grounded in ethical evaluations. It was generally held that Confucius had incorporated his moral evaluations in his compilations of the *Spring and Autumn Annals.*[25] Incorporating this makes history both descriptive and prescriptive.[26]

We can see the above mentioned two-fold approach to historiography continue from Confucius's time throughout the classic period. For example in the *Shu jing*, the reason for the change in the mandate of heaven from one dynasty to the next is always couched in moralistic terms. How far the old ruler had fallen from the Dao is publicly proclaimed by the soon to be founder of a new dynasty. I do not wish to entertain an evaluation of the validity to the claims made of moral and administrative corruptions here as it is not pertinent to this study. Nor am I going to delve into the arguments regarding the dates and historic accuracy of various parts of this text. What is significant is the fact that historiography had as one of its corner stones moral considerations. As noted by Burton Watson, "The function of history… is twofold: to impart the tradition and to provide edifying moral examples as embodied in the classics."[27]

Time was seen as being cyclic particularly after the

yin/yang and five agents theory was applied to historic thought. This coupled with the theories of the ten heavenly stems (*tiangan* 天干) and the twelve earthly branches (*dizhi* 地支) provided the Chinese with a complex system of measuring the passing of time.[28] Further, foundational concepts also influenced the Chinese historian's thinking about history. This included "conceiving of history as a series of great deeds by great men."[29] The establishment of the "golden age" as a measure for all succeeding dynasties with respect to harmony, unity and order played a continuing role in their historiographical approaches.[30] Even a critical thinker such as Sima Qian (Ssu-ma Ch'ien 司馬遷) praised high antiquity,[31] while being very critical about other topics that had both symbolic and historic significance. Yet his criticism did not extend to the problems associated with memory, either personal or collective, as he used memories to help establish the "history" of the five early emperors.[32]

One last point that is pertinent to this discussion is the significance played by the ritualistic aspect of the respect paid to ancestors. From prehistoric times, the Chinese have accepted the idea that providing the family ancestors with ritual offerings would be reciprocated by the ancestors who would bring blessings into the family.[33] Certainly, this ritualistic role was also part of the impetus to maintain family genealogical records. This in turn made history both familial and formal for everyone. Official histories were the records of great men and their great deeds. The written family genealogy made history personal, not just about the doings of the emperor and other great men.

Chinese Buddhist Histories

The above shows that there were many points of interface between the Indian Buddhist historic tradition and the key features found in Chinese historiography. Both laid emphasis on the ethical aspects of events, had "golden age" mentality and saw time as cyclic. Both saw history as the record of great men and events and the role lineage would play was significant. Although the articulations of these notions were different in China than in India, there was a congruity of concepts as Buddhism moved into the land of Chin.[34] We will see below how these concepts played out in the maturation of Chinese Buddhist historical records. Before we do, it is interesting to note that the use of memory in Chinese Buddhist historical writing is in line with Chinese usage disregarding the Indian Buddhist critique explained above. We find for example, that in the *Biographies of Eminent Monks* (dated 519), Huijiao (慧皎 497–554)[35] consulted respected elderly people with regard to oral history.[36] This example was followed by such other authors of collected "biographies"[37] as Daoxuan's[38] (道宣 dated 665) and Zanning's[39] (贊寧 dated 988).

Although at times a brief account of master-disciple relationship is provided in the various "biographies," the accounts mainly focus on the great man and his great deeds. The information does not approach the use of lineage in the way that will be outlined below in the Chan tradition. With the Song dynasty material we find more use of lineage in the ritualistic sense amongst Buddhist historic writers than in the previous dynasties. This was perhaps due to the Chan influence.[40] The pertinent point is that the "biographies" were composed as accounts of great men and sometimes women.

Their use was clearly to act as a model for future generations be they monastic or imperial/bureaucratic.[41] The question that arises is exactly what type of model was intended to be relayed?

In his study of Song transmission records, T. Griffith Foulk states that these records were religious mythology that served polemical, ritual, and didactic functions in the Song,[42] refers the reader to the study by Yanagida Seizan[43] and offers the following points to support his position:

1st Various Dunhuang texts demonstrate conclusively that Song depictions are compilations.

2nd Hagiographies and discourse records do not appear among contemporaneous Tang materials.

3rd The literary quality is typical of fiction.

4th The Chan concept of lineage is a religious not historic category.

He later states that succeeding "flame histories" used the information from earlier accounts and added material on recent prominent Chan masters.[44] His main point is that these "biographies" should be read as literary fiction instead of as histories. However, his approach leaves unresolved several problems.[45]

Certainly, the recent additions of masters who may have been known by the readership in the successive "*Transmis-*

sion of the Lamp" collections would have to take into account actual historic events. Further, at least some of the earlier accounts of Chan masters were based on information gathered from records closer in time to the individual in question and thus offer some possible historic information. Reading these materials as fiction leaves us with no method for trying to separate the mythic layers from the historic as has been pointed out by Mario Poceski:

> To some degree, the introduction of these kinds of critical perspectives has been useful in terms of moving scholarship away from naive reliance on traditional sources and interpretations. It has also helped shed light on slanted historical reconstructions of Chan history in terms of normative interpretative templates or ideological supposition that exude latent sectarian biases. However, at times these trends have led to broad mischaracterizations of key features of Tang Chan, which usually go together with a tendency to gloss over the actual lives and contributions of notable historical actors. While it is, of course, important to trace the development of key literary transmutations of major Chan figures such as Baizhang, or of the movements they belonged to, that should not lead to scholarly neglect of historical analysis of their lives and teachings, set against the backdrop of the appropriate social, religious, intellectual, and institutional contexts. In addition, we cannot fully understand or appreciate the Song (or

> later) perceptions and imaginings of Tang Figures—or of the whole of Tang Chan as the tradition's golden age—if we do not have adequate knowledge about the historical actualities of Chan monks, or if we are unable to ascertain the contours of their teachings, as they existed during the Tang era.[46]

Foulk does focus scholarly attention on the externals to the "biographies" such as their political use, institutional authority, *et cetera* instead of the internal information found therein. This is extremely important for contextualizing the collections. Yet, whatever the dynamic may have been between the master and the disciple in the Tang era, the narratives told of them allowed certain repetition of themes that were woven into the parameters of the Chan "biographies," indicating more than an external focus is needed. Further, the use of these "biographies" in the Song period with the extracting of the *gong'an* and *huatou* (話頭) as a form of praxis moved these themes from literary devices to personal encounters with the ancestors.

Because of the emphasis placed on ethics in both Chinese and Buddhist histories, the "biographies" of different masters were didactic as stated above. They were more than just examples of how good monks ought to act.[47] For example, in one of the accounts of Śubhakarasiṃha, he shares a room with Daoxuan at a monastery in the capital. The unkempt Indian master comes home every night drunk and vomits on the floor. Daoxuan's eyebrows are raised because of this. Śubhakarasiṃha criticizes Daoxuan, a vinaya expert, for killing a flea. Looking at this story simply as a lesson in morality, a myth, polemical or fiction would not allow one to fully understand the implications of the story. The unkempt Indian is not just some monk but a Vajrayāna master. His unkemptness is in keeping with the tantric yogins then very popular in India.[48] His drinking is also understandable within the paradigm of advanced tantric yoga. This story is not merely about morality nor is it merely a myth although those elements are present. It is also a statement about tantric realization. The "biography" goes beyond being morally instructive; it is actually a small section of a larger depiction of liberation in this world as understood in the tantric forms of Buddhism. By fully comprehending the symbolism within the depiction one actually enters into the liberation process as defined in that particular system. Thus, these are psychodramas. This helps explain why the *gong'an* and *huatou* could be extracted from such accounts and used as they were in meditation.

Reading the "biographies" as psychodramas also does not provide a method for distinguishing the mythic from historic. There are other methodologies which can tease out that information. However, it does provide us with a way of refocusing scholarly attention to the internal formation within the "biographies."[49] This should be seen as an addition to the external focus that Foulk's approach brings out and Poceski's critique which refocus attention on the truly historic. These points become significant below wherein I will finish this chapter with an analysis of the Pure Land lineage and the Chan lineage as two examples of compositions.

The Pure Land teachings in China were very dynamic and had many different developments within. Certainly the promotion of Pure Land teachings by the Tiantai tradition was extremely important in making Pure Land activities a ubiquitous feature of Chinese Buddhism.[50] However, the line that is most discussed in scholarly works because of modern Japanese influence is the tradition that stems from Tanluan (曇鸞 476–542). In his *Collection (of Passages Concerning Birth in the Land of) Peace and Bliss*, (安樂集)[51] Daochuo (道綽 562–647) provides a list of six masters of the Pure Land. These are: Bodhiruci, Huichong (慧寵), Daochang (道場), Tanluan, Dahai (大海) and Fashang (法上).[52] Shinko Mochizuki thinks that Huichong is an alternative name for Daochong (道寵) the founder of the Dilun (地論) tradition, Daochang was a scholar of the prajñāpāramitā literature, Dahai is the same person as Huihai (慧海) a Pure Land follower, and that Fashang was also a Maitreya devotee and a disciple of Huiguang (慧光) the founder of the Southern Dilun tradition.[53] A number of these individuals are not counted in the Pure Land lineage as they belong to other teaching traditions. Of the remainder, some seem to have been fellow disciples of Bodhiruci along with Tanluan. According to *The Collection of Biographies of Buddhist Masters in the Pure Land Tradition in the Three Countries*,[54] Dahai was Tanluan's disciple and Fashang studied with Dahai.

To isolate some of the important features of Pure Land histories, I provide below a very brief account of the most important masters to emphasize the connection or lack thereof between them. Much more could and has been said about each of these individuals. In fact, the "biographies" providing materials on these masters have been extensively studied and presented to the community of scholars, followers, and critics.[55]

Tanluan's teacher was the famous Bodhiruci (5th–6th c.) who had produced a translation of Vasubandhu's *Discourse on the Pure Land (Sukhāvatīvyūhopadeśa?)*[56] as well as other texts. Tanluan wrote a commentary to Vasubandhu's work wherein he also shows influence from Nāgārjuna's thought.[57] The next master mentioned is Daochuo. However, he was not a direct disciple of Tanluan but was inspired by Tanluan after a visit to the Xuanzhong Temple (玄中寺).[58] He was one of the most influential Pure Land teachers in the history of Pure Land in China. Shandao (善導 613–681) first achieved the Amitābha *samādhi* based on the *Pratyutpanna* and later became a disciple of Daochuo. He was extremely influential in the spreading of the Pure Land teachings.[59] His direct disciple was Huaigan (懷感 7th–8th c.). The next important master was Shaokang (少康 ?–805). However, he was not a direct disciple of Huaigan but was inspired by Shandao.

What seems important with regard to this list of masters of the Pure Land teachings is that there is no attempt to delineate a continuous master to disciple lineage. In fact, the texts indicate breaks in the succession. With all of this "biographic" literature, we see accounts of great men and great events. In some, there is the further addition of cause and effect being demonstrated, in this case with the cause engaged here on Earth, and the effect taking place with birth in the Pure Land of Amitābha. There are some moral aspects to these "biographies" and some depictions of masters living in the world. However, even these last two are not greatly emphasized. A good example of this is found in the *Wang sheng si fang jing tu rui ying zhuan* (*Wang-sheng hsi-fang ching-t'u jui-ying chuan* 往生西方浄土瑞應傳) by Shaokang in the ninth century.[60] This account provides "biographical" information on approximately 50 individual Pure Land followers. Masters both lay and monastic, male and female are given space. Yet in all of this there is no attempt to provide an unbroken succession of master to disciple relationships.

We find a complete different picture when we turn our attention to the Chan lineage.[61] Starting with the Dunhuang manuscript the *Chuan fa bao ji* (*Ch'uan fa pao chi* 傳法寶紀),[62] although the record is partial, we can trace a very different developmental approach to history than with the Pure Land tradition. This important text was compiled by Dufei (Tu-fei 杜朏) in the first part of the eighth century. It seems to be one of the earliest extant records associating an Indian lineage with the Chinese Chan lineage. To be certain, it is not the final version that would be accepted as authoritative, but many of the final elements are found within this text. Moreover, it draws from earlier sources like the *Da mo duo luo chan jing* (*Ta-mo-to-lo ch'an-ching* 達摩多羅禪經)[63] and *Xu gao seng chuan* (*Hsü kao-seng chuan* 續高僧傳).[64]

In this text, one finds only the suggestion of a link going back to the historic Buddha with the Preface providing a list of the Indian patriarchs and the following chapter listing Chinese masters. This text does not establish an unbroken patriarch succession yet we do find the presentation of the first five Chinese "Patriarchs" as it will become authoritative in later texts. Here again, the text is primarily about great men and great deeds with some exemplary morality and brief indication of Chan awakening in the world.[65] Another Dunhuang text entitled the *Leng qui sh izi ji* (*Leng-chia shih-tzu chi* 楞伽師資記)[66] and dateable to or before 741, although not listing Indian Patriarchs, does provide numbers to the Chinese masters. In the *Li dai fa bao ji* (*Li-tai fa-pao chi* 歷代法寶記),[67] dateable to about 780, one finds a list of the 29 Indian Patriarchs followed by the six Chinese Patriarchs ending with Huineng (Hui-neng 惠能 638–713). It continues listing the masters of the Chuji (Ch'u-chi 處寂 669–732), Wuxiang (Wu-hsiang 無相 684–762) line. Although some aspects of the "history" as given in the *Li dai fa bao ji* will not become part of the authoritative tradition, there is much there that will. Finally, the version of the history of Chan that does become authoritative is found in the *Bao lin chuan* (*Pao-lin chuan* 寶林傳).[68]

For the most part, the Indian Patriarchs listed are in fact taken from the Sarvāstivāda vinaya transmission list also known to us from Tibetan sources,[69] along with various great luminaries including those in the Mahayana. There seems to me to be little chance that Bodhidharma was greatly influenced by Sarvāstivāda as his homeland was the strong hold of the Mahāsāṃgika.[70] The foundational doctrinal concept of Buddha-nature so important in Chan in its formative period is closely associated with the Mahāsāṃgika. So here we have the creative use of lineal information in the formation of Chan's history. What is of significance is the manner that the Chan histories used the idea of the unbroken lineage to tap into the very Chinese idea of lineal succession and the spiritual blessings that it can bestow on the descendants.[71]

Conclusion

This chapter has shown that according to modern psychological research, there can be serious problems with the formation and recall of memories. Such problems were understood in ancient India Buddhist circles and thus they were critical of the role of memory in intellectual pursuits.

There was a strong negative position with regard to the materials that are normally employed for the creation of histories in the early sutras. Further, doctrinal points such as impermanence, the world being like a dream, and *śūnyatā* have been taken into consideration with regard to their effect on the growth of Buddhist historiography. This section concluded that it is surprising that history as a genre developed in Buddhism.

We then explored the use of several types of literature such as the avadānas, vinaya accounts of the life of Śākyamuni and the arhats, vinaya lineages, and commentaries to show that there were other forces that came to the fore in the maturation of Buddhist historiography. Moral edification, instilling doctrinal understanding and depicting the awakened in the world all helped in fostering Indian Buddhist history as a pedagogical tool. It is this position as embedded in Indian Buddhist historic writings that was translated and studied in China.

This chapter also presented a brief overview of the important features of traditional Chinese historiography that were pertinent to the undertaking of this study. This included the use of memory, the ethical orientation, the use of "golden age" mentality and history being an account of great men and great events. All of these elements played a significant role in the development of Chinese historiography in classic times. Moreover, a discussion of the merging of Buddhist and Chinese notions in the formation of Chinese Buddhist historiography followed the above and examples of the continued use of memory in these writings were provided. A comparison between the use of history by the Pure Land tradition and Chan tradition was then presented.

The comparison concluded that the Pure Land tradition did not surpass the traditional position in Chinese thought regarding history nor explore new approaches in historiography but instead stayed true to the format of such works in the *Biographies of Eminent Monks.* Pure Land histories demonstrate the elements of: "golden age" thinking, ethics, the great person and great deeds, how the masters live in the world, and showed cause and effect. The source of spirituality is Amitābha and uses of supposed historic events are subordinate to that source. Sinicization took place along general lines with the acceptance of memory as a valid source and an emphasis on elements mentioned above according to Chinese values.

With the Chan histories, we find that the major distinguishing features is the use of the idea of the unbroken lineage acting in a ritual context, which is within keeping with Chinese cultural norms. This formed a new trajectory within the Chinese Buddhist historic genre. The Chan histories also include cause and effect depictions, "golden age" thinking, ethics, great persons and great events, and how the awakened live in the world. However, by bringing together the information from primarily the Sarvāstivāda vinaya and other sources with the notion of patriarchal succession, Chan was able to tap into a powerful source in Chinese traditional culture.

By the Song dynasty when the *gong'an/huatou* became an assigned contemplative technique, each aspirant would personally engage in an intimate relationship with the ancestors in a manner previously unknown in Chinese Buddhism. From then on, the encounter with the lineage was not just a formal bow to the founders and a ceremony held to pay respect and show gratitude to them (an event in every Chan monastery). In addition, the ancestors bestowed their blessings and assisted in one's personal awakening project. But most importantly it was a living encounter with the lineage members' Chan mind.[72]

Chapter Two

What Self?

Introduction

This chapter is an exploration into the notion of "self" that was understood and often assumed within Chinese Buddhism. The understanding that grew indicates considerable movement from its source within the Indian spiritual tradition. The chapter will first provide the Hindu context that will summarize the general Indian spiritual dialogue. It will proceed by providing the Buddhist critique of the Hindu understanding as expounded upon within India. Next, the chapter will delve into the general Chinese context with regard to their notions of "self." The brush strokes in this section are broad in order to keep this discussion at a generalist's level and it is somewhat restricted to viewing the concept as expressed in the materials that have been previously mentioned thus providing continuity. Finally, the last major section will be an investigation into various Chan Buddhist advancements with the idea of demonstrating examples of this aspect of sinicization but not being a comprehensive study.

In India

To study the Indian notion of "self" one has to also take into account the general context of reincarnation and liberation. The self suffers not only in this lifetime with whatever mixture between happiness and suffering that a particular life entails, but also lifetime after lifetime. It is the endless parade of reincarnated lives (from hell dweller to heavenly god) that was seen as an overwhelming collection of suffering. This suffering is driven by desire which itself is possible because of a fundamental misunderstanding or ignorance (*avidyā*).[1] It also offers the possibility of liberation. By reducing desires we can reach understanding, or better, realization, and put to an end the cycle of reincarnations. However, most of the discussions of "self" in the Hindu tradition usually does not take into account the social context which plays so large a role in the production of suffering and determining one's personality. This dimension is introduced here so that comparisons with the Chinese notions of "self" can be more productive in addition to addressing a major component that is lacking in other discussions. As noted by A.L. Basham:

> "...the *Dharma* of class and stage of life" (*varṇāśrama-dharma*), which in the golden age of the remote past was self-evident and uninfringed, but which is now vague, misunderstood and partly forgotten, and which the brāhmaṇs interpret and the king preserves and enforces. The implication of this phrase is that Dharma is not the same for all. There is indeed a common Dharma, a general norm of conduct which all must follow equally, but there is also a dharma appropriate to each class and to each stage in the life of the individual. The dharma of men of high birth is not that of humbler folk, and the dharma of the student is not that of the old man.
>
> This thoroughgoing recognition that men are

> not the same, and that there is a hierarchy of classes; each with its separate duties and distinctive way of life, is one of the most striking features of ancient Indian sociology. Criticisms of the pretensions of the higher classes were heard from time to time, and equalitarian propositions were occasionally put forward, but in general this concept has held its ground from the end of the Ṛg Vedic period to the present day.[2]

It is indeed difficult to get a feeling for a life wherein the majority of significant factors that will affect one's course through the years have all been predetermined at conception. How your childhood will be passed, your education, the section of the city or which village you are permitted to live in, your friends, your occupation, the group from which your mate will be selected, how society at large will treat you, your economic standing; all these factors and more, which constitute the fabric of one's life and which psychologists inform us are significant in the maturation of one's personality—all determined before you were born.

This rigid hierarchical structure calls on religion and the glorious past for its justification. It is karma that drives this system and as such, it is only through karma that one can possibly find a way for improvement. Generally, any improvement in one's station only happens in some future life. In this life, there is no hope of making significant changes for most people. Yes, there have been occasions where a particular individual or a particular family has been able to not let the solidity of the system prevent them from their goals, but these were rare exceptions. By following your group's taboos, undertaking your group's duties and by generating religious merit, in a future life one will be in a different station. So, too, for those who refuse to uphold their obligations, a future life could bring them a birth lower in the system.

This in no way means that the Indian social stratification system, in all its divisiveness, was stagnant for more than a couple of millennium. It did change on subtle levels and grew in complexity as the centuries passed. However, the basis for the hierarchal system, its presuppositions and its general outcome in the formation of an individual maintained its centrality buoyed by religious justifications.

Sanskrit has an array of terms that roughly relate to the idea of the person in some aspect or another as presently understood in the West. *Puruṣa*, "person, man"; *manuṣya*, "human, man, husband"; *aham*, "I"; *ahamkāra*, "self-cosciousness"; *strī*, "woman"; *jana*, "person"; *kāya*, "body"; *vyakti*, "personality, individuality"; *pudgala*, "personal entity"; *jīva* "life, living being" and more all indicate the need for sophistication in understanding "person" in the largest possible context. These terms, however, treat the person in his or her life with all of its accompanying intertwining. The general usage of these terms, taken individually or collectively, do not actually constitute the real self as spoken about in scriptures but only the self or aspects thereof that are enmeshed or, better, enslaved, in the samsaric realm. The real self—the *ātman*, is the subject of much religious literature and the freeing of that self from its enslavement in samsara is the goal of the spiritual quest. What, then, is the Hindu notion of the self and the predicament in which it is embedded?

By the time Śākyamuni gathered *kuśa* grass and sat under the Bodhi-tree, the Upaniṣads had been the dominant spiritual literature for several centuries. This group of spiritual texts has plenty to say about the self (*ātman*). In fact, the descriptions and list of attributes or qualities is indeed extensive. Here, the most important of these are provided as a way of forming the context for the Buddhist ideas.

This self (*ātman*) is radiant (*tejas*), immortal (*amṛta*), a trail (*sītā*) to the world, the internal restrainer (*antarya*), stands apart from the four elements, stands apart from: ether, the atmosphere (*antarikṣa*), the sky (*div*), the sun (*āditya*), the quarter (*diś*) of the sky, the moon and stars (*candratāra*), the darkness (*tama*), all beings (*bhūta*), the vital force (*prāṇa*), speech (*vac*), sight (*cakṣus*), hearing (*śrotra*), mind (*manas*), the skin (*tvac*), perception (*vijñāna*) and semen (*retas*). It is beyond hunger (*aśanāya*), thirst (*pipāsat*), sorrow (*śoka*), delusion (*moha*), old age (*jara*) and death (*mṛtyu*). It is imperishable (*avināśa*), indestructible (*aśīrya*), ungraspable (*asaṅga*), unbound (*asita*), not injured (*rish*), does not tremble (*vyath*) and does not stick (*sañj*) to anything. This self is Brahman.[3]

There is, of course, much more that could be said but the above list should suffice. The general idea was to first understand that these attributes describe the self and usually through yoga, to come to realize that this self is the Brahman. However, the true self is not something that can be perceived for it is the ultimate perceiver and as Brahman it is all.

Finally, this concept held sway, in one way or another, throughout classic times with various schools of thought presenting often subtle differences. Because of the fact that the Upaniṣads are considered sacred writ, Hindu philosophers could not see the merits of the critique that Buddhist and others offered of their doctrine. They did, however, take account of these criticisms in attempts to better bolster their position.

Several schools of thought arose contemporaneously or following the time of Śākyamuni that each had influence on the progress of Buddhist thought. However, the general trajectories of both the Hindus and the Buddhist were initiated in the Upaniṣadic period.

Early Buddhism

As is well known, the Buddhist, from the very beginning of their tradition, held that there simply was no *ātman*. However this idea of *ātman* was understood within the general milieu of early Indian thought, there is no such entity for Buddhist. Because the *anātman* theory forms one of the cornerstones of Buddhist doctrine, I will not attempt to produce a comprehensive delineation of all the sources and commentaries. However, a brief survey of important points is provided below. Śākyamuni taught:

> A man has the following view: "The universe is the Ātman, I shall be that after death, permanent, abiding, ever-lasting, unchanging, and I shall exist as such for eternity." He (*i.e.*, a person learning of no-self) hears the Tathāgata or a disciple of his, preaching the doctrine aiming at the complete destruction of all speculative views…aiming at the extinction of "thirst," aiming at detachment, cessation, Nirvāṇa. Then that man thinks: "I will be annihilated, I will be destroyed, I will be no more," so he mourns, worries himself, laments, weeps, beating his breast, and becomes bewildered. Thus, O bhikkhu, there is

> a case where one is tormented when something permanent within oneself is not found.[4]

Buddhism being the thorough going application of the idea of impermanence within samsara, the acceptance of a permanent self, soul or ego is philosophically impossible. This not only had significance doctrinally but also with regard to the meditational tradition as pointed out by Conze.[5] Rejecting any notion of a self the Buddhist put forth a theory of five aggregates the elements of which have a tendency to compound. These five are: form, feelings, volition, perceptions, mental predispositions (*saṃskāraskandha*) and consciousness. These five are constantly changing and thus nothing permanent is found. The false notion of a self is imputed on to these five with no real entity being referenced. The possible relationships between a self and the aggregates are each presented and rejected in the abhidharma literature. Probably the most famous explanation of this theory is the chariot simile from the *Milindapañha.* The master Nāgasena leads the Greek King Milinda to discover that there is no permanent self by comparing the "self" with the idea of a "chariot." The chariot is not found in each of the parts or in a random combination thereof.[6] The outcome of this speculation then is that even though there is no person, self or soul who acts, things happen. Thus for the Buddhist, things never really exist as such but are continually becoming. Yet, even given this strong position taken by the sutras, there arose what later authors considered a heresy with a group that Vasubandhu called "Pudgalavādins."

Pudgalavādins

Buddhism consolidated its doctrine, enlarged upon the various connotations and coined its experiential language within a body of teachings. From these teachings we can delineate at least five major problems of note associated with the no-self (*anātman*) doctrine.

The Teachings of *anātman* are experientially grounded but that experience is not of something lacking or even a blank nothingness. Even though a self is not experienced, there is a pristine awareness (sometimes called consciousness) as explained in the *Pabhassara Sutta* of the Aṅguttara Nikāya that is ever present and referentless. The first of these problems then is how to discuss this awareness.

The second problem is that some statements in the sutras do not support the more radical position of absolute no-self. Perhaps the best example is found in the *Bearer Sutra* wherein it states both in the prose and the concluding verses:

> … And oh monks, what is the bearer of the burden (*i.e.*, the five aggregates)? It is the *pudgala*…

and:

> Indeed, the burden is the five aggregates,
> The bearer is the *pudgala.*
> Burden bearing in the world is suffering,
> To lay it down is bliss.
> Laying down the burden,
> Another burden not taken up.
> Extracting the thirst with its root,

Cravingless he is completely liberated.[7]

There are other references in the Pali literature to the *pudgala* but let this suffice. Clearly here, one cannot uphold a position of absolute no-self given these rather straightforward statements in the sutras. Such statements in the sutras present significant intellectual challenges for upholding a thoroughgoing or absolute no-self doctrinal position.

The next three problems are much more doctrinal in nature. First, if there is no *ātman*, then how do we account for one's passing from life to life and who then experiences the liberation of nirvana? Second, if all aspects of being are constantly changing and there is no *ātman*, how can we account for memory? Third, if there is no *ātman*, who experiences the positive or negative karma made by the person?[8] Each of the various early schools had to struggle with these issues. Although a complete survey of the various philosophical positions taken by the different schools would be illuminating, I will only present in summary form those developments that are germane to our discussion.

The Theravāda school posited the notion of a *bhavanga* consisting of unawareness (*avidyā*) and karma. This being the substratum of life it explains memory, karma retribution, rebirth, *et cetera.* The Mahāsāṃghika put forth the theory of a root consciousness (*mūlavijñāna*) that addressed these concerns. The Mahīśāsakas held that functioning through multiple lives there was an aggregate which dissipated only upon liberation.[9]

"Pudgalavādin"[10] is a collective term for any of the followers of various Buddhist schools in India who accepted the position of the idea of a *pudgala* or "person." All of these schools were descendant from the Sthaviravāda, one of the two main early divisions. The schools classified as Pudgalavādin are: Vātsīputrīyas, Sāṃmitīyas, Dharmottarīyas, Bhadrayānīyas and the Ṣaṇḍagarikas.[11] There are only four treatises now preserved in Chinese from the Pudgalavādins. These are: *San fa du lun* (*Tridharmakaśāstra* 三法度論),[12] *Si a han mu chao jie* (四阿鋡暮抄解)[13] another version of the previous text, *San mi di bu lun* (*Sāṃmitīyanikāyaśāstra* 三彌底部論)[14] and *Lu er shi er ming liao lun* (*Vinayadvāviṃśatividyāśāstra* 律二十二明了論).[15] There are also a number of secondary works that provided information on these schools and their doctrine.

Kuiji (窺基), Xuanzang's disciple, informs us:

> The self exists in reality, neither created nor uncreated. But it is neither the same as the aggregates nor separate from them. When the Buddha said that there is no self, he meant only that there is none that is the same as the aggregates or separate from them, like the selves imagined by the *tīrthikas* (the non-Buddhist philosophers). All of those (selves) are non-existent, but not the inexpressible self which is neither the same as the aggregates nor separate from them. Since it is inexpressible, its shape, limits, size, and so on also cannot be stated. This self continues to exist until one becomes a Buddha…[16]

After a careful philosophical analysis of the sources, Leonard Priestley concludes:

> We are now in a position to form a reasonable picture of the Pudgalavādin doctrine of the self. The self or *pudgala* forms a unique category of being, situated between the three categories of created *dharmas* (past, present and future) and the category of the uncreated, which is Nirvana. It is supported by the created, and therefore impermanent, *dharmas* of the five aggregates, as a fire is supported by its fuel. Since it is supported by impermanent *dharmas*, it cannot be said to be permanent, when the series of *dharmas* which supported it has come to an end with Parinirvana, it is no longer existent. On the other hand, it does not share the impermanence of its supporting *dharmas*, for it continues through life after life, and even in Parinirvana cannot be said to be non-existent. It is thus not the same as the five aggregates, since it continues as they arise and pass away, nor is it separate from them, since its existence is not independent of them.[17]

In the Mahayana too, there were attempts to produce a solution for the five problems listed above. The Yogācārins advanced the idea of the storehouse consciousness (*ālaya-vijñāna*). This idea was also expounded in some of the tantras. Perhaps more importantly, there was the idea of *tathāgatagarbha*, *buddhadhātu* and similar ideas which we now turn to.

Tathāgatagarbha and Related Ideas

Tathāgatagarbha, *buddhadhātu*, and related doctrinal points are first posited in a number of sutras that research indicates originated with the Mahāsāṃghikas in the Krishna River area of Andhra.[18] The earliest two sutras in this group are probably the *Tathāgatagarbha Sūtra* and the *Śrīmālādevī*. These two were "published" around the third century. In addition, sutras such as the *Mahāparinirvāṇa*, the A*vataṃsaka* and the *Laṅkāvatāra*, all of which have *tathāgatagarbha* teachings as an important theme, amongst others arose shortly thereafter. The *Laṅkāvatāra* had an impact on the Chan tradition in its early years and quotations from the *Mahāparinirvāṇa* were often used by Chan teachers.

After the Buddha Śākyamuni caused countless buddhas sitting on beautiful lotus flowers to appear before his attending audience, the petals withered. The buddhas were still radiant within the putrid flowers. This opening is how the *Tathāgatagarbha Sūtra* begins to explain *tathāgatagarbha.* It continues:

> "Good sons, it is similar to the Buddha's conjured innumerable lotus flowers suddenly wilting yet the immeasurable transformation buddhas inside the lotus flowers, their characteristics are dignified and august as they sat in the lotus posture. They radiated great brilliant light and of all who saw this rarity none did not offer respect …" So like this, good sons, when I, by means of my Buddha eye, behold all sentient beings, in all of their pol-

> lutants of greed, desire, anger and foolishness, there have the *tathāgata's* wisdom, *tathāgata eye*, the *tathāgatakāya*, sitting cross-legged in the lotus position majestic and unmoved. Good sons, all sentient beings although living in the polluted body's realm, have *tathāgatagarbha*, constantly without defilements and completely provided with virtuous characteristics, like me without a difference."[19]

The general idea is that one is already an awakened being. Adventitious pollutants obscure this fact. Those pollutants and the container world are of our own making and when we stop manufacturing them, we will see the buddha within.[20] However, this idea of a buddha within displaying excellent qualities such as wisdom and compassion appeared to some to be moving too close to the idea of a *ātman.* This was a concern of the *Śrīmālādevī* and the *Laṅkāvatāra.* Queen Śrīmālādevī states it this way, "Lord, the *tathāgatagarbha* is neither self nor sentient being, nor soul, nor personality."[21] The *Laṅkāvatāra* also shows concern about this point. It states:

> The Tathāgata is like this (a potter making different objects from the same clay), with reference to the dharma of no-self (*anātman*) separated from all false thought characteristics. By various wise and skillful means, sometimes I talk about *tathāgatagarbha* and sometimes I talk about no-self. Because of

> this reason, it is not the same as the non-Buddhist who explain a self (*ātman*).[22]

The doctrinal subtlety that is displayed in the *Laṅkāvatāra* and *Śrīmālādevī* to clearly distinguish between the *tathāgatagarbha* and the *ātman* or *pudgala* seemingly move to the background in another very important text that was influential in the Chan tradition. This is the Mahayana version of the *Mahāparinirvāṇa*. Although showing concern about distinguishing between the non-Buddhist position and its own teachings, it displays a vocabulary that adds to the confusion and those who take a radical *anātman* stance could easily take issue as will be seen in the quotations below. However, it is precisely these terms that will become significant when these teachings leave the parameters of the Indian spiritual dialogue and enter the dynamic intellectual tradition of China.

> All things (*dharma*) are without *ātman* really are not without *ātman*. What is *ātman*? Supposing some *dharma*, it (the *ātman*) then is real, it is true, it is permanent, it is sovereign, and it is in accord with the nature which is immutable. This is called *ātman.* Similar to those great doctors who well know milk medicine, the Tathagata also is like that. For the sake of sentient beings, he says in all *dharmas* truly, really, there is an *ātman.* You four classes (of disciples) ought to cultivate this teaching (*Dharma*).[23]

The sutra even goes further in a conversation explaining

the distinction between the Hinayana nirvana and the Mahayana "great nirvana," it states: "Why again is it called great nirvana? Because of having the great *ātman* it is called great nirvana."[24] The goal of great nirvana being equated with a great *ātman* having the attributes of being real, true and permanent is a stark statement. However, the term "great *ātman*" also shows up in other sutras such as *Angulimālīya Sūtra*[25] and in various commentaries like the *Mahāprajñāpāramitā Śāstra*,[26] *Buddha Nature Treaties*[27] and the *Mahāyānasūtrālaṁkāra.*[28] The great *ātman* is equated with the true *ātman* or true self (*satyātman*) and it is these terms that will be used in the Chan tradition. These terms as such are apparently not used in the Guṇabhadra's translation of the *Laṅkāvatāra*,[29] the most referred to sutra in the traditional explanations of Chan.

In China

Before Buddhism entered the Middle Kingdom, there was the idea that an individual, a self, was part of the fabric of the whole that constitute the world view of the Chinese. China never having anything approaching the Indian caste system, in all of its complexities, did not produce a philosophy with such rigidity that most of an individual's life was determined at birth. Instead, the view of the self was understood more like a beautiful silk tapestry; each self was interwoven into the whole. The self was unique in that that person, and that person alone, held a particular position in relation to all the other threads that made up the tapestry and each individual was in part defined by the relations in an ever widening circle but the various relations were also defined by that particular individual.[30] As with any elaborate tapestry, there are many centers and endless relations to the whole. As noted by Roger Ames:

> The classical Chinese assumption is that personal, societal, political and even cosmic orders are immanental, coterminous, and mutually entailing. Thus to the extent we understand order in any one aspect of the human experience, we have a direct insight into other areas of experience as well.[31]

In reading through much of the Chinese Buddhist literature one gets the feeling that one of the foremost aspects of the dialogue was not about leaving the horrors of samsara although that is certainly there, but more so arriving at completion or perfection which is much more in line with Chinese thought. Here, I leave aside the monastic emphasis stemming from the vinaya because of its *śrāvaka* foundation with its renunciative base and excluding some understandings of the Pure Land teachings which clearly was vested in the horrors of samsara (as witnessed by their emphasis on the hell realms) and the need to flee to a perfect realm.[32] This pursuit of completion may help explain why the Mahayana became the dominant form of Buddhism in China. This idea is well explained in two passages from the *Zhuangzi:*

> The understanding of man is paltry, but although it is paltry, it must rely upon all those things that it does not understand before it can understand what is meant by Heaven. To un-

> derstand the Great Unity (*dayi* 大 一), to understand the Great Yin (*dayin* 大陰), to understand the Great Eye (*damu* 大目), to understand the Great Equality (*dajun* 大均), to understand the Great Method (*dafang* 大方), to understand the Great Trust (*daxin* 大信), to understand the Great Serenity (*dading* 大定)—this is perfection. With the Great Unity you may penetrate it; with the Great Yin, unknot it; with the Great Eye, see it; with the Great Equality, follow it; with the Great Method, embody it; with the Great Trust, reach it; with the Great Serenity, hold it fast.[33] Therefore, the Holy Man hates to see the crowd arriving, and if it does arrive, he does not try to be friendly with it; not being friendly with it, he naturally does nothing to benefit it. So he makes sure that there is nothing he is very close to, and nothing he is very distant with. Embracing virtue, infused with harmony, he follows along with the world—this is what is called the True Man. He leaves wisdom to the ants, takes his cue from the fishes, leaves willfulness to the mutton.[34]

These general points have bearing on the notion of self and the need for liberation within the Chinese context.

Translating "*ātman*"

Early on, the Chinese had already advanced the idea of souls. In short, there were two groups of souls that make up an individual while living. These are the three *hun* (魂) souls and the seven *po* (魄) souls. These groups of souls are always associated with each other and thus can be treated as simply two groups. The three *hun* are what moves on after the death of the individual to their future life with the ancestors and the seven *po* stay with the body at the grave. We only find two terms used to translate the Sanskrit *ātman* using compounds that include *hun*. However, these are not often encountered.

Another possibility for translating *ātman* could have been *shen* (神). This term can mean "spirit" but also something like one's personality. However, there were problems with this term too as noted by Maspero:

> The whole quarrel arose out of the word *shen*, "spirit," which each party (Confucianists, Taoists, and Buddhist)[35] used in a different sense. For the Taoists, the spirit was a material element … During life it was what governed man, possessed awareness, what caused man to act well or badly. The Confucian literati were not concerned with the origin of the *shen*, or its role within man, taking account of it only after death for the purpose of funerary sacrifices. It is probably because this Confucianist word seemed to them most adequate that the Buddhist, seeking a Chinese term to designate that uncertain element which transmigrates from life to life (the Me not being permanent), defined it sometimes as *shih-shen*, the Knowing Spirit.

> However, as they become aware of the plurality and the unimportance of the Taoist souls, they had to abandon the word which they had originally selected.[36]

Thus, this term did not become the dominant translation for *ātman*.

Still there were many different attempts to translate the Sanskrit *ātman* because of its central importance to Buddhist doctrine and praxis. What made matters worse is that some of the same Chinese terms were used to translate both *ātman* and *pudgala* which added to the confusion and perhaps indicates that some Chinese were not particularly interested in the fine philosophical points of differences.

Further, because of the tendency in Chinese to not distinguish grammatical number and case as is clearly delineated in Sanskrit, further ambiguities are indicated with some translations. The best example is *wo* (我). This word was often used to translate *ātman* for example in the quotations above in both the *Mahāparinirvāṇa* and *Laṅkāvatāra* passages. The original meaning was either a weapon or a rake of some sort. The character later developed into the meaning "I, me, mine" or "we."[37] Often identified as the first person pronoun, *wo* can be translated as first person singular "I" or "me" or plural "us" or "we." Moreover, it can also be used as the first person singular possessive "my" or as the plural possessive "our." We find a spectrum of uses for this term from the first person singular to the plural possessive in the writings of Confucius. The Sanskrit word can be declined in the singular, dual or plural and case endings added to make the genitive or possessive rendering. However, a single word with a comparable range of ambiguity as the Chinese *wo* was not possible in Sanskrit. Given these considerations it is surprising from certain perspectives that *wo* became one of the most used translations for *ātman.*

Other terms frequently encountered to translate *ātman* are *shen* (身), *ji* (己) and *zi* (自). "*Shen*" originally this character meant "being pregnant" and came to mean the physical body. The extension of this concept is "oneself, in person, I" or "me."[38] The fact that *ātman* was something embodied and not the body indicates that the contextual field between these two terms did not overlay much. "*Ji*" originally meant the individual strings or threads in a net. From this idea of an individual, the notion of "self" or "I" grew.[39] "*Zi*" originating as a pictograph meaning "the nose," borrows the meaning "oneself." It also has the connotation of "being naturally oneself," and from this the term came to include the meaning of "natural" and "spontaneous."[40]

In general, "The classical Chinese conception of self does not entail superordination, where superordination is the assumption of some formal and unifying identity or agency that entertains experience, and that is able to objectify both its experiences and itself."[41] There simply is not the reification of a self (*e.g.*, a soul, a rational self, *etc.*) that develops in China as it had in the either the Indian subcontinent or in the West, which in fact are both linguistically and culturally linked in certain ways. Thus in approaching the Chinese notions with regard to the conveyance and translation of Buddhist idea of no-self one has to be cautious.

The position of a "self" is elaborated in the *Zhuangzi:*

> Tzu-Ch'i (Ziqi 子綦) of South Wall sat leaning on his armrest, staring up at the sky and breathing—vacant and far away, as though

> he'd lost his companion. Yen Ch'eng Tzu-yu (Yancheng Ziyou 顏成子游), who was standing by his side in attendance, said, "What is this? Can you really make the body like a withered tree and the mind like dead ashes? The man leaning on the armrest now is not the one who leaned on it before!" Tau-Ch'i said, "… Now I have lost myself (*sangwo* 喪我)." …. Joy, anger, grief, delight, worry, regret, fickleness, inflexibility, modesty, willfulness, candor, insolence—(is like) music from empty holes, … Let it Be! [It is enough that] morning and evening we have them, and they are the means by which we live. Without them we would not exist; without us they would have nothing to take hold of. This comes close to the matter. But I do not know what makes them the way they are. It would seem as though they have some True Master, and yet I find no trace of him. He can act—that is certain. Yet I cannot see his form…[42]

Here not only is the idea of action without actor supported, but the notion of self is made relative with the words, "Now I have lost myself." What is more, the notion of a self that is continually in transformation is indicated with the saying that the man who began the action is not the same as the one who is with Yen now. One more story from *Zhuangzi* will be instrumental in our inquiry. Confucius asks Laozi if a philosophical debater can be a sage. Laozi replies:

> "A man like this is a drudging slave, a craftsman bound to his calling, wearing out his body, grieving his mind. Because the dog can catch rats, he ends up on the leash. Because of his nimbleness, the monkey is dragged down from the mountain forest. Ch'iu (Confucius), I'm going to tell you something—something you could never hear for yourself and something you would never know how to speak of. People who have heads and feet but no minds and no ears—there are mobs of them. To think that beings with bodies can all go on existing along with that which is bodiless and formless—it can never happen! A man's stops and starts, his life and death, his rises and falls—none of these can he do anything about. Yet he thinks that the mastery of them lies with man! Forget things, forget Heaven, and be called a forgetter of self (*wangji* 忘己). The man who has forgotten self may be said to have entered Heaven."[43]

Chan

In this section, I wish to explore what was the Chan idea regarding the self and how it is connected with general Chinese ideas and is distant from the Indian position. This section begins with an important selection from the "teachings of Bodhidharma." This selection will then be compared with the teachings in the *Zhuangzi.*

There is a collection of texts often called the *Long Scroll*, or sometimes the *Bodhidharma Anthology*, that purports to be the teachings of the illustrious founder of the Chan tradition in China—Bodhidharma. Although scholars have long found this attribution dubious, the collection does represent material from the early developmental phase of Chan. Because of this, the material is useful for gaining insight into the seminal orientation regarding numerous topics taken up in the Chan tradition. Number twenty-five is particularly pertinent to understanding the notion of self. It reads:

> Q: Among the people in the world, there are all sorts of learnings, please explain how they do not obtain the Dao.
>
> A: Because they view an individual/self (*ji* 己) is the reason they do not obtain the Dao. If they were able to not view a self, then they would obtain the Dao. The individual/self (*ji*) is the "I" (*wo* 我)! The means by which the sage meets with suffering and is not grieved or experiences joy without taking any pleasure therein is because he/she does not view a self. The means by which he/she does not experience suffering and joy is because of losing (*wang* 亡) the self. Obtaining the extreme space, the self is also naturally lost so what further things are not also lost? How many under heaven are there that lose the self? If one is able to lose the self, at that time, all from the root will not occur. The self arbitrarily produces resistance and opposition, then one is affected by birth, old age, sickness, death, grief, sadness, suffering, vexation,

> cold, heat, wind, rain and all kinds of things not as one wishes. They all together are manifestations of false thought. Accordingly they are like magical conjuring—the self does not control going or staying in this life. Why? Arbitrarily producing resistance and opposition one does not understand going or staying. Hence, having afflictions because of holding on to a self, one then has going or staying. For those that know going or staying are not controlled by the self, then "mine" is a magical conjuring of dharmas, and is not able to delimit you. If you do not oppose magical conjuring, touching any affairs will not hinder you. If you are able to not oppose transformations, touching any affairs you will not have remorse.[44]

In the above question and answer the term *ji* is used for "individual/self." However, the text itself states that *ji* (individual/self) is *wo* (self = *ātman*). The key term for our understanding is "losing" (*wang* 亡) in the phrase "losing the self." Returning to the conversation between Confucius and Laozi, the key term is "forgetting" (*wang* 忘) in the phrase "forgetting the self." In both cases the character *ji* was used to mean "self." Further, the character used to mean "forgetting" is composed of the upper portion *wang* (亡) and the lower portion *xin* (心). *Xin* means "heart" or "mind." *Wang* the upper portion of "forget" and *wang* the character meaning "lose" are the same. In Zhuangzi's other story too, we have "lose self (*sangwo* 喪我)." *Sang* is a synonym of *wang* to lose. In Bodhidharma's answer given above, by selecting the characters "losing (*wang*) self (*ji*)" and by first explaining that self (*ji*) is self (*wo*), he is able to immediately connect his reply with the two stories from the *Zhuangzi*. However the connections go further.

The conversation between Ziqi and Yan is in regards to the fact that the real sage is not moved by either positive or negative sentiments. Further, although one seems in control of things the controller cannot be found. The conversation between Confucius and Laozi is in regards to suffering in life and the lack of control. In both cases, Zhuangzi informs us that the solution to the problem is to lose or forget the self. Bodhidharma's reply tells us that we have suffering because of our belief in a self and that the controller is lacking. The person of Dao is free from being moved by either positive or negative experiences. To be such a person one needs to lose the self. The author of the Buddhist text cleverly connects the Chan teachings with both stories in the *Zhuangzi* by means of thematic expressions and linguistics.

For our purposes, the connecting of Chan with these two stories from the *Zhuangzi* also allows us to understand that the Chan tradition in its early phase did not actually relate to the Indian notion of a self enslaved in samsara but was closer to the Chinese notion of self. One could argue that in the Chan text because of making reference to various forms of suffering they have incorporated some of the Indian notion. However, given the tenor of the Chan text, it would appear that the weight is given to the Chinese stance. This is inferred because the way to go beyond suffering in the various Chinese texts above, is not to end thirst (as often found in Indic texts) but to be balanced in such a way that one is not moved by either the positive or negative. There is no discussion of renunciation of desire as is usual in Indic material.

True self

As noted above, the notion of a "true self" becomes influential in Chinese Buddhism and one finds use of this term in Pure Land, Huayan, Tiantai, Chan and just in general. Some of the diverse texts that utilize the term "true self" are: *Fo shuo wu shan gyi jing* (?*Anuttarāśraya Sūtra* 佛說無上依經),[45] *Da fa gu jing* (*Mahābherīhārakaparivarta Sūtra* 大法鼓經)[46] and *Chang a han jing* (*Dīrghāgama* 長阿含經),[47] to mention a few. Although the term is found in some Buddhist translated texts, perhaps the most influential of these was the *Mahāparinirvāṇa* and we have viewed how "true self" is used in that text. In short, the true self is the self that is no self and not connected with the five aggregates that constitute our being. That the *Mahāparinirvāṇa* was influential in the Chan teachings is well attested to in various compositions.[48]

In Chan texts too, there is ample evidence of the sustained use of the term "true self." Both the *Zhong hua chuan xin di chan men shi zi cheng xi tu* (中華傳心地地門師資承襲圖)[49] and *Chan yuan zhu quan ji du xu* (禪源諸詮集都序)[50] by Zongmi (圭峰宗密 780–841), the *Zong jing lu* (宗鏡錄)[51] by Yanshou (延壽 904–975), and *Fa yan chan shi yu lu* (法演禪師語錄;[52] cir. 12th c.) verify this. The idea of the "true self" is associated with the related concepts "true nature" (*zhenxing* 眞性), "true mind" (*zhenxin* 眞心) and other such terms in the Chan literature. "True nature" was first used by Bodhidharma in his *Two Ingresses and Four Courses* and its use continued throughout Chan history. The person who realizes his/her true nature has discovered the true self. In particular, "true nature" allowed the Chan tradition to further connect with Chinese native materials regarding the concepts of one's nature as found in both Confucius' and Zhuangzi's works. Regarding the true self, in a discussion distinguishing between natural (naive) thought and *śūnyatā* teachings, Zongmi says:

> … to have a self and no-self are different. In the *śūnyatā* teachings thereby having a self is called false and no-self is called true. In natural (naive) thought (*xingzong* 性宗) thereby no-self is called false and having a self is called true. For this reason the *Mahāparinirvāṇa Sūtra* says, 'No-self is called birth and death, having a self is called "Thus come" (*i.e.*, awakened). Also it says, 'with the concept of self then no-self is delusional." Even if you attain an extensive breakthrough of the two vehicles (*śrāvakayāna* and *pratyekabud dhayāna*) into the views of impermanence and no-self, it is like being at a spring-fed pool holding gravel and calling it jewels …Even if you attain what is stated to be no-self, in that dharma you still have a true self.[53]

This is in stark contrast with the Pure Land tradition. In one sutra entitled: *The Ten Going and Being Reborn in Amitābha Buddha's Realm Sūtra* (*Shi xing sheng a mi tuo fo guo jing* 十往生阿彌陀佛國經),[54] it simply states that the true self is one who has confidence or faith in the sutra and upholds it. It would appear that for this sutra the need was felt to mention that followers can know this true self without having to mention the realization of one's true nature.

In ancient times, one could not read the term "true self" without thinking about "true person/man." Zhuangzi's idea of a "true person/man" (眞人) has been compared favorably with the Confucian superior person (*junzi*) and with the perfect person (*zhiren* 至人). Zhuangzi states in chapter one, "… the Perfect person has no self, the spiritual person has no merit, the sage has no fame."[55] In the same book, chapter six we find a long presentation about the qualities of a true person which are desireless, lacking pride, not planning, not regretting, unafraid, without care, indifferent to life and death.[56] In chapter 13, there is a conversation between Confucius and Laozi. Confucius wanting to place his teachings in the Zhou library has to get Laozi's help. They have a conversation about the content of the books. Confucius tells him the books are about benevolence and righteousness and Laozi asks about these. Confucius replies, "benevolence and righteousness are the true person's nature…"[57] Laozi goes on to show him the error of his thinking proclaiming that being natural and simple is one's true nature.[58]

Conclusion

This chapter began with presenting information on the general notion of a self within the Indian spiritual setting. This was supported by textual information from the Upaniṣads. The idea of self was connected with the system of social stratification that is so dominant in Indian culture. There was further information presented on the lexicon used within the Indic literature that presents an idea of a self with the emphasis on the term "*ātman*." The basic idea in the Indian spiritual dialogue is that the self is enslaved in the cycle of samsara with its endless suffering.

A short exposé of the general Buddhist position on no self "*anātman*" doctrine began the sub-section on Early Buddhism followed by a lengthier presentation on the Pudgalavādins, a group of different early Buddhist schools that later writers such as Vasubandhu considered heterodox but which lasted for several centuries. This section also delineated the circumstances that led to a doctrine like the *pudgala* to have arisen. With the above as a foundation, a discussion of the *tathāgatagarbha* and related ideas were put forward with special emphasis on the textual sources. In particular, the *Mahāparinirvāṇa* and its terminology of "true self" and "great self" were argued to have been significant in the progression of Buddhist thought. Although the terminology of "great self" and "true self" are not unique to the *Mahāparinirvāṇa*, it is the most influential in this regard.

Next, I opened a discussion regarding the Chinese ideas of self drawing on information from Confucius but more extensively on Zhuangzi. The basic Chinese idea of a self is one wherein this self was a unique thread woven into the tapestry of life both defining the circles around it and being defined by those circles. I illustrated that the Chinese, lacking the idea of a self enslaved in the endless cycle of suffering as envisioned in India, were not particularly focused on the suffering aspect of life as a motivational or even doctrinal point. Instead it was the quest for wholeness, oneness, and unity with the great Dao that seemingly garnered their spiritual energies particularly in Chan. This was supported with an exploration of the Chinese terms used to translate the Sanskrit terms for "self" with a focus on the etymology of these terms in pre-Buddhist China.

The sub-section on Chan began with a translation of

Question twenty-five from Bodhidharma's *Long Scroll of the Treatise on the Two Ingresses and Four Courses.* It showed that this teaching in the early Chan tradition was closely connected with two stories found in the *Zhuangzi* which allowed the reader to see how the Chan teachings were utilizing the Chinese notions of "self" instead of the Indic notions. In addition, a sub-section on True Self as understood in Chan and deriving from the *Mahāparinirvāṇa* was presented for consideration. We viewed what Zongmi had to say on this point and contrasted this briefly with the position in one Pure Land sutra. Next, the connections between a true self and the true person referred to in the *Zhuangzi* were delineated.

From this lengthy exposé it has been determined that as Buddhism was being assimilated within the Chinese contextual framework, the Chinese notion of self prevailed. The Mahayana form of Buddhism allowed greater flexibility in one's orientation toward the goal. This in turn permitted the Chinese desire of "being in the Dao" (*i.e.*, return to completion) to be the language of choice shying somewhat from the Indian penchant to discuss fleeing from suffering in certain genre. This is particularly the case in the Chan School. We have also seen how early Chan was using very sophisticated means to reassure the audience that the discussion on the *tathāgatagarbha* that forms the base of Chan was in line with their own ancient sages' wisdom.

Chapter Three

Dragons, Lions and Buddhas

Introduction

This chapter examines two related but separate types of performing arts. The first is the Dragon Dance and the second is the Lion Dance. In general, the aim of this chapter is to view sinicization through the lens of both adaptation and creation. In particular, the Dragon Dance existed in China before the rise of Buddhism. It was in the addition of the pearl (see below) to the dance that we see adaptation taking place. The Lion Dance was the creation of Buddhist culture of the Tang dynasty and thus we see creativity in formation of this performing art form.

Because this section looks into these two performing arts as cultural phenomena the journey at times is less direct as multiple factors need to be introduced. It is often the case that these factors are of equal significance or at least are historically of the same time period such that order is not always achieved by lineal progress through either time or cultural space. Yet, the compilation of information does allow us in the end to come to an understanding of each of these dances.

Well-loved and performed throughout China with many local variations the Dragon and Lion dances are notable elements of Chinese communities across the world. The Dragon Dance and the Lion Dance are distinct from each other and yet they function in the same general cultural space. Although both of these performing arts are dances, they are superficially very different types of dances. The Dragon Dance is essentially a puppet show with multiple puppeteers. The

Lion Dance is a two person masked dance. However at a deeper level, both are in effect rituals performed to bring about good fortune in all of its connotations and forms by means of symbolic magic. The dragon is the more potent symbol and to illustrate this perhaps a personal story is not out of place.

A couple of years ago, I was accompanying the Golden Dragon troupe at a dance inside a casino on Chinese New Year. It was a combined Dragon and Lion Dance. There was an open space for the performance by the lions followed by the costumed dancers walking through the casino. The lions gathered again in the open area just as the dragon made its appearance. They performed together for a while and the dragon as well as the lions went their separate ways through the crowd. What was interesting was that the patrons were happy to see the lions and welcomed the good luck, but they were literally falling over themselves trying to touch the dragon as it weaved through the casino. There is luck and then there is luck!

The Dragon in China

Theories on the origin of the dragon including the following: that they are an extinct animal's image that became mythologized, an amalgam totem, crocodiles that became mythologized. There are other theories almost as numerous as the multitude of dragons one encounters in Chinese tales. Surely a more perfect symbol would be hard to find. Combining different animals' parts to represent power, wisdom, fertility, wealth, and more, the dragon has had such a powerful effect on the whole of East Asia, speaking to its people from six thousand years ago to the present. A symbol of abundance, good fortune, protection, prosperity, wisdom, power, excellence, bravery, preservation, spirituality, nobility in general and specifically the imperial family, the dragon represents all good things. Although malevolent dragons are known, the focus is on the positive image. Closely connected with all bodies of water, seas, lakes, rivers, waterfalls, *et cetera*, much of the symbolic "good fortune" associations surrounding the dragon can be understood as derivatives of a good harvest which requires sufficient water. Further, the fact that dragons mount the sky allows the symbol to be connected with spirituality, nobility, yang forces and of course, the emperor.

Symbols of dragons have been found in the cultural artifacts of the microlithic peoples in what is now China dating from around 5,000 to 4,000 BCE. The duration of this symbol, as meaningful within this geographic region, is matched by few symbols in the human vocabulary. Dragon lore had become so profuse that in classical times, not only were dragons subtyped but the term (*long* 龍) became a category for dragon-like creatures such as the winged dragon (*yinglong* 應龍), scaly or hornless dragons (*jiaolong* 蛟龍), fish dragon (*longyu* 龍魚), fire or torch dragon (*zhulong* 燭龍) as well as other such creatures. The dragon's appearance was standardized by the Han dynasty (206 BCE–220 CE) as found in Wang Fu's (王符, c. 78–163) description of the three joints (head, mid-section, tail) and nine resemblances: head of a camel, horns of a deer, eyes of a devil, neck of a snake, abdomen of a clam, scales of a carp, claws of an eagle, paws of a tiger, ears of a cow. Pre-Han depictions of a dragon's heads are less camel-like and other characteristics may be different from the post-Han depictions.[1] In a later addition, the dragon must have a *chimu* or protrusion on its head for it to be able to fly.[2]

The dragon is the only mythic animal to be placed in the twelve year cycle zodiac. It is one of the animal guardians of the four directions (along with tiger, turtle, and the phoenix). It is connected with the theory of five elements and the combination is used to evaluate various things from periods of time to personality types. They are placed into five subtypes: Celestial Dragons (which guard the gods' palaces), Spiritual Dragons (ruling wind, rain and floods), Earth Dragons (cleansing rivers and deepen oceans), Treasure-Guarding Dragons (protecting precious metals and stones), and Imperial Dragons (five clawed and solely associated with the imperial family). However, as noted by Marinus Visser, the notion of the dragon in East Asia was influenced by the Indian notions of nagas and that from the Buddhist perspective.[3]

In the Yuan dynasty (1271–1368), the dragon kings proper were divided by color. The number of claws increased from the Tang dynasty's three claws to the Ming dynasty's (1368–1644) five claws, but also as the number of claws increased dragons were differentiated by class: five clawed—imperial,[4] to three clawed—common.[5] Like the lion, the dragon has five basic colors: green or azure (spring, East), vermilion or red (summer, South), white (autumn, West), black (winter, North) and golden or yellow (center). The combination of the Indian Buddhist *nāga* ideals with the native Chinese ideas not only strengthened the image and the cult of the dragon but extended it as well. For example, it seems that the idea of dragons' shape-shifting ability was from the amalgamation of the Indian ideas regarding the *nāga* with that of the Chinese dragon.

The *Nāga* in India

The Indian nature spirit called a *nāga* is associated with bodies of waters such as pools, wells, seas, *et cetera*. One of the earliest examples in literature is the story of how the god Indra defeated Vṛtra the *nāga* holding back the monsoon rains in the *Rig Veda*. Also representing fertility, wealth, and the guardians of treasures, they can impart good fortune but also withhold their aid causing drought and misfortune. These nature spirits have popular cults of their own and their images are found associated with Viṣṇu, Śiva, Gaṇeśa and other gods. Usually depicted as cobras, they have the power to shape-shift becoming totally human like or half human – half snake. Some are said to live in the subterranean city of Bhogavatī.[6] Of interesting note is the fact in the Buddhist Gandharan art they show up shaped like dragons and not snake-like.[7]

<u>Nagas in Buddhism</u>

We see from the textual sources a close connection between Buddhism and the *nāga* cult that emerged at the beginning of the tradition when the Buddha gained his awakening. For example the *Mahāvagga* relates:

> Shortly after the Buddha Śākyamuni gained his liberation he had moved from the Bodhi-tree to the Ajapāla banyan tree and then to the Mucalinda tree, where he sat for a full week. However, a storm cloud appeared bringing with it rain, cold and darkness. The nāga king Mucalinda encircled the Buddha's body with

> seven coils and extended his cobra-hood over the head of Śākyamuni. After the week long storm passed Mucalinda changed his nāga form into that of a young man. He pays his respect to the Buddha and receives a teaching on the joys of realizing no-self.[8]

In addition, the future Buddha Śākyamuni was even born as a *nāga* on several occasions. For example, Śākyamuni was the *nāga* Atula who received a prophesy from Vipassa Buddha in a previous life. In Buddhist texts the nagas maintain their association with prosperity, rain, and particularly wealth (especially with the wishing-granting gem: *cintāmani*).

Nagas' characteristics are described in various Buddhist texts. Nagas have four types of birth. The lowest is egg-born, next womb-born, moisture-born and the highest is born without two parents. One can be reborn as a *nāga* from double-dealing in a previous life. One can also be born a *nāga* because of fostering a wish to be born in their realm. They are fair and live happily,[9] they live in oceans amongst other places,[10] and they are often in the retinue of a buddha.[11] There are both male and female nagas and they can mate with humans. They have extraordinary powers, can fly and may have poisonous breath. The Virūpakkhā, Erāpathā, Chabyāputtā and Kanhagotamakā are royal tribes of nagas. Other *nāga* tribes like the Kambalas and the Assataras are known.[12]

Further, they are listed as protectors of the Dharma along with devas, yakṣas, gandharvas, asuras, garuḍas, kiṃnaras and mahoragas. The four gods of the directions called lokapālas includes Dhṛtarāṣtra, the king of the gandharvas,

Virūḍhaka, the king of the gods, Kubera, the king of the yakṣas and finally Virūpākṣa, the king of the nagas. *Nāga* is also a word used for greatnes.[13] and even the Buddha like others in Buddhism who have accomplished the goal of their activities, is called a *nāga*.[14] One also finds that at the beginning of the Mahayana the cult of the *nāga* continues its presence. In addition to the other symbolic meanings, because the nagas keep the wisdom sutras, they also become associated with wisdom.

Nāgārjuna is considered by all of Mahayana as one of the founding fathers. His life story both in the Chinese and in the Tibetan accounts show very strong connections with the *nāga* cult. Born into a brāhmaṇa family he was able to master the Vedas as a child. Later, he became a Buddhist monk and mastered the Tripitaka. Still having questions, in his travels he met an old monk who taught him Mahayana. Nāgārjuna's association with the nagas is noted by Shohei Ichimura:

> Unable to understand the doctrine (of Mahayana) fully, he further ventured to visit the Nāga king's palace in the bottom of the ocean and studied the innumerable Mahayana texts at his library in search of the profound insight for ninety days.[15]

In most accounts of Nāgārjuna, the texts he studied and eventually brought back to the human realm were the prajñāpāramitā sūtras. He systematized these teachings to create the Mādhaymika branch of Mahayana philosophy. This connection between various elements of the Mahayana and the *nāga* cult continues into the tantric period.

Nagas are mentioned in various Mahayana texts including complete texts like the *Sāgaranāgarājaparipṛcchā Sūtra* (dealing with extrasensory perception) and sections in important texts like the *Avataṃsaka*. Within this last named sutra's opening scene, the reader is informed that there were ten named *nāga* kings including three very famous ones: Virūpākṣa, Sāgara, Takṣaka, as well as a host of other nagas in attendance. Further, section one presents the teachings realized by various nagas. This is significant because the *Avataṃsaka* had an extraordinary impact on Tang dynasty Buddhism and Chinese culture as noted.

One of the other Mahayana sutras that became instrumental in Chinese culture and in the formation of one of the major Chinese Buddhist traditions was the *Lotus Sutra*. This sutra was used by the Venerable Tiantai Zhiyi (Tien tai Chih-I 天台智顗 538–597) for the foundation of the Tiantai tradition. The *Lotus Sutra* idea of an all-encompassing approach called the "one-vehicle," which includes all other vehicles (*i.e.*, approaches to Buddhism), was overwhelmingly appealing to members of a culture steeped in holistic thought. In addition, the symbolism from the *Lotus Sutra* influenced and extended the vocabulary of the Chinese. The same three famous *nāga* kings mentioned in the *Avataṃsaka* are also mentioned in the *Lotus Sutra* as well a host of other nagas. For our purposes, the most important section of the *Lotus Sutra* is entitled "Apparition of a Stupa." This will be taken up in greater detail below.

The Dragon Dance

Documented in the Han dynasty and perhaps much earlier as a rite propitiating rain, the Dragon Dance grew in popularity and complexity in the succeeding dynasties. In general, as the ultimate symbol of good fortune, this dance featuring the dragon and the rarity of the performance guaranteed it the highest respect. By the Tang dynasty we have dragons of various colors each symbolizing something different. The last major change to the dragon was the addition of the five claws in the Ming dynasty.

The Dragon Dance is usually made up of at least one large dragon puppet and a pearl. The dragon can have as many as one hundred people manipulating it but the usual number is nine. The head is fashioned out of various materials including cloth, hair, bamboo, *et cetera* but in ancient times could even be carved out of wood. Traditionally the head is slightly larger in proportions to the body. The head is suspended on a pole through the skull portion allowing the lower jaw to be open. The head is attached to a cloth body internally containing assorted hoops to give it a round shape with poles suspended in even intervals and a large decorative tail also having a pole. The poles are held by the puppeteers who are plainly visible (unlike the Lion Dance where the people are covered).

The dance is actually the tracing out of different symbolic patterns of steps weaving around, then swirling and opening up again. The dragon moves in an undulating motion and it should never look like it is dead. Thus, the puppeteers must keep the dragon shimmering with slight movement at all times, giving the illusion of life. Considerable practice is needed to not only memorize the multiple dance patterns but to simply handle the dragon in a way that makes it look more lifelike. Parading with the dragon is also common in which case the dragon moves in a slithering motion and periodically moves through one of the dance patterns as it progress.

There are also considerable taboos in dealing with the dragon. As with buddha statues and the lions used in the dance, a new dragon must undergo an eye opening ceremony. While the dragon is in motion it is never to touch the ground and traditionally one was not permitted to step over the dragon. Usually, martial artists formed the dance troupe although any group could form a team for the common dragons of the green, three clawed variety. Only Shaolin martial artists were permitted to carry the Imperial Golden Five Clawed Dragon. Like the better known Lion Dance, the Dragon Dance is accompanied by drums, gongs and cymbals. However, the music played is different than the music played for the lions and the drum is smaller and of a different shape. The gongs and cymbals are the same. Although this is a very entertaining performance, much loved by the Chinese people for centuries, it is still a rite of magic with the music and the dance patterns all designed to bring wealth, good fortune, wisdom and prosperity for the community and its posterity.

In addition to the dragon there is also a flaming pearl suspended on a pole as part of the Dragon Dance. This element was only added in the Tang dynasty, before that the Dragon Dance did not have a pearl. Customarily, the pearl is called a "wisdom pearl" and like in various buddha and bodhisattva statues (*e.g.*, Avalokiteśvara, Maitreya, and Kṣitigarbha) wisdom is indicated as flames emanating from the pearl. In the case of the Dragon Dance, the pearl is a ball suspended on a pole. The ball will have flames painted on it, be multi-colored, or have silk streamers attached representing the flames. The puppeteer holding the pearl is actually the performer who is leading the dance as the dragon must follow the pearl both in its waving motion and in the movement through the dance patterns. It is most curious that the pearl was added in the Tang dynasty at the height of Buddhist influence on Chinese culture.

The identification of the wisdom pearl's meaning has been disputed in the literature for a century. Various hypotheses on its symbolism include: spermatozoa entering the ovum, a common gem, thunder, lightning, the sun and the moon.[16] All of these can either be dismissed outright or seems to be of late attempts to explain its meaning. The spermatozoa theory mistook the wisdom flames' tails as the tails of the spermatozoa. A common gem would not have flames issuing from it. Thunder is depicted as a drummer or a winged creature in Chinese myth and lightening is often depicted as a mirror. Finally, there is a beautiful hanging tapestry taken from a pre-Buddhist tomb in Hunan (c. 186 BCE) showing multiple dragons and the sun and moon. None of the dragons are in relation with the sun and moon except spatially.[17] It is really within Buddhism that we find the identity of the flaming pearl.

The Chinese were cultivating pearls before the Current Era and they came to symbolize beauty, purity and preciousness. They were thought to be maturated by means of moonlight. However, there seems to be no connection between pearls as symbols of wisdom or spiritual power in association with any of the Chinese gods or the dragon before the arrival of Buddhism. The flaming gem is a pan-Indic symbol and can even be found in exquisite depictions of Viṣṇu.[18] As we now move to explore, the flaming gem is sourced from the Indian concept of the *cintāmani*.

Cintāmani

The *cintāmani* (lit. *cintā*: thought, care, anxiety and *mani*: gem, jewel) is the most precious jewel that dragons possess. They guard it very carefully and become anxious when it is misplaced. The jewel itself is able to grant all that one wishes and thus is often translated as "wish-granting jewel." It can grant mundane requests such as food, clothes, housing, wealth, good health and is able to purify water. It is mentioned in Pali texts but the potency of this symbol is more fully advanced in the Mahayana branch of Buddhism wherein it comes to be a symbol for the teachings of the Dharma.

In India it is depicted as tear-drop shaped, oval or as a cut jewel although a *mani* is simply any type of precious or semi-precious gem and thus its shape is not dictated by the term. It can be found at least by the Six Dynasties period (220–589) in Chinese Buddhist artwork and thereafter.[19] Further, Tang Dynasty images of the gem are found on the cave walls of Dunhuang.[20] In purely Chinese depictions it is usually portrayed as pear-shaped, although the more Indic style is not unknown. The use of the pearl image probably is because the term *cintāmani* was translated into Chinese using the word pearl as part of the compound. Chinese translations include: *ruyi-zhu* (如意珠) "wishing pearl," *ruyi-bao* (如意 寶) "wishing jewel," *ruyi-baozhu* (如意寶珠) "wishing precious pearl," as well as others.[21] The connection between the dragon and the wisdom/wish-granting pearl is beautifully illustrated in a short story found in the *Lotus Sutra*.

The sutra states that Mañjuśrī having been asked if he knew of anyone who was adept in the *Lotus Sutra* speedily gaining buddhahood, answered that the eight year old daughter of the dragon king Sāgara has so applied herself. Following the dragon girl's appearance, the inquisitor Śāriputra, states his disbelief because a female cannot become a buddha amongst other stations.[22]

> At that time, the dragon girl had a wish-granting pearl, whose value was the [whole] thousand-millionfold world, which she held up and gave to the Buddha. The Buddha straightway accepted it. The dragon girl said to the Bodhisattva Wisdom Accumulation and to the venerable Śāriputra, "I offered a wish-granting pearl, and the World-Honored One accepted it. Was this quick or not?"
>
> He answered, saying, "Very quick!"
>
> The girl said, "With your supernatural power you shall see me achieve buddhahood even more quickly than that!"[23]

She then proceeded to transform into a man and immediately gain buddhahood. Metaphorically, she presents her wisdom to the Buddha who acknowledges it and she then achieves final liberation. This brings dragons, their wisdom/wish-granting pearl and the Buddha together into one eloquent story.

The fact that there was no precedent for a pearl in association with the dragon or gods in pre-Buddhist China is an important factor. The introduction of the pearl into the Dragon Dance in the Tang dynasty when Buddhism was so influential in the culture is likewise important. That there was already a close association between the wish-granting gem and the Indian *nāga* and that this wish-granting gem is depicted as a flaming jewel in Indian iconography points to India as the source. The popularity of the *Lotus Sutra* in the Tang dynasty with its story of a dragon girl giving her wish-granting gem to the Buddha as well as other accounts in popular Buddhist texts all helped to crystallize the connection between the dragons, wisdom pearls and Buddhism at that time. This allows us to correctly identify the ball on a pole used in the Dragon Dance as the wish-granting pearl or wisdom pearl.

The Lion

From the western shores of Spain to India, the range of the lion in ancient times allowed for the Indo-Europeans to marvel at this unique creature and transform it into a universal symbol of kingship, nobility, bravery and strength. Even today, in the twenty-first century, the lion symbol is still ubiquitous ranging from the symbol of British monarchy to the flag of Sri Lanka and many more powerful emblems are all graced with lions. Even given this range both in the geographic distribution and in symbolic meaning, the lion only played a minor role in China before the influence of Buddhism

.

The Lion in China

The lion appears in China as a borrowed symbol of protection from mid-eastern sources and does not take on any significant role in the Chinese symbolic world during the early dynasties. The earliest use of the lion symbol as a protector was in the Eastern Han dynasty.[24] However, how distinguishable those early forms are from the chimera is disputable. In fact, there really was no place for the lion in the symbolic lexicon of the Chinese. The symbolic position of a fierce predatory cat was filled by the tiger which was a yin-earth symbol of strength and courage. The markings on the tiger's forehead were seen as the Chinese character for "king" and thus the tiger is the king of the animals and was seen as the protector of the wilderness. Although some stone lions decorated official buildings and were used by important people to "safeguard" their abodes, it was not until the Tang dynasty that the lion's roles expanded and this was completely in connection with the popularity of Buddhism.

The Chinese knew of the lion and a few people had seen living examples which arrived in the Middle Kingdom as gifts from other kingdoms. However, these were rarities and kept in the imperial compounds as part of the emperor's collections of rarities and thus were not well known beyond the palace walls. The *Hou ha shu* (後漢書) notes that both the Kushans and Parthians sent lions as gifts.[25] In trying to show that a lion was a gift from some kingdom in the area of Eastern India and into South-east Asia, William Hu wishes to connect the ancient term "*suanni*" (狻猊) with lion and although possible his argument is not conclusive as it is also likely that some other cat-like animal might be indicated.[26] Later commentators connecting the *suanni* with lions may have simply confused one unknown animal with a little known animal. Some of the early "lion" depictions lack the central horn familiar to us from the Chinese chimera but this lacuna is consistent and thus not an indication of a lion as a distinct animal. Thus, we find limited exposure to lion lure in China before the arrival of Buddhism that is provable.

The Lion Dance

There is also a case made that there was some sort of Lion Dance during Han times.[27] However, at best it was probably a single person in a lion costume and may have had shamanic connections. Although earlier precedents may have existed, the Lion Dance as we know it today had its origins at the end of the Sui or early Tang dynasties and clearly indicates continued and increased communications with the kingdoms west of China and in particular India. It is interesting to note that in analyzing the nine stories of the origin of the Lion Dance provided by Hu, when those stories purely of a local origin and those of post Tang dynasty dates are eliminated two of the remainder indicate a Buddhist connection and the third contains an improbable historic event.[28]

The first story reports that once in the border region, some lions were menacing the people and every attempt to kill or capture the lions failed even by great heroes. A Buddhist monk came along, went into the wild, found and tamed the lions and sent them as a gift to the Emperor. The Emperor enjoyed the addition of the lions in his collection and when they died, he had costumes made and the Lion Dance created in imitation of the real lions.[29]

The second story reports that once one of the Tang Emperors had a dream of a large Buddhist temple. On each side of the front gates were two black guardian lion statues. After the Emperor entered the temple the lions came down off their pedestal and frolicked in front of him. Later, he ordered a search of the empire for black lions. This search failed but created difficulties for the population. Finally, the fairy Eluanxianzi offered the Emperor a gift of a black lion disguised as a house cat. The Emperor did not recognize the gift for what it was and rejected it. Depressed by these turn of events the Emperor became ill and the Lion Dance was created to lift his mood.[30]

Evidence of the Lion Dance in the Tang dynasty is found in *A Record of Buddhist Monasteries in Loyang* (*Luo yang qie lan ji* 洛陽伽藍記) wherein it claims that the statues leaving Changqiu Temple (長秋寺) to join the statues from all the other temples and monasteries in Loyang which were then paraded through the city on Śākyamuni's birthday, were accompanied with a procession of entertainers including man-made lions.[31] The statues gathered at the famous Jingming Monastery (景明寺) in the southern suburbs and then proceeded in procession through the city gate. This is very similar to the juggernaut, an activity that Buddhists as well as Hindus in India undertook showcasing their icons for worship during these same centuries. The whole city turned out for the parade and the emperor would scatter flowers as an offering to the Buddha. The pre-main event procession from Changqiu Temple was considered one of the better events to see.[32] The other man-made creatures in this procession were considered to be able to ward off negative influences and promote auspiciousness. The Lion Dance would have been seen in the same light, a function that still survives.

Guarding lions protecting government offices, temples and the home of the powerful are distinguished as male and female. The male has a ball under his front paw and the female has a small cub often upturned under hers. There are also other distinguishing features such as the number of curls in the mane (distinguishing rank) that grew over the centuries. Most of these elements were not present in the Tang dynasty. The ball would continue its importance in the dance from its early phase into the present.

The lions are made from a costume with a highly stylized head, a cover with a tail sewn on, and because it takes two people to fill the costume, two sets of leggings. Sometimes false cloth lion's paws may be tied over the performer's shoes. The lions of the dance can be divided into the five colors in general, but others may be added. New lions have to undergo an eye opening ceremony the same used for consecrating a new Buddhist statue. The numbers of lions used in the dance commonly are some lucky number like five or eight. They dance around focusing on the four directions and the center or the eight directions, acting like playful Pekingese dogs. They may or may not use platforms, large balls to stand on, roll on the ground and other stunts. The actions of the performers are very energetic and require skill, strength and dexterity which probably explains why professional performers and martial artists are the usual dancers in the lion costume. Usually firecrackers explode and drums and cymbals play martial sounding music all of which are used to scare off negative influences. The dance ends with the lions throwing "lucky candy" to the crowd. This last item is probably a more recent addition as no mention of it is found in the Tang accounts.

In addition to the dance which is performed in one place, the lions can also parade down the street doing some of the same stunts as in the dance along with various dance movements. Progress down the street is usually slow as the lions walk and dance from side to side. Usually, at the end of the parade in front of a temple or some other edifice, a dance will be performed as a concluding act of the whole show. In addition, there is often a large-headed Buddhist monk (a man dressed in a Buddhist robe with a large false head covering his own) carrying a palm fan who assists the lions in distributing (fanning) the good fortune. The Big Headed Monk is also a post Tang addition. Several descriptions of the Lion Dance from the Tang dynasty exist. The dance is mentioned in the *Jiu tang shu* (舊唐書), *Xin tang shu* (新唐書), Du you's (杜佑 735–812) *Tong dian* (通典) and the *Yue fu za lu* (樂府雜錄) by Duan Anjie (段安節 c.894–898). There is also archaeological and art historic evidence for the dance during the Tang.[33]

However, in the Tang dynasty the parading lions would also have handlers holding tethers tied to the necks of the lions. The artwork from the period indicates that one handler was common but more were sometimes used. These individuals named "lion boys" are key to identifying the lions and help in determining the origin of the Lion Dance. Handlers sometimes are still part of the dance but at some point the tethers were no longer used. The curious thing is why the handlers are called "boys." One would not expect a child to be handling a dangerous beast, as this is not a realistic depiction although not beyond possibilities, there probably is a more reasonable answer which we turn to below. As the *Jiu tang shu* informs us:

> The T'ai-p'ing-yueh, a musical composition, was written during the reign of Emperor Wu in the second half of the Han dynasty (140–87 B.C.) and was also called Wu-fang-shih-tzu-wu (Lion Dance of the Five Directions). The lion is a violent and bloodthirsty animal

> and comes from southwest India and surrounding areas. Variegated cloth and fur was used to construct a lion costume to be manipulated and worn by two persons. These dances would imitate various up and down movements … Two handlers holding onto ropes and whisks tease the lion as they lead him out. Each of the five lions are (*sic*) positioned in specific places. A chorus of one hundred forty men sings the tune of the T'ai-p'ing-yueh as the lion is coaxed to dance while being held with ropes.[34]

The Lion and Buddhism

From the early days of Buddhism in India, there has been a continuous association with lions as symbols and used in metaphors. Śākyamuni's teaching of the Dharma is called the lion's roar in various early materials such as the *Udumbarika Sīhanāda Suttanta,*[35] *Cakkavatti Sīhanāda Suttanta,*[36] *Cūḷa Sīhanāda Suttanta*[37] and the *Mahā Sīhanāda Suttanta.*[38] The connection between the Buddha and his teachings with the lion was used by Emperor Aśoka in an artistic rendition –the lion capital, which now graces the official seal of India. When Śākyamuni lays down on his right side it is called the lion's posture.[39] Approaching the Buddha is said to be like approaching a lone lion.[40] This symbolic connection continues in the Mahayana sutras. For example, lion thrones are mentioned in the *Vimalakīrtinirdeśa*, *Avataṃsaka* and the *Mahāratnakūta Sūtra* to name a few.

In India beginning in the Vedic period, there are descriptions of gods' associated with certain animals such as Surya with the horses drawing his fiery chariot. Not every god is associated with a particular animal mount (*vāhana*) as we now know them. The details of many of the gods associations with animals are actually advanced in the Purāṇas. It is in the Puranic period, fourth century to the sixteenth century, that we find the majority of the gods being affiliated with one animal or another. This impetus also had its effects on Buddhism where, for example, the Bodhisattvas gain animal mounts.[41] The standard list of Mañjuśrī with his lion, Samantabhadra with his elephant and Avalokiteśvara with a dragon, phoenix, or other animals is well known. These iconographic details are transferred to China from India during this time period. In particular, because of the close association of Mañjuśrī with the lion we will look at the acquisition of his cult in China.

With compassion and wisdom as two cornerstones of the Mahayana, Mañjuśrī's role of representing wisdom was soon crystallized. There are many canonical texts that have Mañjuśrī as an important figure as is to be expected with a great bodhisattva of the highest stage. For example, the *Susthitamati Devaputra Paripṛcchā Sūtra* wherein Mañjuśrī attempts to kill the Buddha with his sword as a skillful means was translated into Chinese by Dharmagupta in the early fifth century. The sutra which teaches the "one course *samādhi*," a teaching that was important in the Chan tradition, is the *Saptaśatikā*. This sutra is also known as *The Prajñāpāramitā as taught by Mañjuśrī.* It was translated from Sanskrit into Chinese by Mendrasena (502–557). Mañjuśrī also has an important role in the *Lotus Sūtra*, a text already mentioned in regard to the dragon. The *Mañjuśrīparinirvāṇa Sūtra* translated into Chinese in the third century, speaks of Mañjuśrī living on the Gandhamādana Mountain accompanied by five hundred ṛṣis. The *Mañjuśrī Dharmaratnapiṭaka Dhāraṇi Sūtra*, translated into Chinese by Bodhiruci (8th c.) states that the bodhisattva lives in Mahācīna (*i.e.*, China) on a five peak mountain.[42]

One of the sutras that had a significant impact on the Chinese elite was the *Vimalakīrtinirdeśa.* It presented the teachings on non-duality in a conversation between a layman and Mañjuśrī. There are several depictions of this conversation in Dunhuang cave art. At that location, images of Mañjuśrī span from the fourth to the tenth centuries. Tang dynasty and later images often show him on his lion along with Samantabhadra on his elephant.

Most importantly, the *Avataṃsaka* was translated by Buddhabhadra (5th c.), Śikṣānanda (7th c.) and Prajñā (8th–9th c.). The final portion of this sutra collection is the *Gaṇḍavyūha Sūtra*, the Sanskrit text that demonstrates one of the most skillful employments of the language found within the Buddhist genre. The sutra is about a young man seeking to train in the Mahayana and describes all the teachings he accumulates. The whole of his trip is assisted by Mañjuśrī.

The *Avataṃsaka* became the foundational text for the Huayan tradition. Tuxun (杜順 577–640), Zhiyan (智儼 602–668) and Fazang (法藏 643–712) are considered the founding fathers of this tradition. This later master had enormous influence on the court and was involved in a number of major Buddhist projects. In fact, the Huayan tradition was one of the most significant branches of Buddhism in the Tang dynasty. Because of the important role that Mañjuśrī plays in the *Avataṃsaka* this was an important contributing factor in the growing cult of this Bodhisattva. Fazang wrote the *Essay on the Golden Lion*, an exposé on the one-in-all and all-in-one doctrine. This sutra also provides a list of eight mountains in the eight directions each associated with a bodhisattva. A ninth mountain is associated with Mañjuśrī.

In China, Wutai Shan is considered the mountain home of Mañjuśrī. Exactly when this mountain became associated with the bodhisattva is difficult to ascertain. In the mid fourth century there seems to have been no Buddhist establishments on the mountain. There are three major records regarding this mountain as a miraculous place: *Gu qing liang zhuan* (古清涼傳 7th c.),[43] *Guang qing liang zhuan* (廣清涼傳 11th c.)[44] and *Xu qing liang zhuan* (續清涼傳 11th c.).[45] There are also notes about this mountain by Fazang and many more reports.[46] There are legends stating that Emperor Aśoka, King Mu of the Zhou (周穆王), and King Ming of the Han (漢明帝) all built structures there. The Emperor Xiaowen Hong (孝文宏 467–499) built a temple on Wutai Shan (五台山) in the fifth century which may have been the first Buddhist establishment.[47] It also seems that by this time there was some association of this mountain with the bodhisattva Mañjuśrī. By the Tang dynasty, there was a thriving monastic community with 72 temples on the mountain which acted as the center of the Mañjuśrī cult. Every tradition of Chinese Buddhism had a representative monastic complex on the mountain by the Tang dynasty. The Huayan tradition was one of the most active as noted by Mary Anne Cartelli:

> Although Mount Wutai was considered the pure land of Mañjuśrī and the Center of the Avataṃsaka school, it also attracted the monks and pilgrims of Amitābha's Pure Land sect, along with those of the Tiantai, Chan, and Tantric schools.[48]

In addition to Fazang promotion of the cult of Mañjuśrī, Amogavajra (705–774), a famous tantric master working in China, was also a promoter of this cult. He even wrote a letter requesting the Emperor to promote Mañjuśrī as China's national protector.[49] This tantric master is closely associated with the Jinge Temple (金閣寺) located on the southern peak of Wutai Shan.

Eventually the whole of the Buddhist world accepted that Wutai Shan was the earthly home of bodhisattva Mañjuśrī. Pilgrimage to the earthly home of the great Bodhisattva became an extremely popular feature of the Chinese landscape. In fact, it was even criticized by Chan master Wuzhu (無住 714–777) as noted by Wendi Adamek, "…Wuzhu mocks those who make pilgrimage to Mt. Wutai, at a time when Bukong (*i.e.*, Amoghavajra) was involving the state in massive expenditure at this site in order to glorify China as the domain of the bodhisattva Mañjuśrī."[50]

The translations of texts wherein Mañjuśrī is a key figure, the establishing of an internationally recognized cultic center, the accounts of miraculous occurrences along with the support of the nobility and elite in China during the period from the Sui dynasty to the Song dynasty indicates the continuing growth of the popularity of this bodhisattva during this time frame. This is important in our research of the Lion Dance. As noted above, the Lion Dance emerges in the Tang dynasty exactly when all of this activity associated with the cult of Mañjuśrī was at its height. When the Lion Dance first appears there is one or more "lion boys" or handlers who held tethers to the lion. Who then are these "lion boys"?

In the tantric period of Buddhism in India (beginning roughly in the 7th c.), a number of iconographic forms of Mañjuśrī are found. Each of these forms is provided with a ritual text and these texts give details on the iconography of the bodhisattva. In the textual description of Mañjughoṣa (another name for Mañjuśrī), it says that the bodhisattva sitting on a lion is accompanied by Yamāntaka (trans. "Death's termination") and Sudhanakumāra. The last named individual is the same young man seeking teachings in the *Avataṃsaka.* Siddhaikavira Mañjuśrī (another form) is said to be accompanied by Jālinīprabha (or Sūryaprabha), Candraprabha, Kaśinī, and Upakśinī.[51] The *Mañjuśrī Dharmaratnapiṭaka Dhāraṇi Sūtra* says that Mañjuśrī is accompanied by Sudhana, Vasubandhu, Vimalakīrti and King Udayana. Other depictions have eight youths associated with him.[52]

It is pertinent that one of Mañjuśrī main attendants is noted in multiple texts to be the youth Sudhana. In general, we see in Chinese Buddhist iconography that attendants to important figures who themselves may also be bodhisattvas are depicted as youths. The *Long Roll of Buddhist Images* by Ding Guanpeng (丁觀鵬) is a Qing dynasty copy of Song dynasty scroll showing over 2000 figures.[53] There are youth attendants associated with images of Guanyin, Mañjuśrī and Virūpākṣa, in Bhaiṣajyaguru's assembly, in Vimalakīrti's assembly and in Śākyamuni's assembly. This leaves little doubt that the "lion boy" is actually Sudhana the main attendant of Mañjuśrī known to us from the *Avataṃsaka.* In time the lion lost its tether and the lion boy replaced it with a ball as is found under the foot of the male lion statues. The function of the boy is to tease and play with the lion. If more than one lion boy is involved the additional youth is probably one or another of the individuals mentioned above as the customary attendants of the bodhisattva.

Conclusion

In the field of Buddhist Studies, it is common for researchers to view the activities of the elite particularly in China. This would include not only the famous foreign monks but also translators, native masters, founders of movements, emperors and the literati to name some of the most significant contributors. There are far less studies on the activities in the sphere of folk customs. The Dragon Dance and the Lion Dance grow out of this later sphere and in maturing become significant even to those elite members of society.

This section discussed two cases of sinicization found in the folk arts, both of which occupy nearly the same ritual space. That is both the Dragon Dance and the Lion Dance are magical acts that bring about good fortune. The Dragon Dance being the more potent of the two.

The origin of the dragon image has not been conclusively determined but a number of theories exist. The significance of the symbol is beyond question, has lasted for several millenniums in China and is one of the longest used symbols in the human lexicon. The Dragon Dance is documented to have existed as far back as the Han dynasty and began as an act of rain-producing magic. These early Dragon Dances did not include the pearl. The pearl was added in the Tang dynasty.

The Chinese were cultivating pearls from early times but there are no known examples of pearls being associated with either Chinese gods or mythic spiritual creatures in a significant manner. Further, there seems to be no example of flaming pearls in the early dynasties either. However, the wish-granting gem (*cintāmani*) was associated with the Indian nagas from early times. Nagas have a long association with Buddhism and the Buddha Śākyamuni was even born as a *nāga* in previous births. Nagas continued to by symbolically represented and provided narrative space in Indian Buddhist arts. The Sanskrit term *cintāmani* was often translated into Chinese using the word "pearl" (*zhu*). The usual Indian depiction of the *cintāmani* is a cut jewel or a pear shaped jewel with flames. In addition to the nagas being associated with good fortune they are also associated with wisdom in Mahayana Buddhism because of being the keepers of the prajñāpāramitā sūtras. Iconographically, the flaming gem is encountered not just with nagas but with buddhas and bodhisattvas holding one in their hands often while seated in meditation.

With the amalgamation of the complex Indic *nāga* cult with the equally complex native Chinese dragon (*long*) cult, the flaming wisdom pearl was added to the Dragon Dance in the Tang dynasty. A dragon being most anxious about his/her wisdom pearl and the pearl having the magical ability to move, the pearl comes to be the lead of the dance with the dragon following its every twist and turn. Buddhist literature influential in the Tang dynasty connects the pearl, dragons, the Buddha, bodhisattvas and awakening.

The Lion Dance was the creation of the Tang dynasty. The lion not being native to China comes to have the symbolic role of a playful creature although it can be fierce. In the Tang and Song dynasties the "lions" used in the dance were accompanied by handlers referred to as "lion boys." These "boys" were identified as members of Mañjuśrī's retinue as understood in those centuries. The most important member of this group being Sudhana, a young man seeking to learn the Mahayana with the aid of Mañjuśrī in the *Avataṃsaka*, which was one of the most influential sutras in the Tang dynasty. The Tang dynasty saw the extensive propagation of the cult of Mañjuśrī by both foreign and native Chinese masters with the Chinese Wutai Shan being internationally recognized as the earthly home of the bodhisattva. A popular bodhisattva mentioned in numerous texts, he was associated with the lion in India. The lion has a long association with the Dharma.

The Dragon Dance is an excellent example of sinicization as it adapted the Indian *nāga* cult which includes the wish-granting gem with the Chinese dragon cult. From the Tang dynasty onward, the dance includes the wisdom pearl as its lead. The Lion Dance is an example of sinicization taking place through the creation of a new folk cultural form based on Buddhist literary and mythic precedents. Both of these dances are understood as bringing about prosperity and thus they function in similar manners.

Chapter Four

Buddha's Play

The All-seeing for the sake of leading call
this Lions' Play leading to the stages.
This!—which leads in the reversal of pasturing in impurities and,
In explanations for whichever is meritorious
and unmeritorious.[1]

Introduction

The *Nettipakaraṇa* an important Pali text for Buddhist teachers, and assumed to have come to Sri Lanka sometime in the first five centuries of the Current Era, contains a wealth of information beyond the method of exegesis that it illuminates. It is supported by a commentary by none less than Buddhaghoṣa (5th c.) the famed expounder of Theravadin orthodoxy. According to the textual tradition, Mahā Kaccāyana was the author and upon finishing its utterance, the Buddha Śākyamuni approved it. This text was recited and approved at the first council. Most scholars think this work is a composition well after the time of the Buddha.

The *Nettippakaraṇa* explains that the "lions" in the above verse are the buddha, pratyekabuddhas and the arhats. They are so called because they have destroyed desire, hatred and delusion by their play. That play consists of: the four means of reaching the goal (*paṭipadā*: *i.e.*, unyielding, yielding, self-control, equanimity[2]), the four applications of mindfulness (*satipaṭṭhāna*: mindfulness of body, mind, sensations, phenomena), the four meditational states (*jhāna*), the four stages (*vihāra*), the four appropriated exertions (*sammappadhāna*: non-generation of and abandoning of unwholesomeness, generating and maintaining wholesomeness), the four marvelous signs (*acchariyā abbhutā dhammā*),[3] the four resolutions (*adhiṭṭhāna*: to gain insight, gain truth, abandon unwholesomeness, to master oneself), the four ways of cultivating concentration (*samādhi-bhāvanā* based on impulses, mind, effort, examination), the four dharmas that deal with happiness (*sukhabhāgiya*: restraint of faculties, abstinence, meritorious dharmas, cultivating factors of wisdom) and the four measureless (*appamāṇa*: compassion, sympathetic joy, equanimity, loving-kindness). It also consists in cultivation, in verification, and in discontinuation. Play is connected with the faculties and with reversal (*vipariyāsa*). The faculties of energy, pasturing in the Good Dharma (*saddhammagocara*) and pasturing in the reversal of impurity (*kilesagocara*).[4]

Therefore, we can see that "play" is an important concept in understanding what the awakened do but more importantly how those activities are perceived by them. That is these are not odious tasks but play ("The all-seeing …call this play"). The Pali word translated as "play" above is *vikkīḷita.* The Sanskrit equivalent is *vikrīḍita*, which is composed of *vi* probably acting as an intensifying prefix and *krīḍ* meaning play. This word is encountered in a variety of non-Buddhist texts and generally relates to the activities of humans and animals but also of the wind and waves. With the prefix "*vi*" it is rare in the Pali texts but "*kīḷita*" and "*kīḷā*" are more common. The Majjhima Nikāya uses the notion of play (*kīḷita*) in a simile drawing a comparison between an elephant playing a game (*saṇadhovika*) in the water with how Saccaka a son of Jains intends to play with the Buddha Gotama and defeat him in spirited discussion.[5] It is further found in the Dīgha Nikāya where Śākyamuni explains a previous life as the great King Sudassana. He speaks of when he was a sporting (*kīḷikā*) youth followed by becoming the viceroy.[6]

The Sanskrit *krīḍ* is also the origin of the Pali *khiḍḍā* which has the same meaning. In this form, it is also found in a number of canonical and post-canonical texts. The *Brahmajāla Sutta* speaks of gods who are debouched by sport (*khiḍḍā-padosikā*).[7] The Aṅguttara Nikāya relates a story of a foolish cat who thinks he can play in a deep pool like a bull elephant being similar to a person who has not achieved concentration (*samādhi*) wishing to live alone in the jungle.[8] A number of other examples in the post-canonical literature are also found.

An example from the post-canonical literature should suffice. The *Vimānavatthu Aṭṭhakathā* is a commentary on the *Nettipakaraṇa* composed by Dhammapālatthera (post 5th c. Buddhaghoṣa, but date unknown). It provides extensive additional information on the material in the primary text. A quotation in this text both illustrates the use of "play" in the commentarial tradition and will act as a transition, as will immediately be seen. The quotation is part of a longer explanation of "*devī*." It reads,

> …"The meaning moreover is—she games (*dibbati*) with power attained from merit—plays (*kīḷati*) and lulls (*laḷati*) in the five sense pleasures enjoying herself, or as said above she is splendid, radiant, she goes in her sky-chariot, thus "*devī*."[9]

This quotation is important as it distinguishes different types of amusement. *Dibbati* is playing usually by throwing dice and hence gaming. Whereas *laḷati* is related to the Latin *lallo i.e.*, "lull." These are distinguished from general play (*kīḷati*). Given this, why use terms that mean play/sport when referring to some of the activities of buddhas and other awakened individuals?

Play

Although every reader has engaged in play, when we look at the psychological literature on play there is a wide divergence on just exactly what type of phenomena is being presented. Terry Marks-Tarlow in reviewing the neurological genesis of play by other researchers, presents information on the mammalian "open neural wiring." In his article, he indicates that only play and care of the young which are main sets of social instincts, act as the point of delineation between the mammalian and reptilian brain. It is by play that mammals can be "proactive, adventurous and inquisitive."[10] Play has both neural and neurochemical distinction which allows for particular expressions and hence allows for differences due to culture (human *vs*. canine; Japanese *vs*. Norwegian) and other factors. Play openness enhances vitality whereas negative emotional states are limiting. As he states, "...play enhances the intrinsic motivation to engage in activities for their own sake, that is, for the pleasure, enjoyable, and/or absorbing experience of the process, rather than as a means to outside ends."[11] As pointed out by Berk, Mann, and Ogan, play is an important mechanism in developing self-regulation which in turn is understood as the "foundation of choice and decision making, for mastery of higher cognitive processes, and for morality."[12] Singer and Singer state, " But the production of a socially defined creative product, whether it takes the form of an artistic, scientific, or business achievement, calls for specific skills and knowledge, high motivation and effort, and the capacity of a playful consideration of many possibilities."[13] In discussion on the importance of play, based on experiments performed by Panksepp, Marks-Tarlow mentions that, "play arises from subcortical areas without any need for cortical involvement underscores how play can arise implicitly…"[14]

The distinction between general play and gaming noted in the Pali terms is supported by Schwartzman in listing the general characteristics used in the definitions of play. She states, "Play is first of all assumed to be pleasurable and enjoyable, to be characterized by freedom and spontaneity, and to elicit active (as opposed to passive) engagement by players.[15] She further continues in her discussion to explain why games must be distinguished from general play based on the effects of the rules of the game on the activity.[16] Schwartzman states that "play is an activity that is very much alive and characterized always by transformation and preservation of objects, roles, actions, and so forth."[17]

Many when viewing various animals in their early development playing, see in play the preparation for their mature life. Lion cubs pouncing on sticks, prepares them to pounce on game as adults. This thinking is also applied to human children. This approach sees the physical aspects of child play as the development of motor skills and the make-believe as socio-psychological modeling all of which is in preparation for the adult life. There may well be truth to some extent or another in this analysis as to the function of play in children, but play is also something that adults, even senior citizens, engage in quit readily. Pellegrini and Bjorklund draw a distinction between these two ways of understanding play by noting that fantasy play has an immediate function whereas object play has a differed function.[18] Others see in play behavior that the means are more significant than the ends. That is play is unpurposed. And some researchers have argued this holds true for both human and non-human play.[19]

"Play, music, and dance, alongside laughter, can interrupt proper orders that hinder access to the flourishing of the self, to the enjoyment of life. Festive elements of life such as these can vivify another imaginary, the good."[20] Certainly, the labeling of particular "spiritual" activities that the Buddha engaged in as "play" removes a heaviness with which such activities are imbued. This is fun, this is breaking of the norms by opening up. This is not rote but imaginative. It is a relaxing into and not a beating down or regimentation. The "flourishing of the (no)-self" becomes possible. Things are not as they are said to be but fluid.

To summarize and leave to the side the neurological and neurochemical aspects, play for us is proactive, adventurous and inquisitive. It enhances vitality, motivation to engage in activities for their own sake and is pleasurable or enjoyable. It can be absorbing whether general play or gaming. Its characteristics are freedom, spontaneity, eliciting active engagement, and transformation.

The Mahayana Texts

Students of the Sanskrit tradition will find numerous passages speaking about play in various contexts. So the technical terms continue being used across the traditions. Here a few quotations will be provided arranged according to their usage of the technical terms in the sense that the text is referring to the simple play of individuals or if the text is using the term to denote some higher processes. The first passage comes from the *Lotus Sutra*, chapter two.

> Children playing here and there
> Who with intent made heaps out of sand
> Raise up stupas for the Jina
> They all obtain becoming awakened.[21]

Here we read *krīdisu* in what one would expect being the most normal of usages. Children playing in the sand. Although, they may not have a profound spiritual practice of erecting monuments or even manufacturing small reminders of monuments, they have intent but only in play and only for amusement. Yet, they too even by such a token arrive at awakening. This is part of the profound teachings of the *Lotus Sutra* which most scholars would place somewhere before or slightly after the beginning of the Current Era for "publication."

The next selection speaks of the wonders of Amitābha's Sukhāvatīvyūha realm. In that majestic place, the beings who are reborn are said to be very similar to the Olympian gods (*trāyastriṃśa*). In many ways, Sukhāvatī seems a combination of the characteristics of the sphere on top of Mount Meru combined with known features of great kings' pleasure parks. In such a wonderful place, the people who are reborn enjoy their lotus flowers, in which they are born, as the gods enjoy their palaces. The following passage comes from the Larger *Sukhāvatīvyūha Sūtra*.

> Indeed, such as the gods called the 33 or Yamas enter into celestial places that are 50, 100, or 500 *yoganas* in extent, sport, dally and promenade, So too, Bhagavan, I see there in the Sukhāvatī world realm these men dwelling in the receptacle of illustrious lotuses.[22]

One final passage bearing greater purport to the issue under investigation comes from the *Aṣṭasāhasrikā.* In this passage, the Buddha Śākyamuni is explaining to Subhūti that the positive meritorious karma created by providing many beings the necessities of life is surpassed by a person who cultivates the perfection of wisdom for merely as much as a fraction of a second. He continues epitomizing the perfection of wisdom in various ways.

> Venerable Subhūti, a bodhisattva mahāsattva wishing to attain the excellent complete perfect awakening, wishing to go to the supreme position of all beings, wishing to become a refuge to the unprotected beings, wishing to attain the sphere of a buddha, wishing to emulate the buddha's manliness, wishing to sport the buddha's sport, wishing to roar the buddha's (lion) roar, wishing to acquire the buddha's accomplishment, wishing to teach the Dharma to the three thousand great thousand world realms, that bodhisattva mahāsattva should undertake the perfection of wisdom.[23]

Chinese Translations

The translation into Chinese of the Sanskrit "*krīḍ, vikrīḍita*" and various derivatives produced a variety of attempts to capture the notion. More often than not, this produced a two character translation that was much less specific than the original. Some examples would be 自娱 (*ziyu*: self-amusement) found in the *Madhyamāgama* translated by Gautama Sanghadeva at the end of the fourth century,[24] 歡樂 (*huanle*: pleasure and happy) found in the *Dīrghāgama* translated by Buddhayaśas also at the end of the fourth century,[25] and 歡娱 (*huanyu*: pleasure and amuse) found in the early translation by Dharmarakṣa of the *Lotus Sutra* [26] third to fourth century. In the same source one finds 娱樂 (*yule*: amuse and happy),[27] and 歌舞 (*gewu*: sing and dance) found in the 古來世時經 (*Gu lai shi shi jing*) translated by Anshiguo in the mid-second century.[28] However, Chinese translators more accurately translated *krīḍ, etc.* as 戲 (*xi*: play) but even this term has limited overlap with the Sanskrit connotative field. One also finds two character translations where one element is *xi* such as, 戲樂 (*xile*: play and happy), 歌戲 (*gexi*: sing and play), 嬉戲 (*xixi*: fun and play). These various attempts register that the Chinese translators were struggling with the concept of play with all of its Sanskrit connotations and perhaps in particular in association with such an august person as a buddha.

In the rather large collection of primary texts that define the Confucian tradition, on occasion, one can come across one or another element in the two character translation noted above but not both. However, as for *xi*, I was able to find several exemplary uses. One is a citation in the *Analects*

(Book 9, 17)[29] wherein Confucius states he was playing or sporting with his previous words. In the *Shi jing* or *The Classic of Poetry*, the Qi Ao section, we read the following:

> Look at the other bank of the Qi River,
> The green bamboo like a curtain
> There is the recusant prince,
> like gold or pewter
> Like a princely tablet or princely badge.
> Lenient—generous, bravo! Regarding his charioteering,
> Good at playing tricks—, but not cruel.[30]

Laozi famous work seems to yield no result after a search for these terms. However, Zhuangzi also employs the word *xi* in various settings. Two examples should suffice. In the first he discusses the virtue of introspection and human nature. He states, "…their authority is like an emperor but they are unable in their nobility to be haughty to people, their wealth includes all under heaven but they are unable with that wealth to play people."[31] The second example comes in a section talking about having extraordinary skill in swordsmanship with the king. It reports this part of the conversation, "The king said: 'Master, cease then go to your lodging and wait my command. I will arrange to play (*i.e.*, a sword fight) then invite you.'"[32]

In Chinese Buddhism

As noted elsewhere in this volume, one of the important works to influence Chinese Pure Land thought is the *Wu liang shou jing you bo ti she yuan sheng jie zhu*. This is stated to be an explanation of Vasubandhu's *Sukhāvatīvyūho-padeśa.*[33] This later is claimed to have been translated by Bodhiruci a well-known translator from central India who translated the *Diamond Sutra,*[34] the *Laṅkāvatāra Sūtra,*[35] the *Daśabhūmikasūtraśastra*[36] along with thirty-five other texts. Scholars have raised doubts about the authenticity of this work being ascribed to Vasubandhu but none the less, it along with Tanluan's commentary has been greatly influential in East Asian Buddhism.

Near the conclusion of the *Wu liang shou jing you po ti she yuan sheng jie zhu* (無量壽經優婆提舍願生偈註), Vasubandhu's verses present information about five Causative Entrances (Approach, Assembly, Dwelling, Room) associated with the Pure Land. The fifth one is the Gate of the Garden-grove Playground (遊戲地 *youxidi*). Tanluan's commentary explains after entering: the Mahayana, Awakening, the Pure Land, The Tathāgata's Assembly, Settling of Samsara (*vyupaśama*), Accomplishment (*siddhi*), one "should arrive at the stage of Teaching Others. The stage of Teaching Others is the bodhisattvas' stage of enjoying play (自娛 *zi yu*)."[37] A few lines further, Tanluan explains that "playing" means spontaneously bodhisattvas ferry beings to nirvana. Further, it means ferrying without someone ferried.[38]

An interesting note is that the term ferrying (渡 *du* 度 *du*), although both written forms are found, the first is properly "to ferry" or "a ferry." The second looks similar and the pronunciation is the same in Mandarin. However the second really means: "a limit, measure, rule, degree," *et cetera.* In the current text, the second is used to mean "ferry." Here it is a translation of the Sanskrit *pāramitā.* The Sanskrit has been translated as "perfection" but actually means "gone (*ita*) to the other side or bank (*pṛ*).[39] In the Buddhist context, this term is used with reference to nirvana being the other shore to samsara. This concept implying that sentient beings need a way across and hence a ferrying. Unfortunately, the Chinese term has been wrongly translated as "salvation" causing much confusion in general and specifically with the Pure Land materials wherein this term is frequently encountered. Further, it thus gives the impression that there is both a concept of salvation and a point of true comparison with Christian theology. Such a doctrinal position however, is incomprehensible given Buddhist posit that there is no self or soul to be saved and that no buddha can take one to the goal but one must accomplish awakening for oneself. The bodhisattvas spontaneously assist sentient beings to get across not by saving them but by providing them with teachings often referred to as a vehicle.

The famous Pure Land master Daochuo (道綽 562–645) uses the term "play" but seems to add nothing to the conversation.[40] Shandao (善導 613–681) in his *Zhuan jing xing dao yuan wang sheng jing tu fa shi zan* (轉經行道願往生淨土法事讃)[41] uses the term *xi* but only in a rather mundane context. In the passage just below, he is discussing the transmutation of severe negativity as found in the hell realms into characteristics of the Pure Land. The texts explains:

> The eighteen karmic wind swords like the fire and iron chariot when released cut the body. Because of the possibility of burning compelling me, it is appropriate to say this. Obtaining a beautiful flower, refreshing trees below which you can romp and play there is no similar joy. When you have this thought, Avici's 84,000 various maleficent sword forest is

> transmuted into jeweled trees, with rows of abundant flowers and fruit present in front. The great burning fire's flames are transmuted into lotus flowers below the trees. Vile people look! It is that vow by which I obtain this fruit.[42]

Huaigan (懷感 7th–8th c.) was a disciple of Shandao after first studying the Yogācāra teachings. He is claimed to have achieved the *Buddha anusmṛti samādhi* which in this line of development is connected with the *Buddha Amitābha Meditation Sutra* (*Guan wu liang shou fo jing* 觀無量壽佛經).[43] Shandao was a major force in Pure Land thought, and his disciple also contributed by composing an important text entitled: *Treaties Elucidating a Multitude of Doubts Regarding the Pure Land* (*Shi jing tu qun yi lun* 釋淨土群疑論).[44] In that work, he connects "play" with spiritual powers. The treaties reads:

> I say again, the Mahayana Dharma bliss, continues without decline, is transferred. Without limit the course of the vow, moment by moment, increasingly advances. Quickly proving impearled correct kind of Bodhi. Again the people who wish to be reborn and renounce this foulness and sorrow for the joy of seeking nirvana, the initial bliss of departing in the western direction is the course of the Bodhisattva's practice. This already has the joy of the intention of renouncing. Furthermore, it is the place of birth without reversal. How must it be when sorrows entangle the

> body then the arising thought of cessation? Again it is the bliss of seeking nirvana, not only renouncing sorrows. Perhaps you hear about all the Buddha's inconceivable merits, or hear about the six pāramitās, the Dao, or the classes of dharmas. Perhaps you view all great bodhisattvas romping and playing in spiritual powers. Perhaps the smelling of excellent scents or the tasting of delicious foods, all of which can advance the Dao and hasten seeking nirvana. For these reasons one turns his back on birth and death and is inclined toward cessation. It is not merely a path and one cannot just say "without sorrow" and then is able to renounce. The consequences would probably not be the joy of seeking nirvana.[45]

Both Shandao and his disciple Huaigan use the same combined term, "romp and play" (*youxi* 遊戲). This Chinese term is another translation of the Sanskrit *krīḍ* and its derivatives. But the context is very different between the two Chinese authors. From reading Shandao's passage, one get the impression that the people in the Pure Land are relaxing and enjoying themselves in the shade of the jeweled trees. This is rather like what one would envision the manner in which the nobility enjoyed themselves in their pleasure gardens in India. This however, is not out of place here. As mentioned the ideal found in the Pure Land sutras in terms of the physical description is a combination of Indian ideas of what the god's home Mt. Meru is like combined with the real world of pleasure gardens connected with the ostentatious palaces that dotted the Indian landscape. Those gardens were specifically constructed to mitigate the unyielding heat of the Indian summer. Thus, the canopy of trees overhead, artificial lotus ponds, and various decorations to catch one's eye were common elements. It seems inconceivable that Shandao would be unaware of the connection between "play" and spiritual powers given he was versed in several sutras and composed commentaries. Thus, here we can venture that it is the narrative of the passage that is driving the exclusion in mentioning it.

Huaigan on the other hand specifically connects "romping and playing" with the spiritual power in his discussion of motivation to seek awakening and a means to it. He lists a number of items that draw people to seek and in particular to seek the way of the Pure Land. His list of things that draw people to seek includes both negative motivational factors as well as the positive ones. Thus, leaving behind sorrow is coupled with the Amitābha Buddha's merit, the six pāramitās, the Dao, and more. It is in this context that he speaks of the bodhisattvas romping and playing in spiritual powers.

Chan

Anyone conversant with the wealth of "biographical" stories of the Chan masters knows that a great many masters were very playful. Pang Jushi better known as Layman Pang (龐居士 740–808) repeatedly exemplified this playful nature. For example,

> One day the Layman asked the Chan master Ma-tsu (Mazu Daoyi 馬祖道 709–788), "A

> man of unobscured original nature asks you please to look up." Ma-tsu looked straight down. The Layman said: "You alone play marvelously on the stringless ch'in." Ma-tsu looked straight up. The Layman bowed low. Ma-tsu returned to his quarters. "Just now bungled it trying to be smart," then said the Layman.[46]

One would therefore assume that *xi* would appear throughout the tradition in various contexts. However, this is not the case. Bodhidharma's *Two Ingresses and Four Courses*, Huike's reply letter, *Confidence in Mind Inscription* allegedly by Jianzhi Sengcan (鑑智僧璨), and the other Patriarchs works seem to not use this term.

Further, the *Xu gao seng zhuan* or *Continued Biographies of Eminent Monks* (mid-7th c.) by Daoxuan,[47] *Chuan fa bao ji* or the *Annals of the Transmission of the Dharma Jewel* (early 8th c.) by Du Fei,[48] the *Leng qie shi zi ji* or *Records of the Masters and Disciples of the Laṅkā(vatāra Sūtra)* (early 8th c.) by Jingjue,[49] do not seem to use *xi* in their lengthy compilations. Yet, these very texts contain extensive materials from the early and formative periods of the Chan tradition.

One eighth century exception to the above is the *Li dai fa bao ji* or *Record of the Dharma Jewel Through the Generations* (late 8th c.) wherein *xi* appears in several passages. In an account of the Venerable Hongren the text states that "(when) all the trainees were frivolously playing, he remained silent without joining."[50] Further for example, in the account of Master Zhishen in retelling about the behavior of the unusual childhood it states, "(he) did not engage in youthful play."[51] One final example, in a section recounting the discussion between some Daoists priests and Master Wuzhu, they were discussing the differences between Laozi's and Zhuangzi's teachings and the Buddha's Dharma. Wuzhu states, "(The Buddha) is not like this, he taught that both causation and spontaneousness are called play discussions."[52]

Historically next is the famed *Platform Sutra of the Sixth Patriarch.* This text has an informative passage which reads,

> The person who has seen his/her nature, whether he/she establishes something and obtains it or not, he/she comes and goes freely, without obstacles or restraints. He/she acts according to necessity and replies according to others' discussions. Always manifesting his/her physical form, without separating from his/her self-nature. Immediately obtaining mastery of super natural powers and romping and playing in *samādhi*. This is called seeing one's nature. Zhicheng again asked the master, "How is this not establishing meaning?" The master replied, "The self-nature is not false, not foolishness nor confusion. Thought after thought wisdom illuminates. Continually leaving behind dharmas' characteristics. Although sideways it is entirely obtained. With what can anything be established? Self-nature is self-awakened, sudden awakening is sudden cultivation and without gradualness. All dharmas are tranquil and extinct. With what is their gradation?"

> Zhicheng offered reverence saying, "I promise to attend and serve you morning and night with no remiss."[53]

The use of the term "romp and play" is not found in the Dunhuang version of this text but only in the above classical edition.

Further, the use of the term *xi* increases as we progress historically through the literature. For example we find the use of *xi* in the twelfth century *Blue Cliff Records* (*Bi yan lu* 碧巖錄) in a number of passages.[54] The exact significance of this development is not known at this time.

Conclusion

We have seen that it is well recognized that the buddhas are liberated from samsara by means of their play (*krīḍ*). For the buddhas, pratyekabuddhas and arhats, this play consists of the four means of reaching the goal (*paṭipadā*: *i.e.*, unyielding, yielding, self-control, equanimity), the four applications of mindfulness (*satipaṭṭhāna*: mindfulness of body, mind, sensations, phenomena), the four meditational states (*jhāna*), the four stages (*vihāra*), the four appropriated exertions (*sammappadhāna*: non-generation of and abandoning of unwholesomeness, generating and maintaining wholesomeness), the four marvelous signs (*acchariyā abbhutā dhammā*), the four resolutions (*adhiṭṭhāna*: to gain insight, gain truth, abandon unwholesomeness, to master oneself), the four ways of cultivating concentration (*samādhibhāvanā*: based on impulses, mind, effort, examination), the four dharmas that deal with happiness (*sukhabhāgiya*: restraint of faculties, abstinence, meritorious dharmas, cultivating factors of wisdom) and the four measureless (*appamāṇa*: compassion, sympathetic joy, equanimity, loving-kindness).

Here then we must understand that it is not in the make-believe fantasy fun of one's youth that is being referred to by the above quotation but the attitude that the buddhas have towards various aspects of cultivation. It is not the case that either the Sanskrit or the Pali traditions do not recognize different ways of playing or types of play and therefore lacked terms to express these differences, but that the textual tradition is making a clear distinction between how a buddha engenders these aspects and how the unawakened might mistakenly engender the same aspects.

The Sanskrit *krīḍ* and its derivatives has its Pali equivalents and derivatives. These various references to "play" are sufficiently abundant in the Buddhist literature for us to gain a clear idea of what was intended by the term. Further, different types of playing are noted in this literature differentiating between games, theatrical plays, lulling and so on have been pointed out.

After, this chapter investigated the notion of "play" as explained in modern psychological literature. It has noted that neurological aspects and the role that "play" has in distinguishing behaviors between mammals and reptiles. We have found that "play" is proactive, adventurous and inquisitive and allows for different cultural expressions. Of particular note, "play" being self-fulfilling increases our desire to engage in particular activities simply for its own sake. It is pleasurable, absorbing and improves self-regulation. As such it can be the foundation of choice, significant in mastering higher cognitive processes and has both connections with morality and social-psychological modeling. The festive element fosters the good and yet, disjoins the given order. "Play's" characteristics include freedom, spontaneity, active engagement, transformation. Imaginatively relaxing into the embellishing and fluidity of no-self. In general, it indicates that the means are more important than the ends or as Pellegrini and Bjorklund termed it "play" is unpurposed.

From these findings we can link a buddha's activity in spiritual discipline with the enjoyment of life that comes about through play. A buddha is proactive in his pursuit of spirituality stemming from being inquisitive. He finds these activities as enjoyable, because they are spontaneous, and transforming. They further develop his cognitive powers, his morality and they are absorbing. So, "play" is not only found in the Pali canonical and post-canonical literature as seen in the quotations provided, but continues to be used in the Mahayana texts as well. I have pointed out uses in the *Lotus Sutra*, *Sukhāvatīvyūha Sūtra* and *Aṣṭasāhasrikā* as examples by providing a translation for each from the original Sanskrit.

Next our attention turned to the Chinese texts. This section began looking at the notion of "play" in Chinese by first viewing the many different ways that the Sanskrit *krīḍ* and its derivatives were translated. In particular, I continued by focusing on the Chinese *xi* as perhaps the most important of the Chinese terms being used both alone and in combinations with other words providing a more nuanced understanding. This was followed by looking at the use of "play" in pre-Buddhist literature in China. The *Analects* and the *Zhuangzi* were both cited as examples of early uses.

Beginning with an investigation into Vasubandhu's *Sukhāvatīvyūhopadeśa* and its sub-commentary the *Wu liang shou jing you po ti she yuan sheng jie zhu* by Tanluan. The Indian master Vasubandhu identifies five Causative Entrances associated with the Pure Land. The last of these is the Garden-grove Playground. This level is characterized by teaching others. This teaching is termed "bodhisattva play" in the text. This is further explained as the bodhisattva's spontaneous ferrying beings to nirvana.

The next Pure Land master's work investigated for this chapter was Shandao's *Zhuan jing xing dao yuan wang sheng jing tu fashi zan* wherein the author uses "romp and play" a term frequently seen. This was followed by viewing Huaigan's *Treaties Elucidating a Multitude of Doubts Regarding the Pure Land* (*Shi jing tu qun yi lun*). In this text the author makes a clear connection between "play" and spiritual powers of bodhisattvas in the Pure Land. It was noted that although Shandao and his student Huaigan both used the term "romp and play" Shandao merely indicated the more mundane idea of someone having fun in the cool shade of the trees. Huaigan uses the term as a possible positive motivational factor for seeking the Pure Land in contrast with listed negative motivational factors.

Early Chan texts being primarily practical (instruction manual and confirmation letter *etc.*) do not use the word "play." As too with a number of compilations presenting materials on the early masters and their teachings. Although the *Li dai fa bao ji* (8th c.) does use the term *xi*. One can also find it used in the famed *Platform Sutra of the Sixth Patriarch*. Of particular note is the phrased "romp and play" also appears herein and thus this is not a peculiar expression limited to the Pure Land texts. The information on the use of *xi* or "play" in Chan literature ended with a note on its increasing usage in later texts.

Here we must be sensitive to the difficulties that the Chinese faced in trying to understand the India contextual setting behind even the most basic of Buddhist terms. As noted elsewhere, few Chinese working on importing Buddhism in ancient times actually worked with or encountered an Indian master. So probing questions on the unexplained cultural background to the Buddhist concepts could only be gleaned from the literature in many cases. In the West too, at the introduction of the term "Buddha" people often were confused into thinking that it was some sort of god or Christ-like figure.

The Chinese world that Buddhism was introduced into well knew about the different categories of beings. Gods already populated the Chinese thoughts of heaven and monsters occasionally harassed and brought devastation to the people. Fairies (仙女 *xiannu*), ghosts, and sages (聖 *sheng*) assumed different roles in many a Chinese tale. So, the Indian gods such as Indra, mentioned in the sutras could easily be understood. The apsaras and gandharvas are not too far from the fairies. The Confucian sages with their unassailable deportment and the Daoist immortals (仙 *xian*) with their mystic powers and highly idiosyncratic personalities acted as models in understanding the arhats and great masters. However, a buddha was a new and altogether different category of being.

The august nature of a buddha may well have been understood conceptually by comparisons with Confucius or Confucian sages. Although that seems to have been one of the inspirations, the barefoot begging vagabond portrayed in many a sutra and the vinaya prevented too close of a comparison. The magical powers of a buddha may well have allowed comparisons with the immortals, but his more down-to-earth personality was not portrayed as highly idiosyncratic. Even the standard Chinese character for "buddha" was newly minted but other attempts were made. 浮陀 (*futuo*)[55] "to float, drift, exceed" and "steep bank, rough terrain"; 浮圖 (*futu*)[56] "to float, drift, exceed" and "diagram, chart, map"; and others but eventually the Chinese settled on 佛陀 (*fotuo*). The first character consists of the radical for person, man on the left and the phoneme on the right providing the sound quality but in its own right meaning, not or negative. The first two examples listed just above, were not attempts to translate the word "buddha" but merely attempts at transliteration of the Sanskrit. *Fotuo* the last example, which now has been shortened to the first character *fo*, was also an attempt to transliterate. Yet the question as to why the early translators felt they needed to create a new character for this concept remains unanswered. Some have attempted to ascribe a particular meaning based on the elements of the character *fo,* but these arguments are unconvincing. The fact that there were several attempts made to transliterate the Sanskrit but a new character was created suggests that the Chinese were struggling with this all important word.

A similar struggle may be postulated with the attempts to understand the Sanskrit *krīḍ.* The various translations were attempts to better capture the nuance of the word particularly in the context of a buddha's mastery in gaining liberation. How is one to understand that the profound insight, mastery of advanced meditational states, and the slipping of the bonds of samsara along with the august presence, could be "play" for the humble barefoot vagabond? These attempts at translation demonstrate Sinicization, documenting the process of negotiating the differences in the contextual fields between the two languages. The employment of *xi* and in particular *youxi* as a means of approximating an accurate translation and the further use of this two character term within the understanding of heightened spiritual abilities incorporates much of the Indian understanding and develop the subtleties behind the concept.

Chapter Five

A Comparison of Ritual Creation and Use of Chan and Pure Land Art in China[1]

Introduction

Gregory Schopen, working in the field of Buddhist Studies,[2] and John E. Cort, working in the arts,[3] have both illuminated the shortcomings of the approach where one accepts the Protestant assumption of locating religion in texts. Indubitably, the field of Buddhist Studies would be very different if more attention were paid to the significant amount of knowledge which could be garnered from culturally based studies in such areas as art, archaeology and anthropology to mention but a few.

I hope to present in this chapter an analysis of two different types of Chinese Buddhist art forms, both in terms of the ritual production and the ritual viewing as an exploration into culturally significant points that are relevant in understanding the traditions that produced the artworks under investigation. Following preliminary remarks I will begin by presenting the Indian Buddhist stance as a foundation for viewing the differences and similarities in the Chan and Pure Land forms of art. For the latter I will be utilizing methodological considerations presented by John Elsner's explanation of Paursanius' "Description of Greece" where he discusses ritual in viewing non-Christian art.[4] Elsner states, "… the ritual appreciation of an image may be seen as a kind of alternative (not necessarily an exclusive one) to what we would regard as a more straightforwardly art-historical response."[5] According to this usage, authenticity is determined by ritual and magic in relation to the image. This will be connected with the developments in Pure Land art. For the former, I will be analyzing Chan art from the point of view of the major philosophical position that drove the advancement of this tradition. The difference in approach to these two art forms is due to the very differences in the schools themselves. While Pure Land Buddhism, in the sub-tradition under investigation, expounds a simple doctrine based on preparations for one's future birth, Chan focuses on a direct and immediate encounter with the awakened state.

Additionally, I will also be discussing both the ritual production of art in both cases, as well as the ritual viewing of art in both traditions. This ought to provide solid information on the ritual use of art within the context of Chinese society demonstrating sinicization of Buddhism in the process.

Darśanic Buddhism

Scholars interested in Indian spirituality are usually impressed with the universal and sophisticated imagery found through the millenniums. Rich imagery played an important role in the Vedic tradition and all that followed it. The gods' power was focused in the images, verses dedicated to the gods (*e.g.*, the *Rig Veda*) and in those who were able to see the gods in all their awesome glory. These seers of the gods became the objects of devotion and their mystic powers are legendary.[6]

The *ṛṣi* (seers) in the period before and during the composition of the Upaniṣads were not only the paragons of spirituality and were granted their position by their practice of austerities and the consumption of *soma*[7] which allowed them to see the gods. However, this "seeing" was not understood as a hallucination brought on by the psychedelic effects of the drink. "Seeing" was a means of gaining power much as we find in Shamanism. Seeing the gods allowed the seer to enter the world or realm of the gods and the sub-cult of a particular one like Indra. Thus, "seeing" is far more than a visual observance, it comes to be a "viewing" accompanied with the spiritual power that "view" can bring about. This viewing is not limited to those who are spiritually gifted for it is granted to all who approach with the intention to see. Whether the object approached is a symbol of the god, a statue wherein the god's power may be focused or channelled, the visualization and more, the power comes through and allows the mere mortal to touch the sacred. As noted by Diana Eck:

> The central act of Hindu worship, from the point of view of the lay person, is to stand in the presence of the deity and to behold the image with one's own eyes, to see and be seen by the deity … Since, in the Hindu understanding, the deity is present in the image, the visual apprehension of the image is charged with religious meaning. Beholding the image is an act of worship, and through the eyes one gains the blessings of the divine.[8]

Darśana (behold or view) in Buddhism is well attested

to in the Pali canon. The *Mahāparinibbāna Sutta* story of Mahākassapa activities around the *parinirvāṇa* of Śākyamuni is understandable from the position of *darśana* and without it one is hard pressed to explain some of the major elements of the story. In short, The Buddha Śākyamuni passes away while Mahākassapa is traveling and those present cannot light the funeral pyre because the gods prevent it; Mahākassapa appears in person and unwraps the feet of the Buddha and pays respect,[9] and finally, the pyre spontaneously combusts. Further this story is connected with the teachings on the stupa given in the same text.[10] It is taught that the stupa will grant spiritual advancement to those who "see" it because of the nirvanic power emanating from Śākyamuni's physical remains housed therein. Both of these examples show the darśanic complex of ideas at work in this sutra. Buddha *darśana* is a spiritually based nirvanic power. With Mahākassapa being considered the most important arhat in the period immediately following the *parinirvāṇa*[11] and the fact that one of his activities was buddha *darśana*, then *darśana* in Buddhism is to be considered a core activity.

The story of Vakkali also demonstrates that *darśana* was an important element in early Buddhism. Vakkali was an arhat of Brahman origin from Śrāvastī. He sees the Buddha Śākyamuni and becomes overwhelmed by the awe from his form. He attempts to stay continuously in the presence of Śākyamuni to bask in that awe. Following a retreat, he is sent away from the Buddha's presence. The Buddha was acting out of compassion and had explained to Vakkali that seeing the Dharma was seeing the buddha and seeing the buddha was seeing the Dharma. Feeling dejected Vakkali traveled to Vulture Peak. Śākyamuni, fearing that Vakkali would commit suicide by throwing himself off the mountain, appeared to him in a blinding light. Receiving the Lord's *darśana*,

Vakkali is awestruck and gains arhathood.[12] This story provides us with two important points. First, most students of Buddhism probably have encountered the teachings that seeing the Dharma is seeing the buddha meaning that if one understands and applies himself or herself to the teachings one can gain awakening. Second, the other part of this couplet points the practitioner in a very different direction. If one can see the buddha, one will understand the Dharma.

A further example of *darśana* in the pre-Asokan period is also found in the *Sutta Nipāta's* "Pārāyanavagga" chapter.[13] An example of a post Aśokan account of *darśana* is found in the story of Upagupta tricking the god Māra (who actually met Śākyamuni) into assuming the Buddha's form so he could have *darśana*.[14] From these accounts we can determine that the *darśana* complex of ideas in Buddhism consists of *śraddhā*, the use of laudatory verses, and vision. Also these accounts leave clear that one can gain awakening through this approach. There are accounts of *darśana* taking place not just with Śākyamuni but with some of the arhats and Maitreya in non-Mahayana forms of Buddhism. Further, one finds in the early Mahayana texts like the *Lotus Sutra, the Pratyutpanna*, *Avataṃsaka*, *Aṣṭasāharikā*, *Sukhāvatīvyūha Sūtra*[15] and others significant examples of the *darśana* complex of ideas. Thus, *darśana* was an important element in Mahayana Buddhism from its formative period onward.

One important point stemming from this material is that the "viewing" of the physical body (*rūpakāya*) of a buddha or others was not necessary. For example *darśana* was possible for Vakkali by seeing the projected image of Śākyamuni. Seeing a *stūpa* or a visualized image of a bodhisattva like Maitreya also has the ability to grant *darśana*; that is entering into the nirvanic power. Since in India, it is commonly thought that a plastic or painted image can act as a focal point for the god's power, it is likely that Buddhist art also functioned in this respect. Thus seeing the image of the buddha allowed one to enter into the nirvanic power within the *darśana* complex making worship all the more efficacious and spiritually uplifting. Anyone with some sensitivity can certainly feel the calming effects that transpire when viewing a statue of Śākyamuni meditating. Thus, we have not lost our abilities to enter, however slightly, into that nirvanic power.

Chinese Buddhist Art

The early legends of the origin of Buddhism in China mention the significance that art played in the transmission of this spirituality to the Middle Kingdom. For example, in 120 BCE, the Han general Huo Qubing (霍去病) found that the defeated Hsiung-nu (Xiongnu 匈奴) worshiped a golden human statue with incense and bowed to it but made no sacrifice. It was claimed that these were buddha statues. Another story informs us that Emperor Ming sent out an envoy after dreaming of a golden man. Upon their return they brought with them Buddhist masters, books, and images which were set up in the first monastery named "White Horse" in the capital city.[16] The historical accuracy of these stories cannot be verified, but the recounting of the legends clearly indicates that art played an important role in the early days of the spread of the Dharma into Chinese society.

Buddhist art in China, like its literature and philosophy, would eventually become a mixture of Indian and Chinese elements when viewed in its entirety. For example, in viewing Chinese images, the elongated ear lobes on the Buddha Amitābha are of Indian origin, the high cheek bones, eyes and mouth of the Buddha's face are clearly Chinese. In order for Buddhist art to be effective it had to speak in the language of the native traditions of art in addition to introducing new forms and motifs.

In the area of rituals there are a wide variety of activities associated with Chinese Buddhist art. For example, scenes of grand possessions of imperial patrons to places of worship are immortalized in both stone[17] and cave paintings at Dunhuang.[18] Entire arrays of buddhas and bodhisattvas statues housed in temples were found scattered across the country such as at Foguang si (Fo-kuang Ssu 佛光寺)[19] where offerings were made. Pilgrimages were made to places like Wutai Shan[20] and Putuo Shan (普陀山)[21] where visiting the richly decorated temples was the main focus. One last example would be the use of Buddhist art in death rituals.[22] All of these testify to the continuous association of Buddhist art and ritual in Chinese society.

Pure Land Art

One of the major lines of Pure Land tradition runs through the masters Tanluan[23] Daochuo and Shandao as mentioned above.[24] Within this tradition one finds the use of art for both pedagogic and inspirational roles.[25] Paintings of the Pure Land were popular in Shandao's home district.[26] The luminary Shandao was inspired to pursue the Pure Land path by a painting he saw. He was also famous for making over one hundred Pure Land paintings. One of his main contributions to Pure Land doctrine was that the *samādhi* leading to a vision of the Pure Land was not necessary for rebirth in Amitābha's Pure Land, the goal within this tradition. The *samādhi* being necessary had been the earlier traditionally accepted position. The Pure Land follower only needs to recite the name of the Buddha Amitābha to achieve the state of being assured of rebirth in the Pure Land, according to Shandao.[27] Thus, in this ideology, paintings were teaching tools used to illustrate what the Pure Land was like and art objects used in worship aimed to inspire individuals similar to the manner Shandao received inspiration. This is in stark contrast to the use of paintings as meditative props in China by other Pure Land systems not associated with Shandao and in the Vajrayāna tradition of both China and Tibet.

Shandao's paintings were used in a distinctively ritual way. As inspirational art for followers to gain a longing to be reborn in Amitābha's Pure Land and in this connection, the setting of offerings (incense, lamps, food, water, flowers, *etc.*) in front of such paintings. However, since the *samādhi* was not needed for the goal, then a visionary experience associated with the art was not needed. We find a description of a very different type of ritual use of Pure Land art from the Song dynastic period originating in a different tradition of Chinese Pure Land thought. The Tiantai Pure Land tradition master Ciyun Zunshi (慈雲遵式 964–1032) claimed that the chanting of the name of Amitābha would grant one protection with the aid of the guardian gods and bodhisattvas; the suffering of afflictions caused by ghosts, demons, *et cetera* would not occur; Amitābha would eliminate the devotees' transgressions and give followers dreams of him and his land as well as other benefits.[28] We also learn that inspired by Zunshi, people would gather in front of the image of Amitābha performing rituals and hoped for visions of him in addition to this and other worldly benefits.[29] Such visionary and dream granting, in association with the darśanic tradition in general, is to be considered a regular feature as attested to in such sutras as *Pratyutpanna*, *Saptaśatikā* as well as countless accounts of masters as preserved in Tibetan Buddhist literature.

We can understand this feature of the Tiantai Pure Land tradition with reference to Elsner's position on the power of the ancient Greek art within the ritual context mentioned at the outset of this chapter. Here the art historic and aesthetic qualities of a form depicting Amitābha were not the main concern just as they were not the main concern in Greece. Like in ancient Greece, it is the spiritual effect generated within the ritual context that concerns us in this use of Buddhist art. The most reasonable explanation of this ritual use within the Tiantai tradition is that they were following the darśanic complex's *modus operandi*. This would have been in keeping with similar occurrences of *darśana* in the Amitābha cult found in Indic material, as well as in Tibetan traditions. One can also see how Shandao's use of Pure Land art for inspiration and merit-making worship radically departed from the Indic model and from other Chinese traditions of the Pure Land.

Although Shandao held that accomplishing of the deep contemplation by means of the method of visualizing the Pure Land was unnecessary, he did not completely neglect the meditative tradition associated with the Pure Land as later followers of his line would. For Shandao, the most important sutra for the meditational tradition associated with Amitābha was the *Fo shuo guan wu liang shou jing* (佛說觀

無量壽經).[30] Shandao wrote a commentary on this sutra discussing various aspects, including the entrance to the Pure Land by reciting the name (*nianfo* 念佛) and the entrance by visualization.[31] A careful reading of the sutra clearly shows that although the text provides a general description of the particulars in the Pure Land, there is much left to be desired if one wished to use it as a meditational guide. Even Shandao's commentary does not provide sufficient details in many cases. This is precisely where a painting of the Pure Land could be most useful. It can depict what the gods mentioned look like, what type of lotus flowers are present and so much more.

There is an Indic text with a commentary in the Pure Land sub-tradition of Shandao that helps us in understanding the ritual involved. Shandao's predecessor, as noted above, was Tanluan, who wrote a commentary to Vasubandhu's *Vow for Birth: A Commentary on the Amitāyus Sūtra* (*Sukhāvatī-vyūhopadeśa*).[32] In that text, Vasubandhu mentions both calm abiding (*śamatha*) and insight (*vipaśyanā*) meditation: the two main ritual forms of meditation in Buddhism. Tanluan explains the first as "stopping," which is of three kinds: 1) single mindedly focusing on Amitābha's land and name stops all (general) negativity; 2) the peace and bliss of the land stops negativity of one's body, speech and mind; and 3) Amitābha's awakening stops one pursuing lower Buddhist paths. Thus, by visualization meditation one enters calm abiding. He further explains that insight meditation is of two kinds: 1) contemplating the Pure Land's "suchness"[33] adornments leads to insight and 2) seeing the Buddha in a future Pure Land rebirth, one realizes the pure mind of insight.[34] If we are considering a visualization meditation, then, the adornments are visualized and thus not real. This being the case, suchness would be suchness of the imagined. It therefore seems logical that the insight meditation level is primarily understood as taking place in the future Pure Land rebirth.

The visualization system in Shandao's thought was more likely understood by him as incorporating both the calm abiding and insight meditations as explained by Vasubandhu and commented on by Tanluan. The combined calm abiding and insight meditation is fairly standard in Buddhist meditational ritual. The distinction between the Pure Land style of visualization in relationship to paintings and Chan use of paintings is not found in the division between calm abiding and insight meditation. It is to be found in the tripartite division of the bodies of the buddha as will be seen below.

The three part division of the bodies of the buddha into *Dharmakāya*, *Saṃbhogakāya* and *Nirmāṇakāya* was propagated by Yogācāra texts like the *Mahāyānasūtrālaṁkāra* and *Mahāyānasaṃgraha.* The first being the ultimate level of understanding, it also represents the buddha's mind in its completeness. The *Saṃbhogakāya* or "reward body" is a form body that appears to bodhisattvas on advanced stages of their careers but is not gross like a physical body. The *Nirmāṇakāya* is the physical form of a Buddha, for example, the historic Buddha while still on Earth.

There were considerable debates as to the nature of Amitābha and his Pure Land with regard to the three body theory. For Shandao *Sukhāvatīvyūha* the Pure land of Amitābha was a *Saṃbhogakāya* manifestation.[35] His interpretation makes sense because 1) since the focus in meditational ritual is on a vision—it must have a form and therefore it cannot be the *Dharmakāya* as that is formless and because 2) Amitābha and his land are not gross physical forms, then it must be a *Saṃbhogakāya* manifestation. Further, because 3) one does not realize the mind of the buddha (*i.e.*, the *Dharmakāya*) until rebirth in the future again, the visualization must be on the *Saṃbhogakāya* level. This understanding is also supported by the fact that Shandao strongly believed, as did his teacher, that this world was too corrupt and thus people's capacity to achieve nirvana (*i.e.*, the *Dharmakāya*) while still in this body is highly limited (see Chapt. 7). This teaching is collected under the doctrine of the Dharma Ending Age—*mofa* (末法). Finally, this concept was one of the major factors in the development of Shandao's tradition away from the visualization meditation to simply reciting the name of the Buddha Amitābha.

Chan Art

Turning now to the ritual use of art in the Chan school we find a very different situation. Chan arts began in China in the Tang dynasty, as noted by Shin'ichi Hisamatsu.[36] Chan painted arts include portraits, landscapes, still-lifes, abstracts, calligraphy and more. There are ritual uses of these forms[37] and a comprehensive coverage of all would take us beyond the confines of this chapter. Although we can clearly distinguish both a pedagogic use in works such as the famous Ox Herding pictures and works aimed at evoking a gestalt-like experience. My remarks will be inclined to the ritual aspect of a limited array with the focus on the experiential aspects of Chan art.

Hugo Musterberg, in speaking of Zen art, stated,

> The works of these artists represent a distinct break from traditional religious painting.

> While the older sects produced religious icons painted in a meticulous academic style and using conventional subjects such as buddhas, bodhisattvas, paradise scenes, and mandalas, the Chan painters used a different style with subjects that reflected Chan teaching.[38]

Further, Winston Fuller notes, "Zen style, it is said, reflects Zen perception."[39] Although the subjects of Chan paintings are often Śākyamuni Buddha, arhats and patriarchs, they have a distinct down to earth feeling to them as contrasted by other schools of Buddhist art. Chan style landscapes differ from the background landscapes found in Pure Land pictures. The mountains, trees and rivers, indicate a ruggedness or raw nature with limited or no human contrivance or fantasy marring them. Animals such as monkeys, birds, or water buffalo and vegetation or fruit have a simple straight forwardness that makes them stand out like an interesting rock.[40]

Francois Cheng, in discussing Chan landscape paintings distinguishes five categories used in analysis: brush-ink, yin-yang, mountain-water, man-heaven, and what he termed the fifth dimension which is the only non-binary level.[41] This fifth dimension is explained as beyond time and space hence, it represents emptiness (*śūnyatā*) and transcending the constructed universe that "carries it towards the original unity."[42] Because of this concept of original unity, Hisamatsu distinguishes seven characteristics in Zen art. These are: no rule (*i.e.*, fixed or perfect forms), no complexity, no rank, no mind (naturalness), no bottom (subtlety), no hindrance (from attachment), and no stirring (tranquility).[43] Ven. Hiu Wan a famous twentieth century painter explains Chan art and the original unity called "Dao" (Way) in paintings. She states:

> All this (various references on the connection between art and meditation) goes to show that art is in conformity with the Way and the Way is in harmony with art, which brings forth from life the flower of wisdom.[44]

There is a strong connection between the creation of Chan art, which incorporates the Dao, and Buddhist ideas of emptiness (*śūnyatā/ kong* 空). This is not accidental; it was a refinement of creative notions in the Tang dynasty models. As Peter Bol notes:

> Because early-eleventh-century *shih* defined their shared values in terms of *wen*, attempts to redefine literati values easily took the form of redefining the nature of "good" *wen*. "Ancient style" writing, inspired by T'ang models, became the vehicle for this movement. Advocates of the new style claimed that *wen* would be good if the composer sought guidance from the Way of antiquity, which had guided the sages in establishing the culture, tradition and civilization.[45]

In other words, the Way (Dao) as understood and expressed by the ancients was the measure of what was "good" by the elites in society. These Tang models arose first in the literary fields by masters like: Bai Juyi (白居易 772–846), Liu Yuxi (劉禹錫 772–842), Han Yu (韓愈 768–824), and

Liu Zongyuan (柳宗元 773–819) all of whom were instrumental in literary movements (*e.g.*, *Guwen* 古文 *etc.*) attempting to reunite spiritual, moral, and philosophical values to literary production.[46]

As noted by William Nienhouser in discussing ideas presented by Georges Margoulies in *Anthologie raisonnee de la literature chinoise*:

> ... definition stipulates that a *ku-wen* piece must have (1) a complete and unique independence and sense, (2) an absolute unity of action with little or no superfluous detail, and (3) the presence of a philosophical or moral idea.[47]

However, the understanding of this genre in the 1920s, when Margoulies was writing, can be glossed to help us in seeing the connections with painting. His second point can be understood within the notion of "spontaneousness," which should be seen as meaning free from contrivance and connected with the ideas of *wuwei* (see below). Point three should be expanded to include spiritual values as well because both philosophy and moral thought are intimately connected with Chinese notions of spirituality.

Guwen and similar movements were also emphasized in the Song and later dynasties among certain circles. As noted by Joseph Parker,[48] the Song saw an upsurge in interest in these movements and the foundational ideas of achieving the Way as accomplished by great sages of the past. Their method of achievement was by means of cultivating spiritual growth through poetry, histories, and philosophical works. However, by this time because of the Chan influence, more direct approaches such as seated meditation (*zuochan* 坐禪) and eventually *gong'an* contemplation were also utilized by some. As noted by Parker:

> The most important criterion for judging the value of literary expression for members of the Ancient Civilization movement (*ku-wen*) was not the mastery of a particular style or the ability to make appropriate allusions, but the degree to which it expresses the Way (Tao) of the ancients.[49]

In the Northern Song, Su Shi (蘇軾 1037–1101), Huang Tingjian (黃庭堅 1045–1105), and others played a significant role in advancing the acceptability of painting inscriptions which tended to be poetry. This along with their other writings, re-valued painting by arguing that they are similar to poems (the traditionally held highest form of literary arts). This, in turn, elevated the status of painting from craft-work to art. Because of the general importance of the spiritual, moral, and philosophical value of literary productions, these values were also seen as being communicated in the painted arts. Arguments were presented on the appropriateness of the painted arts in Buddhism by people like Tung Yu (Dong You 董逌 cir. 12th c.).[50] The connection between "insight" and the creation of paintings is repeatedly spoken about in the Song and later periods. For example, in the writing of Wang Qinchen (Wang Ch'in-chen 王欽臣 11th c.) and Mi Youren (Mi Yu-jen 米友仁 1072–1151) we find such tracts.[51]

Chan art has the double function of being both an expression of the insight of its creator and a method of visually imparting that insight for the viewer. Those forms that are not pedagogic convey something about the awakening and insight it produces. Just as the meditation on a *gong'an* or the master "beating one with a stick" may open the door to Chan awakening, the painting acts as a trigger. To understand this better, we need to delve into the ritual of Chan meditation and what constitutes Chan awakening.

Like other forms of Buddhism, Chan upholds both calm abiding and insight forms of meditation in its tradition. Counting the breaths and "just sitting" are both popular forms of activities that exemplify these two forms of meditation respectively. However, what is the insight gained? This insight is into the experience of "empty of inherent existence or own-being" that is explained in the prajñāpāramitā sutras, which is a genre of literature that forms part of the foundation of the Chan tradition. This quality of being "empty of inherent existence" is termed *śūnyatā.* The realization that forms, sights, sounds, *et cetera* are empty is only the first step one needs to go further making a jump into the "emptiness of emptiness." This "emptiness of emptiness" is the ultimate truth, the *Dharmakāya*—nirvana itself. The distinction between emptiness and the ultimate truth (*i.e.*, emptiness of emptiness) is important for understanding the use of Chan paintings from the viewer's perspective. After all, one of the rules of painting is, "... a third fullness, two-thirds emptiness," as noted by Cheng.[52]

The surface to be painted begins with emptiness and from that the artist spontaneously brings out form based on his or her insight. This process is the manifestation of the fundamental Mahayana principle so eloquently given in the *Heart Sutra*: "Emptiness is form." The artist does not fill the surface with forms but leaves substantial amounts empty. Thus the painting is not a depiction of form but a depiction of both form and emptiness. The viewer, if he or she knows how to view, enters into a ritual relationship with the painting as the prompt for awakening. Just like the *gong'an* moves the practitioner outside the words of the expression, the painting moves the viewer to an insight outside the frame. Because the painting has form and emptiness (thus containing the other leaf of the couplet of the quotation from the *Heart Sutra*: "form is emptiness"), the viewer first captured by the form comes to appreciate the emptiness within the frame. Since both form and emptiness are manifest in the painting, the spiritual observer moves to an emptiness outside of the frame.

Just as with a poem which points outside itself, the Chan painting moves one outside the frame to the other realm—the realm of "emptiness of emptiness." That realm cannot be truly depicted but it is the core of the Mahayana message, as noted by Conze.[53] This experience of moving from the realm of emptiness and form to "emptiness of emptiness" is not like other experiences one normally encounters.

Transpersonal psychologists have coined the familiar term "peak experience." This is the experiencing of something beyond the self and often includes the universal, the holistic and feelings of compassion.[54] Will Adams in an article on one aspect of the peak experience, regarding interpermeation of self and world, discusses the mutability of self and world. This is when the universal energy, life, and meaning flows into one and one's being, consciousness, awareness and self flows into the universal. This leads to a very different understanding of both the "self" and the world.[55] This explanation helps illuminate the experience pointed at by Chan art.

Conclusion

Much neglected by modern western scholarship the notion of "*darśana*" was a prominent force in Buddhism from its inception. This can be demonstrated by analyzing such stories as the Buddha Śākyamuni's *parinirvāṇa*, Vakkali, Upagupta and others. As is well known, to see (understand) the Dharma is to see the buddha, but equally, to see the buddha (even in a vision) is to see the Dharma.

As the *śrāvaka* tradition grew, the importance of *darśana* appears to decline. It again becomes a major force within the overall tradition of Buddhism with the advent of the Mahayana with the "publishing" of sutras like the *Lotus Sutra, the Pratyutpanna*, *Avataṃsaka*, *Aṣṭasāharikā*, *Sukhāvatīvyūha Sūtra* as well as others.

When Indians go to meet their guru, go to a temple, and other such activities they understand these acts as "going for *darśana*." Within Buddhist terms, it is the entering into the nirvanic power of a buddha, arhats, bodhisattvas, and gurus, while in their actual presence, in their visualized presence, as preserved in relics, or focused in works of art. The use of art here is not for appreciation of its aesthetics but for appreciating its ritual function similar to how the ancient Greeks and others approached their religious art in the pre-Christian world.

We have seen how ritual gatherings in front of Amitābha's images, for the sake of benefits in this world and the next, were a regular feature in the early Song period. This is very similar to the ritual activities discussed by John Elsner in relations to ancient Greek ritual and art. It is also similar to the ritual relationship that Indian Buddhists seem to have had with their Buddhist art forms. Similar to this Indic model, we find the use of Pure Land art by the Tiantai School in China to continue this approach. It was also shown that the Pure Land tradition of Shandao and his spiritual descendants radically departed from this aspect. The Pure Land tradition as understood by the line of development passing through Shandao, used paintings of Amitābha and his Pure Land in two distinct ways: as devotional aids when not associated with the meditative vision which he claimed was not necessary, and as visual forms of inspiration fostering in one a longing for rebirth in the Pure Land of *Sukhāvatīvyūha.*

Since a clear vision of Amitābha and his Pure Land was not considered necessary and the main activity from the time of Shandao was to repeat the name of this buddha, then artists were not capturing their own realized vision on various media but simply a scholastic reproduction along prescribed lines. This, in turn, made the production of Pure Land art academic and formalistic and this is why one finds little significant content changes when viewing such art over the various dynastic periods.

Both calm abiding and insight meditation are well implemented in the Chan tradition and painted art expressing this is found. However, the use of art in Chan goes well beyond this application. Chan art begins with the Mahayana doctrine of emptiness and the *prajñā* (wisdom) it instills. From this emptiness forms emerge with the able hand of the artist expressing his or her realization. However, in Chan art much of the painting still retains the emptiness and smaller percentage has forms. This was connected with the prajñāpāramitā sutras' ideas.

The expression of realization in both the production and the viewing of Chan art were presented and the movement from the form and emptiness as expressed in artworks such as landscape paintings was discussed. The fact that the painting contains representations of both forms and emptiness means that the painting had to point to something else for there to be movement. Like with the use of a *gong'an*, the function of the art was to produce a leap in the view of the practitioner. That leap driven by the artist's insight was to the realm of emptiness of emptiness—considered the ultimate in Mahayana writings. This emptiness of emptiness is a synonym of the *Dharmakāya* or the buddha's mind, the *summon bonum* in Mahayana. Thus, the art of Chan had a completely different ritual associated with it than found in other Chinese Buddhist art. A ritual leading to a gestalt transpersonal-like experience as understood in psychological theory both in its creation and in its viewing.

Finally, this chapter demonstrated that sinicization took place not only in doctrinal matters but also in the realm of fine arts. Although the Tiantai school continued the Indian model in the ritualistic approach to the use of art (at least as much as possible in China), the Pure Land tradition running through Shandao radically departed from it in line with their understand of the Pure Land doctrine. The Chan tradition not only opened up new vistas aesthetically with the use of different content, a ruggedness within a naturalistic approach, and the incorporation of both form and emptiness in significant ways, but it also moved art to being a springboard for Chan realization.

Chapter Six

Early Chan Buddhist Activities

Introduction

In 1986 John R. McRae published his famous *The Northern School and the Formation of Early Chan Buddhism.*[1] It has become a standard work in the field and deservedly so. In his "Doctrine" section (sub-section 3) entitled, "The Message of the Letters" he offers three important considerations regarding the "practice" of early Chan according to material he investigated. He focuses on *The Treatise on the Two Ingresses and Four Courses* (identified as the *Treatise on the Two Entrances and Four Practices* in his work). In particular, in the following sub-section he offers some explanation regarding the "four practices" and this is followed by reflections on the "entrance by principle" and "wall contemplation." In this chapter, I will revisit the topic of activities in early Chan as presented in the same materials McRae employed, with an eye on investigating what was selected from the Indian heritage and what, if anything, is unique about early Chan activities. However, whereas McRae provided us with a look at these spiritual activities in a general manner, I hope to be able to tie the various activities to textual sources both Indic and Chinese and provide a more in-depth investigation.

The texts used by McRae and myself are: Tanlin's "Preface" to Bodhidharma's *The Treatises* on *Two Ingresses and Four Courses* (*Two Ingresses and Four Courses*), the complete text of Bodhidharma's famous teachings, the *First Letter* (anonymous), *Second Letter* part A (anonymous) and part

B by Layman Hsiang addressed to Huike,[2] and Huike's *Reply* to the previous. McRae points out that the associated materials have teachings on: 1) ignorance of emptiness (*śūnyatā*) and the Buddha-nature; 2) fixing one's attention on the mind; and 3) penetrating reality and identifying with the absolute. He further informs the reader that numbers one and three are standard Mahayana fair and number two is unique to Chan.[3] The "accesses by principle" McRae summed up with the teachings of faith in one's Buddha-nature. Finally, *biguan* (壁觀—translated as "wall contemplation") is discussed by presenting various interpretations. He concludes with a two-fold approach of a static aspect (becoming a wall) and a dynamic aspect (witnessing one's self and the world).[4]

Buddhism is often understood in the modern context as something you practice. However, one needs to ask what does practice mean in this context? "Practice" in English is ambiguous and possibly implies either doing to improve or doing to show mastery. This does not exactly equate to the Sanskrit Buddhist terms. Many of the Sanskrit words translated with the English "practice" are derived from root *kṛi* such as karma or *kriyā.* This root is the basic "to do" verb in Sanskrit. It lacks either the connotation of "practice to improve" or "practice showing mastery" although a notion of habitual doing could be understood in some contexts. *Abhyāsa* is often translated as "practice" but it actually comes closer to "reduplicate, repeat, add." Another Sanskrit word translated as "practice" in English is *vṛit.* This words means: "to revolve, roll, occur". Perhaps the word that is most often translated as "practice" is *carya* (derived from *car* "to move") which comes close to the meaning of "to course." The English word is derived from the Latin "*currere.*"[5] The verbal usage of "course" is now seldom encountered in English except in such phrases as "coursing through her veins." This lack of significant overlap in the contextual fields also holds true for the Chinese translation of *carya* as *xing* (行). It has the basic meaning of "to go." A few other Sanskrit words, not listed here, can also at times be translated with the English "to practice." Yet, as demonstrated above, the contextual field of these terms usually does not overlap by much the contextual field of the English "to practice" and thus to translate the Sanskrit terms with this English term is to distort the picture to some extent.

This is significant for this chapter because it seems when people speak of Buddhist practices, they are assuming some activity that is going to aid a person in transforming himself or herself along a path leading to the Buddhist goal of liberation. That is, the notion of "practice to make perfect" is emphasized. This, however, leads one to a quandary that is difficult to resolve. Yet, it has bearing on any discussion of systems based on the Buddha-nature teachings such as Chan.

The Eight-fold Path is divided into three major areas: Wisdom (*prajñā*)—appropriate view, intentions or thought; Ethics (*śīla*) -appropriate speech, action, livelihood; and Concentration (*samādhi*)—appropriate effort, mindfulness, concentration.[6] Most people would identify these eight appropriate activities as Buddhist practices. For example, one practices appropriate mindfulness and this helps lead one to nirvana. To elaborate on this, by repeatedly applying oneself to sitting in, walking in and laying in mindfulness one gains mastery of this activity. Thus we can say that one practices to perfect mindfulness. The problem is that the Buddha after his awakening, still sat in, walked in and laid down in mindfulness. Surely, he was not practicing to perfect the activity.

The Buddha-nature materials such as the *Tathāgatagarbha Sūtra*[7] and the *Śrīmālādevī*[8] can be understood as beginning from the position that one is already awakened.[9] Notwithstanding, the naturally free mind is adventitiously covered over with the mud of the kleśas (negative states of mind leading to insalubrious activities, *i.e.*, hindrances) like a golden buddha statue still encrusted in the clay of the casting mold as noted in the *Tathāgatagarbha Sūtra*. Further, since the obscuring factor is one's states of mind which are self-generated, then appropriate activities come down to ceasing to manufacture one's own samsara. There is really no position given here "to practice to perfect." As Bodhidharma states:

> … have deep confidence that sentient beings, average people and sages alike have the one true nature. However, because of adventitious defilements and false coverings, one is unable to manifest it … If then one forsakes the false and returns to the true, one accomplishes fixing the mind in "wall contemplation" which is without self and other and the average person and sage are of one rank. … This is being present in the true principle's mysterious state.[10]

Given the above considerations, I use the term "activity" instead of "practice." In what follows, the determination of what is to be included and excluded as Buddhist activities is somewhat subjective. For example, some could consider the Buddhist notion of no-self to be a doctrinal point or activity. Therefore, in order to provide a more comprehensive picture,

I have listed as many items as seems reasonable drawn from the materials at hand. I begin with the *Two Ingresses and Four Courses* and analyze its content along with most of the information that Tanlin provides in his "Preface." This is followed by analyzing the contents of the remainder of Tanlin's "Preface" and the content of the associated *Letters* listed above. After this, I provide a comprehensive conclusion.

Bodhidharma's *Two Ingresses and Four Courses*

> Now then, as for the ingress to the Dao, it has many roads. In summation, they do not exceed two categories. The first is ingress by principle and the second is ingress by coursing. As for the ingress by principle, this refers to the idea by means of the teachings one realizes accomplishment. Have deep confidence that sentient beings, average people and sages alike have the one true nature. However, because of adventitious defilements and false coverings, one is unable to manifest it. If then one forsakes the false and returns to the true, one accomplishes fixing the mind in "wall contemplation" which is without self and other and the average person and sage are of one rank. … This is being present in the true principle's mysterious state.[11]

Tanlin's (曇林) "Preface" generally follows the *Two Ingresses and Four Courses* in presenting different materials. Some of what he states can be read as a gloss on this text. He does add a few significant items that are not covered in *Two*

Ingresses and Four Courses and those will be presented below in the next section. Here, we will work with his information along with each of the activities that Bodhidharma teaches.

To begin with, readers may think that the expression "two ingresses" (*erru* 二入) is a particular non-sutric and Chinese manner of conceptualizing. *Ru* was used to translate a large number of Sanskrit words including *viś*, *āyatana*, *anugam*, *antarbhū*, and *kram*, to list but a few. Also in two Buddhist works frequently encountered in our studies, the use of the term *ru* (入) is employed in an analogous way to Bodhidharma's work. The *Mahāparinirvāṇa*[12] speaks of ingressing nirvana. More importantly, the *Awakening of Confidence* uses expressions like ingressing nirvana, ingressing true suchness, and ingressing the *Dharmakāya.*[13] Thus, it is possible that either of these works may have influenced the selection of this term in Bodhidharma's treatises.

The tranquil or peaceful mind (?*citta vyupaśama*/*anxin* 安心)[14] is one of the attributes of the ingress by principle provided in the "Preface." Tanlin, after explaining that the Dharma master instructed by means of the true Dao, begins a list of some teachings with "tranquil mind." Further into the text, he calls this "the Mahayana tranquil mind *Dharma*," and clearly states that this is *biguan*. These facts, attest to the centrality of the "tranquil mind" in this tradition. Further, if Tanlin was a disciple of Huike as legend has it, then perhaps the later account of Huike asking Bodhidharma to pacify his mind may be connected with these statements. The tranquil mind is mentioned in a number of texts such as the *Mahāprajñā Sūtra*,[15] *Samantapāsādikā*,[16] as well as others. It is not a term that is unique to the Chan tradition or even to the Mahayana. Although, its exact connotation differs according to the text read.

The *Two Ingresses and Four Courses* is famous for a teaching called *biguan* which has been translated as "wall contemplation." However, what Bodhidharma meant by "wall contemplation" has generated an enduring controversy amongst all those interested in early Chan. Various theories have been postulated about the meaning and in this chapter I will neither confirm nor support one or the other of the existing theories. Nor will I put forward yet another theory. However, to date, no research has shown an Indic original term that could be translated as *biguan* which has a referent having something to do with a "wall" associated with some mental activity. In Sanskrit, "wall" could be *kuḍya*, *prākāra*, *prācīra*, *parisara*, *bhitti* and *sāla* or various derivatives. Yet, none of these words appear in a technical term connected with mental cultivation.[17]

The term *biguan* is associated with a number of qualities, attributes and activities beyond the tranquil mind as explained in Bodhidharma's text. Gaining awakening (*anubodhi/ wu* 悟) by means of direct ingress through the teachings is the first mentioned. This refers to a person being explained the view (*i.e.*, teachings) and his or her understanding leads directly to realization. As will be shown immediately below, the teachings in Bodhidharma's *Two Ingresses and Four Courses* are connected with the *tathāgatagarbha* or Buddha-nature complex of ideas wherein this understanding is found. Awakening is mentioned in the *Śrīmālādevī*,[18] *Mahāparinirvāṇa*,[19] *Laṅkāvatāra*,[20] *Awakening of Confidence*[21] and a large selection of others texts. Thus the actual attributes of this Buddhist activity are known and the questions regarding *biguan* are more about terminology, than about the state of mind.

The teachings of dGa' rab rdo rje[22] an Indian master probably living in the sixth century are preserved in Tibetan. Although this author composed a number of tantric works he was also involved in the Ati-yoga, known as rDzog pa chen po in Tibetan, which is in part based on *tathāgatagarbha* thought. In a work entitled *Tshig gsum gnad brdegs pa*, dGa' rab rdo rje provides the core of these teachings. His first of three points is *ngo rang thog tu sprad* or "One is introduced straightaway to one's own basic nature." Similar teachings are found in the Mahāmudrā approach as noted by Matthes, "Essence *mahāmudrā* leads to the sudden or instantaneous realization of one's natural mind (*tha mal gyi śes pa*)." The Mahāmudrā lineage begins with Saraha in the eighth century.[23] So here in two different sets of Indic teachings appear statements similar to those in the *Two Ingresses and Four Courses.*

The *Two Ingresses and Four Courses* next states that one needs to have deep confidence (*shenxin* 深信) that everyone has the same one true nature (*yizhenxing* 一眞性). One should forsake the false (*shewang* 捨妄) and return to the true (*guizhen* 歸眞), then one can engage in *biguan*. *Biguan* is noted as being in a state without dualities and having stability (*zhu* 住). It is "being present in the true principle's mysterious state (*yuzhenliminzhuang* 與眞理冥狀). It is without dichotomies (*fenbie* 分別) or designations (*weiming* 爲名) and is quiet, tranquil, still (*ji* 寂).

"Confidence" (*śraddhā/ xin* 信) is a key concept in the Buddha-nature material as noted by S.K. Hookham: "… it is as characteristic of Tathagatagarbha as of Tantric and Mahamudra literature that it emphasizes the need to abandon concepts and to rely on faith."[24] The first citation of this term in the materials under investigation speaks of having confidence in Bodhidharma.[25] Confidence is one member of the five faculties (*indriya*) and one member of the five strengths (*bala*). Both of these groupings are part of the thirty-seven dharmas conducive to *bodhi* (*bodhipakṣyā dharma*), an inclusive grouping of qualities and courses found throughout the teachings.

Confidence is extremely important to the *tathāgatagarbha* complex as one of the main activities. As noted above, one of the most important sutras teaching *tathāgatagarbha* thought is *Śrīmālādevī.*[26] Tanlin wrote a commentary to the *Śrīmālādevī* which is no longer extant although quotations from it are preserved.[27] The sutra reads:

> If my disciples are in accord with confidence, increasingly giving rise to it, depend on their vivid confidence in accord with dharmic wisdom, then they will obtain the ultimate ends. In accord with dharmic wisdom, they 1) have insight making known the faculty of false imagination's sphere, 2) have insight into karmic retribution, 3) have insight into the arhat's vision, 4) have insight into the mind's spontaneous joy and the joy of meditation, 5) have insight into the great power of the arhats, pretyekabuddhas and Bodhisattvas noble natural penetration. These five kinds of ingenious expedient insights being accomplished, following my death the future and present generations of my disciples in accord with confidence, increasingly giving rise and

> depending on their vivid confidence and in accord with dharmic wisdom, their naturally limpid, untainted minds, despite the so called afflictions and defilements, yet will obtain the ultimate ends. This ultimate ends is the cause of entering into the Mahayana. Confidence in the tathāgatas has great advantage without detracting from the profound meaning.[28]

"Confidence" is also a very important term in other texts. A great example is found in the *Awakening of Confidence* a text attributed to Aśvaghosha. The Treatise states, "There are four kinds of confidence. The first is the confidence in the Root State. This refers to being mindful with joy of the true suchness of dharmic phenomena."[29] This treatise presents considerable information on "confidence" as it is one of the main themes. However, this is nothing unique to the Mahayana. "Confidence" appears as an important attribute in a number of categories of Buddhist activities as enumerated in the Pali texts as well. Notwithstanding, "confidence" does have a more significance role in the tathāgatagarbha literature than either the earlier materials or some other genres of Mahayana sutras. Whereas "confidence" is discussed in a large variety of texts, the most commonly encountered term is simply "confidence" (*xin*) without modification. Of particular note, the *Two Ingresses and Four Courses* uses the term "deep confidence" as stated above. This particular intensified term is found in the *Mahāparinirvāṇa* using the same Chinese characters.[30]

The one true nature is the Buddha-nature (*buddhatā/ fo xing* 佛性) which is explained as the *tathāgatagarbha* (*rulai-*

zang 如來藏) in the *Tathāgatagarbha Sūtra*.[31] Buddha element (*buddhadhātu*/ *fojie* 佛界), buddha mind (*foxin* 佛心) are also synonyms or near-synonyms encountered in this tradition. These terms appear frequently in sutras such as the *Laṅkāvatāra*, *Mahāparinirvāṇa*, and other seminal texts in the formative period of Chan. The "true nature" is equated with the Buddha-nature in the *Mahāparinirvāṇa*.[32] It is also discussed in the *Awakening of Confidence*.[33]

As mentioned in chapter two, Chinese conceptualization of the Buddhist goal has as much to do with returning to the natural state of the Dao, a positive aim, as it did with leaving behind suffering—the main objective of Buddhism stated in most Indian commentarial literature. Thus "forsaking the false" has to do with leaving behind the samsaric world and "returning to the true" is the movement away from contrived activities (*wuwei* 無爲) back to the Dao. *Wuwei* which is employed by both Confucians and Daoists was selected as the translation for the Sanskrit *asaṃskṛta*. This Sanskrit term is often translated into English as "unconditioned." Regarding this term, the Indic tradition emphasizes states or dharmas that are unconditioned whereas the Chinese tradition emphasis unconditioned or non-contrived activity. Separating oneself from the "false" is mentioned in Buddhabhadra's translation of the *Avataṃsaka*.[34] "Forsaking the false" is mentioned in the Śikṣānanda translation of the *Avataṃsaka*. Selection from this text reads:

> The Noble Eight-fold Path is the bodhisattva way (dao) which means coursing in the true insight Dao. Because one is far distant from all heterodox views one gives rise to correct thought. Forsaking false discriminations,

> one's mind is constantly in accord with all knowledge.[35]

"Return to the true" is similar to some terms encountered in the *Awakening of Confidence.* Therein, we read, "return to true suchness"[36] and "return and be in accord with the true suchness *dharma*".[37] Perhaps even more interesting for this analysis is the phrase, "reject grasping and return and comply."[38] This last example is more usually translated "reject grasping and (take) refuge." The two characters that make up the Chinese translation of "refuge" (*śaraṇa*) literally mean to "return and comply."

Being without self or other (*wuzita* 無自他) is also an attribute of the mentality while in *biguan.* Normally one would expect to encounter *wuzi wuta* and thus this formulation is in an abbreviated format. The abbreviated expression is found in the *Mahāprajñā Sūtra*[39] and the *Avataṃsaka.*[40] The unabbreviated term is also found in the *Mahāparinirvāṇa.*[41] Some of the other attributes of *biguan* are "stability" and "tranquillity," as found in the *Two Ingresses and Four Courses*. "Stability" is used in a variety of contexts and with different meanings in both *Śrāvaka* sutras and Mahayana sutras. For example, it is used in the *Fo lin nie pan ji fa zhu jing* (佛臨涅槃記法住經), a translation made by Xuanzang.[42] Most importantly it is used in a similar vein as the *Two Ingresses and Four Courses* in the *Śrīmālādevī,*[43] the *Laṅkāvatāra,*[44] and *Mahāparinirvāṇa.*[45] It is found also in the *Awakening of Confidence.*[46] The *Two Ingesses and Four Courses* associates stability with "not moving" (*buyi* 不移) or *asaṃkrānti* in Sanskrit. This term is mentioned in conjunction with meditational mental states in the *Mahāparinirvāṇa*[47] and the *Avataṃsaka.*[48]

The first of the remaining qualities of *biguan* that are mentioned is being "quiet or tranquil" (*ji* 寂). This term is also found in the *Laṅkāvatāra,*[49] *Mahāparinirvāṇa*,[50] and the *Awakening of Confidence*[51] as well. The second remaining term is *wufenbie* (無分別), which is the translation of either *nirvikalpa* or *avikalpa.* This term is found in various selections from the *Mahāprajñā Sūtra*,[52] the *Avataṃsaka,*[53] the *Śrīmālādevī*[54] and the *Mahāparinirvāṇa.*[55]

Tanlin particularly mentions four major activities that are Bodhidharma's teachings. The first two are the "tranquil mind dharma," which is *biguan*, and the second is "coursing" (*xing* 行). "Being in accord with things" (*shunwu* 順物) and "skillful means" (*fangbian* 方便) are the last two members mentioned. "Coursing" will be taken up just below. "Being in accord with things" is understood as guarding against derision (*jixian* 譏嫌) and can be connected with the second of four courses in the *Two Ingresses and Four Courses*. "Skillful means" is understood as teaching the above while being unattached (*buzhu* 不著) and can be associated with the fourth course in the *Two Ingresses and Four Courses*. This concludes the activities listed by Tanlin in his "Preface."

Bodhidharma's *Two Ingresses and Four Courses* begins with the division of his teachings into two broad categories, "Ingress by Principle" and "Ingress by Course," as is well known. The division into the two poles of principle and its function (*i.e.*, course) is a standard methodology employed in Chinese thought. However, for me, the important points are that these two exist along a single axis (co-dependent and interconnected). Whatever Bodhidharma's teachings may have been, the structuring of these teachings as found in the *Two Ingresses and Four Courses* is strictly Chinese. Indian thought does not use this bi-polar methodology so prevalent in Chinese thought. The first teaching being "principle," it is undivided. The second being the function of the principle is divided into four courses. "These four subsumes all courses and all ingresses are covered in these courses," according to *Two Ingresses and Four Courses*. Further, this structure is also used in the *Awakening of Confidence.*

<u>*The First Course*</u>

> What is the course of repaying hatred? In coursing while cultivating the Dao, if one experiences suffering, one ought to think this: 'I, from the far past, during numberless kalpas, abandon the root and pursue the insignificant, wandering in the various existences, often giving rise to hatred and ill-will, offending and injuring without limit. Although now I have not violated anything, this is my retribution from the past negative karmic fruit ripening. It is neither from divine nor human agents ... with a willing mind I will tolerate this experience without hatred or complaint.' At the time of producing this kind of mind, one is in accord with principle.[56]

The first course about how one should be traveling in the world, focuses on the topic of "repaying hatred" (*pratyapa kāra/ baoyuan* 報怨). This teaching explains that whenever we experience suffering we should cultivate an understanding that it is the manifestation of our own karma. By recognizing the true cause of that suffering and being tolerant of the situation, we are in accord with the ultimate principle. This technical term is found in various Buddhist materials.[57] These would include the *Abhiniṣkramaṇa Sūtra*,[58] the *Mahāprajñā Sūtra*[59] and the *Yogācārabhūmi Śāstra*.[60] Further, the teaching of repaying hatred as expressed in our text is similar to a teaching on the "Nine preliminary reflections on hate." As translated by Conze:

> If, in spite of the act that he has admonished himself in this way, his aversion is not appeased, he should contemplate the fact that both he and the other are the product of their own deeds. And he should at first contemplate this fact with regard to himself, as follows: 'Now listen, what will you in your anger do to him? Will not this deed of yours, which has originated in hate, be conducive to your misfortune? For you are the owner of your deeds, the heir of your deeds, your deeds are the source of what you are, they are your close kinsmen, they are your refuge. You will be the heir to whatever deed you may do, but this deed of yours will not enable you to achieve the full enlightenment of a Buddha or the enlightenment of a Pratyekabuddha, or the level of a Disciple, or some happy destiny, such as that of Brahmā, Śakra, a universal monarch, a local king, and so on; but it will make you fall away from the holy religion, and lead you into an existence where you will feed on scraps, and suffer the exquisite torments of the hells, *etc*....[61]

Conze's translation is from the Pali collection entitled the Aṅguttara Nikāya. Because this collection considerably predates Bodhidharma's teachings it thus demonstrates that the basic idea expressed in the first course is indeed ancient in the Buddhist tradition.

The Second Course

> Second, the course of following conditions means sentient beings are without self and are revolving in causes from karma. Suffering and happiness are equally experienced all from conditioned production. If I obtain excellent reward, honored reputation, *et cetera*, this is that influence of my past produced previous causes. Although now I obtain it, when the conditions are exhausted and return to nothing, what good is there then to have had it? Gain and loss follow conditions; the mind is without increasing or decreasing. Though a favorable wind blows one remains unmoved, mysteriously in accord with the Dao.[62]

The second course is on "following conditions" (*pratyaya pratītya or yathā pratyaya/ suizhen* 隨緣). This is explained as people are revolving in the conditioned state wherein happiness and suffering are experienced. If one now experiences gains or losses, the mind does not increase or decrease[63] and so the external circumstances are essentially meaningless. Because of this, one should remain unmoved and this is in accord with the Dao. This technical term is found in the *Avataṃsaka*,[64] the *Laṅkāvatāra*[65] and Vasubandhu's *Vijñaptimātratāsiddhi Śāstra.*[66]

This idea is eloquently put forth by Nāgārjuna in his *Suhṛllekha* wherein he advises:

> World-knower, be indifferent to these eight worldly dharmas, loss and gain, fame and disgrace, praise and blame, happiness and sadness.[67]

This idea is similarly expressed in the *Dhammapada* with the story of when the Buddha and his disciples spent a rainy season at Verañjā where they were neglected by the community followed by their time in Sāvatthi where they were well-treated. This story is the source of the eighty-third verse in the *Dhammapada.*

The Third Course

> Third, the course of indifference means that worldly people are long deluded, endless dwelling in the world greedy and attached. This is called seeking. The wise realize the truth; principle is contrary to the conventional so keep the mind peaceful without contrived activity. Forms follow the flow of things, the 10,000 things are empty, so be without desire. Merit and demerit constantly pursue each other. For a long time dwelling in the three realms is like dwelling in a burning house. Having a body is entirely suffering. Who can obtain peace? Understand thoroughly this condition. Because of this reason

> in one's various existences, breath by breath
> the thoughts should be indifferent.[68]

The third course is to "be indifferent" (*anapekṣa/ wusuqiu* 無所求). By keeping the mind peaceful without contrived activity (?*vyupaśama asaṃskṛta*/ *anxin wuwei* 安心無爲), understanding that all things are empty (*śūnyatā*) and understanding that dwelling in the three realms (desire, form and formless) is like being in a burning house, then breath by breath one is indifferent. This term is employed in a wide variety of texts starting from the Madhyāgama collection.[69] the *Qui yu jing*,[70] and most importantly the *Mahāprajñā Sūtra*.[71] In the *Aṣṭasāhasrikā* we read:

> *Sakra*, chief of Gods, then thought to himself: "it is wonderful how much this bodhisattva Sadaprarudita loves dharma, how firm is his sense of obligation, how great the armour he has put on, and how he is indifferent to his body, his life, and his pleasure, and how resolutely he has set out with the goal of knowing full enlightenment, in his desire to 'set (*sic*) free all beings from the measureless suffering of birth-and-death, after he has known full enlightenment."[72]

The above passage well shows the scope of what is to be abandoned by "indifference" within the wisdom tradition.

The Fourth Course

> The fourth course coinciding with the Dharma means the principle of natural purity accordingly is designated the Dharma. According to this principle all characteristics are empty without defilements, without attachments, and without this or that…The wise if they have confidence in their understanding of this principle, ought to course in correspondence with the Dharma. The Dharma corpus is without sparing one's body and life. Therefore course in giving with the mind free of regret or grudges, thoroughly understanding the three emptinesses … assist and transform sentient beings … cultivate coursing in the six perfections.[73]

The final course is "coinciding with the Dharma" (*dharma kīrti/chengfa* 稱法). All characteristics are empty and thus one should trust one's understanding of this and coincide with the Dharma. Not relying on attachment one "assists and transforms" (*nigṛhīta/shehua* 攝化) beings. Not discerning characteristics and doing away with false thoughts (*vikalpa/wangxiang* 妄想) one performs "giving" (*dāna/tanshe* 檀捨) as well as the other five perfections (*pāramitā/du* 度). The term *chengfa* is used repeatedly by Tiantai Zhiyi in his *Jin guang ming jing xuan yi* (金光明經玄義)[74] and *Jin guang ming jing wen ju* (金光明經文句).[75] It is also found in the Saṃyuktāgama,[76] the *Abhidharma dharmaskandhapāda Śāstra*,[77] and many more texts. In the "Preface," Tanlin uses the technical term "skillful means" (*fangbian* 方便)[78] to describe these activities.

The Associated Materials

The anonymous author of the *First Letter* informs us that he upheld Chinese customs, was respectful, and engaged in activities with the hope of realizing the Pure Land but these activities did not produce the desired effect. So he read the sutras and once again began sitting upright "fixing the boundaries of his mind king." He spent considerable time trying to view the characteristics (probably of a buddha). Realizing that all of his previous actions were based on false thoughts, he eventually realized the Dharma nature and experienced suchness. He recommends "seated *chan*" so that people can see their original nature. He states that gathering and melding the mind causes purity, calling up thoughts is wrong livelihood and searching the Dharma with a contriving mind does not remove karma.

The author of the *First Letter* tried to apply various Buddhist teachings before giving up on them. Here I will not discuss all of the activities that the author set aside because they did not produce results. The following activities seem to be connected with the spiritual activities whereby he gained realization. "Still dwelling in subtle tranquillity," "fixing the boundaries of his mind king," embracing a thorough comprehension of the *dharma nature*, experiencing "true suchness," seeing one's "root nature," "seated *chan*," and "gathering and melding the mind."

"Still dwelling in subtle tranquility" (*duanjuyouji* 端居幽寂) consists of two different terms. The first, "still dwelling" (*duanju*)" is mentioned in the *Avataṃsaka*.[79] Although the term tranquility (*ji*) is extensively used in Buddhist literature to translate the Sanskrit *śānti*,[80] the combination with "subtle" being viewed here is rare in the sutra tradition but used in the commentarial tradition in China. For example, Jizang (吉藏 549–623) used it in his *Jin guang ming shu* (金光明疏)[81] and there are other uses but mostly of later dates.

"Fixing the boundaries of the mind king" is a more literal translation of *dingjingxinwang* (定境心王). Broughton translated this as "settled external objects in the kingdom of mind".[82] McRae rendered it as, "fixed my attention on my mind" as noted above. *Dingjing* is the Chinese translation of the Sanskrit *viṣaya samādhi* or more fully, *viṣayatīrṇo samādhi.* This is one of the samādhis taught in the prajñāpāramitā literature. The Tibetan translation makes the slightly vague Sanskrit explicit. It reads "the *samādhi* of the wisdom from going beyond objects."[83] We find this *samādhi* also mentioned in the *Avataṃsaka*[84] and in commentaries like Vasuvarman's *Catuḥsatyaśāstra.*[85] "Mind king" is also used in the translation of sutras from the earliest period and gains in popularity as a technical metaphor over the centuries in the commentarial tradition. Sources such as the *Mahāmegha Sūtra,*[86] *Da cheng ben sheng xin di guan jing* (大乘本生心地觀經)[87] testify to its use in early sutra materials. Locating it in the *Shi mo he yan lun* (釋摩訶衍論)[88] and its use in the *Mo he zhi guan*[89] demonstrates its enduring presence in the commentarial tradition. Most importantly, it is found in the *Mahāparinirvāṇa.*[90] Further, "mind king" may be connected with "self king" in the same sutra.[91] In addition, the *Avataṃsaka* has a Mind King Bodhisattva. [92]

"Comprehending Dharma nature" (*prasamīkṣa dharmatā/ jianfaxing* 鑒法性) is presented in many Mahayana sutras[93] such as the *Aṣṭasāharsrikā.* This sutra reads:

> Whatever, Venerable Sariputra, the Lord's Disciples teach, all that is to be known as the Tathagata's work. For in the dharma demonstrated by the Tathagata they train themselves, they realize its true nature, they hold it in mind. Thereafter nothing that they teach contradicts the true nature of Dharma.[94]

Experiencing "true" (*zhen* 真) "suchness" (*tathā/ ru*), and seeing one's "root nature" (*prakṛiti or dharmatā/ benxing* 本性) are commonly mentioned in various Mahayana sutras.[95] It is interesting to note that the term "seeing one's root nature" listed in this *Letter* is also found in the *Mahāparinirvāṇa*.[96] "Seated meditation" (*zuochan* 坐禪) with the connotation of *dhyāna* meditation is also found repeatedly used in the sutras however, these usually are without any clearly specific Chan school designation.[97] Most importantly it is used in the *Mahāprajñāpāramitā Śāstra.*[98]

The most curious term of note in the *First Letter* is "gathering and melding the mind." This particular expression seems not to be used in the sutra material preceding the *Letters* associated with the *Two Ingresses and Four Courses*. However, "melding the mind" (*rongxin* 融心) is found in the *Mahāratnakūṭa Sūtra*[99] and in the *Mahāyānasaṃgrahabhāṣya*[100] by Vasubandhu.

The *Second Letter* makes an early reference to a story of when Śākyamuni was still a bodhisattva and he heard the god Indra speak eight words called the Snow Mountain verse, "All things are impermanent; this life is *saṁsāra.*"[101] Broughton notes that this story probably came from the *Mahāparinirvāṇa*[102] and is found in the ?*Maitreyābhisaṃbodhi Sūtra.*[103] The theme of this story is about the sage who has an awakening due to this Snow Mountain verse; that is he realizes principle. This short letter also presents information on what is termed "distinguishing the root" (*bianben* 釆本). Here "root" probably refers to idea of the root nature mentioned in the first course and in the *First Letter*. According to this *Letter* distinguishing the root is "without theorizing" (*wujianxiang* 無見相). This last term is found in the *Saptaśatikā*,[104] the *Awakening of Confidence*,[105] the *Mahāparinirvāṇa*,[106] and elsewhere in the canonical collection. In general this *Letter* presents the teachings on emptiness in a fashion similar to the *Diamond Sutra*.

Laymn Hsiang's *Letter* which seeks confirmation of his insight also explains emptiness in a similar manner as the *Diamond Sutra*, but the general tenor of the text harkens back to Laozi. The text of his *Letter* reads, "Removing mental defilements to hasten nirvana is like removing form and searching for shadows." *Chufannao* (除煩惱) or "removing mental defilements" is widely used in the sutra collection. Such texts as the *Mahāvaipulya mahāsannipāta Sūtra*,[107] the *Avataṃsaka*,[108] the *Mahāparinirvāṇa*,[109] and many others clearly demonstrate this. The Patriarch Dazu Huike's *Reply* to Hsiang's *Letter* confirms Hsiang's awakening. It encourages him to be compassionate and then raises a rhetorical question, "Why is it necessary to further search for another remainderlessness?" *Wuyu* (無餘) is the Chinese translation for the Sanskrit *niravaśeṣa*—"remainderless" or nirvana without remainder. This term is used in the *Mahāprajñā Sūtra*,[110] the *Mahāparinirvāṇa*,[111] and the *Avataṃsaka*,[112] as well as others.

Conclusion

Initially, this chapter was designed to use the same early Chan materials that other scholars employed in various studies about the origin of the Chan tradition to try to determine if Indic source materials were available to the Chinese to support these teachings. The overall goal was to identify what was "Chinese" about these Chan texts and what was part of the Indian heritage. Having arrived at such a determination would then allow us to analyze how sinicization developed in the early phase of Chan.

What has been determined regarding the Indic sources of the early teachings in Chan Buddhism? Providing an exhaustive list of all possible sources for the various Buddhist activities mentioned in these pages seems pointless for determining which texts were influential. We may never be able to prove with complete accuracy from which textual source the early Chan teachings were selected. Not because the sources are lacking or that these developments were completely Chinese in inspiration, but because there is an overwhelming amount of possible Indic sources for these Buddhist activities that had been translated before Bodhidharma's dates. However, this was not the point of the exercise. Here we are only trying to indicate which of the teachings listed had a precedent in the Indic materials available in China around the time of the composition of these early Chan works. Herewith, this has been shown. Not only were the general concepts that each teaching was based upon demonstrated to have existed in the canonical literature in Chinese translations before or contemporaneous with the alleged composition of Bodhidharma's *Two Ingresses and Four Courses*, but the actual technical terms could be traced.

I find it interesting that a number of these terms are being used in translations that are made within one hundred years or so of the *Two Ingresses and Four Courses*. This may indicate some popularity with particular usages. I do think there is some significance to the fact that most of these teachings are found mentioned in the *Mahāprajñā Sūtra*, *Mahāparinirvāṇa*, *Avataṃsaka*, and to a lesser extent the *Laṅkāvatāra* and the *Awakening of Confidence*. These texts are known to have been used and often quoted by other early Chan teachers who followed in the wake of its inception on Chinese soil. In other words, one could argue that the early sutra sources used by the first few patriarchs in their teachings on Chan, could well have provided much of the teaching's found in the *Two Ingresses and Four Courses* and associated materials. If we accept that the Chan tradition did have a lineage of master-disciple relationships, regardless of the creative lineage making within the tradition shown to have taken place by other scholars, then this influence of a particular grouping of sutras may not be accidental.

We did not see in the above a preponderance of references to the *Laṅkāvatāra.* Although it could have been the source of some of the teachings, other sutras have a higher probability of claiming first place in use. This further adds to work by other scholars bringing into question the claim that Chan is based on the *Laṅkāvatāra.* In terms of the Buddha-nature orientation of these early works, it seems more likely that it was the *Mahāparinirvāṇa* that was the most influential. Certainly the *Laṅkāvatāra* did have an influence on the development of early Chan but it was probably far less than tradition had claimed.

This study has shown that as for the teachings on Buddhist activities that are recommended or presented in these early Chan documents, there is nothing major that is not traceable to Indic sources. The "ingress by principle" which *prima facie* seems to indicate Chinese inspiration, needs to be analyzed not merely according to the terminology employed but also to the ideas being expressed. The general idea of direct ingress to the awakened state was shown to be found in other Buddha-nature materials such as the Ati-yoga and the Mahāmudrā teachings that originate in India within a few centuries of the origins of Chan. The expression "ingress" was shown to have been used in a similar way in the *Awakening of Confidence* and elsewhere. This direct ingress being largely based on confidence was documented with information from various sutras and commentaries that belong to the Buddha-nature genre.

"Repaying hatred" (*pratyapakāra/ baoyuan*) is documented in both the sutra and the commentarial literature. The course as laid out in *Two Ingresses and Four Courses* is very similar to the type of cultivation for abating and eradicating hatred found throughout the Buddhist tradition. Particularly in the Mahayana, hatred is a grave matter as the foundational social emotion within this branch is compassion. As explained by the Buddha Śākyamuni to Upāli:

> If, while practicing the Mahāyāna, a bodhisattva continues to break precepts out of desire for kalpas as numerous as the sands of the Ganges, his offense is still minor. If a Bodhisattva breaks precepts out of hatred, even just once, his offense is very serious. Why? Because a bodhisattva who breaks precepts out of desire [still] holds sentient beings in his embrace, whereas a Bodhisattva who breaks

> precepts out of hatred forsakes sentient beings altogether.[113]

"Following conditions" (*pratyaya pratītya or yathā pratyaya/ suizhen*) is also documented in both the sutra and commentarial traditions. This teaching has a long history in the Buddhist materials. As noted above, the *Dhammapada*, generally thought to have been composed around the third century BCE, contains verses that reflect the same sentiment as expressed in the teachings on "following conditions." Keeping one's mind level in the face of experiencing the worldly things that drive people, for better or worse, is an important consideration in spirituality.

Anapekṣa (*wuqiu*) or "being indifferent" is also a long used term in the Buddhist tradition. However, the Two *Ingresses and Four Courses* clearly makes this into a Mahayana teaching by connecting it with *śūnyatā* or emptiness. It is insufficient to simply cultivate an attitude of not caring in this course, it is important that the Buddhist disciple apply his/her insight into *śūnyatā* to transcend the entire negative complex associated with attachment.

Dharma kīrti (*chengfa*) or "coinciding with the Dharma" also presents a course that is based on Mahayana teachings. Here having gained insight into *śūnyatā* one is emboldened to enact compassion skillfully and to embrace the other pāramitās or "perfections" as one courses through life. These include "giving" (*dāna*), "discipline" (*śīla*), "patience" (*kṣānti*), "energy" (*vīrya*), "meditation" (*dhyāna*) and "insight" (*prajñā*). As noted in the *Aṣṭasāhasrikā:*

> The Lord: The bodhisattva should adopt the same attitude towards all beings, his mind

> should be even towards all beings, he should not handle others with an uneven mind, but with a mind which is friendly, well disposed, helpful, free from aversion, avoiding harm and hurt, he should handle others as if they were his mother, father, son or daughter. As a savior of all beings should a Bodhisattva behave towards all beings, should he train himself, if he wants to know the full and supreme enlightenment. He should, himself, stand in the abstention of all evil, he should give gifts, guard his morality, perfect himself in patience, exert vigour, enter into the trances, achieve mastery over wisdom, survey conditioned coproduction both in direct and in reverse order; and also others he should instigate to do the same, incite and encourage them...[114]

The first two courses explained by Bodhidharma in his *Two Ingresses and Four Courses* are general Buddhist fare. Although the significance of these teachings are somewhat different in the Mahayana, the teachings themselves fall within the parameters of the common Buddhist heritage. The second two courses are proven to be Mahayana in orientation. The significance of *śūnyatā* as employed in these two courses and the specific reference to the first *pāramitā* as well as a general reference to the others perfections is noted.

The findings in this chapter also disproves McRae's claim that "fixing one's attention on the mind" is something unique to the Chinese development of this tradition. In fact, the *samādhi* mentioned in the passage is well known from various sources. Mahayana Buddhism presents a large array of activities and advance states of meditation with the umbrella word "*samādhi*." As noted above, the prajñāpāramitā literature lists over one hundred samādhis. Other sutras provide us many more. Much of this material awaits further study in the academy.

What, then, is uniquely Chan about these early teachings? In short, it is not in the activities taught in the *Two Ingresses and Four Courses* or what is mentioned in the "Preface" and accompanying materials that something truly unique to the Chinese formulations of the Chan tradition is to be found. The unique aspects of this tradition at its inception are in the structure of the main text and in the selection of teachings that are grouped therein. To understand this let us begin by raising a fundamental question? "What problem is Bodhidharma's text attempting to answer?"

In summation, his treatise informs the disciple of the Buddha how to ingress to the Dao. As noted in the accompanying materials, people wishing to follow the Buddha Dharma engage in a plenitude of activities and attempt to cultivate numerous often subtle sentiments and insights. Nonetheless, one may still feel out of tune with the Dao even though the Dao is imminent at all times. For example, even the great Zhuangzi was at times out of tune with the Dao as is demonstrated in the story about his wife's death. Zhuangzi's friend went to pay his respects after hearing that Zhuangzi's wife had passed away. He found Zhuangzi with legs sprawled pounding on a tub and singing ditties. He was aghast and admonished Zhuangzi. Zhuangzi replied:

> You're wrong. When she first died, do you think I didn't grieve like anyone else? But I

> looked back to her beginning and the time before she was born. Not only the time before she was born, but the time before she had a body. Not only the time before she had a body, but the time before she had a spirit. In the midst of the jumble of wonder and mystery a change took place and she had a spirit. Another change and she had a body. Another change and she was born. Now there's been another change and she's dead. It's just like the progression of the four seasons, spring, summer, fall, winter. Now she is going to lie down peacefully in a vast room. If I were to follow after her bawling and sobbing, it would show that I don't understand anything about fate. So I stopped.[115]

We see that right after his wife's passing, Zhuangzi was not in tune with the Dao and so like everyone else he lamented overcome with grief. Then he again was in tune with the Dao and that is why he was singing.

According to the accompanying materials, meditating on the Pure Land, reading sutras, practicing various meditations and so on, does not necessarily help one become in tune with the Dao because these are contrived activities or, stated another way, these are all compounded dharmas. So Bodhidharma resolves this problem by providing two major ways of staying in tune with the Dao or continually ingressing in true harmony. The first is through direct ingress in keeping with the teachings on Buddha-nature. The second is adhering to the four courses while being in tune. How does a buddha or bodhisattva act? He or she, when encountering negative situations, does not hate but understands the situation is produced by karma. He or she does not become elated with fame or honors nor melancholy with blame or disrepute. He or she understands *śūnyatā* and hence is indifferent. Finally, he or she having insight employs skillful compassion and the pāramitās. The follower of the Buddha should be like him because there is no difference between the sage and the common people. In other words, based on the fact that everyone has the one true nature, these ways of ingressing harmony with the Dao are not ways of practicing to arrive at some goal but are ways of being in the world that is in tune with the Dao just as experienced by the Buddha. "Breath by breath" one is in accord with the Dao.

The way that the *Two Ingresses and Four Courses* is structured is clearly Chinese in my opinion. As discussed elsewhere in this volume, bipolar methodology is a typical way that Chinese intellectuals attempt to place everything in the universe into a harmonious whole. Such correlatives as *you/wu* (have/do not have present in the universe), *ti/yong* (substance/function), *ben/mo* (root/branches) and many more are used throughout the intellectual tradition. The important aspects here are that the two aspects are interconnected and share a dynamic relationship just like yin/yang. Thus, they are the two poles of a singular related system. Here in the *Two Ingresses and Four Courses* this same methodology was employed with principle and course (= function). Why is this structure employed? The Dao is not directly accessible through intellectual maneuverings as noted in multiple sources but perhaps most importantly in Laozi's opening line, "The Dao that is spoken about is not the eternal Dao." The Dao can be understood only through *de* (德); by observing and enacting the power or functioning of Dao is how one comes to understand it. Thus, this idea of a mysterious principle that is known by its activity is well established in Chinese thought. This is why these structures are found throughout the intellectual tradition whether Confucian, Daoist or Buddhist. This familiarity helps bring these initial Chan teachings in line with Chinese cultural expectations.

Second, the selection of teachings is important. Even if one limited oneself to the various Buddhist activities as found in the Buddha-nature materials such as the *Mahāparinirvāṇa*, the *Śrīmālādevī* and other works, the amount of activities found within the pages of the sutras would make a long list indeed. Therefore, the early Chan formulators were not simply following a scripted listing, they were clearly making decisions. As with anyone who makes these types of decisions, one wants the best selection based on the criteria set out. Although we, centuries later, may never know the full extent of the thought process that went into this decision-making, one of the considerations had to be what was appropriate for Chinese disciples. Thus, the Chinese context played some role in this process. This is explained just below.

Zurcher, years ago, had already pointed out the importance of the karma theory to the Chinese. He states:

> But in Buddhism this concept-the universal law or rather process of karmic retribution-was given a different meaning: that of a moral principle working through the universe, mechanical and inexorable too, but resulting from and consequently dependent on man's individual course of thought and action. In

> the same way Buddhism not only changed the morally indifferent Way of Nature into an instrument of supra-mundane impersonal Justice, but also brought this concept to its logical conclusion by introducing the dogma of rebirth, or, as the Chinese generally interpreted it, the "immortality of the soul". "Emptiness and Saintly wisdom," "the retribution of sins" and "the immortality of the soul"—these were the most basic and most controversial principles of fourth and early fifth century Buddhism, and we may assume that these were also the elements which first attracted the attention of the cultured Chinese public.[116]

The theory of *karma* strengthened the native Chinese concept of stimulus (*gan* 感) and response (*ying* 應) by providing the mechanics behind the operation as noted by Zurcher. This enhanced theory was one of the primary concepts of interests in the Dark Learning (*xuanxue* 玄學) and also influential in the Pure Conversation (*qingtan* 清談) movements. Further, it provided an underpinning to the Confucian idea of reciprocity (*shu* 恕) with an individualistic moral imperative. Hence, the first course teaching on how to face the arising of negative karma in one's life and still be in tune with the Dao was on familiar terrain by the time of the "publication" of the *Two Ingresses and Four Courses*.

The third course of "being indifferent" to the eight worldly concerns would have been seen as paralleling teachings of Zhuangzi. He relates:

> Chien Wu said to Sun-shu Ao, "Three times you have become premier, yet you didn't seem to glory in it. Three times you were dismissed from the post, but you never looked glum over it. At first I doubted that this was really true, but now I stand before your very nose and see how calm and unconcerned you are. Do you have some unique way of using your mind?"
>
> Sun-shu Ao replied, "How am I any better than other men? I consider that the coming of such an honor could not be fended off, and that its departure could not be prevented. As far as I was concerned, the question of profit or loss did not rest with me, and so I have no reason to put on a glum expression, that was all ..."[117]

The third and fourth courses are both connected with the teachings of *śūnyatā* and the *pāramitā*. Ever since the introduction of the prajñāpāramitā literature to the Chinese population, it has claimed considerable interest. It heightened internal developments and brought both depth and breadth to the intellectual traditions such as Dark Learning and Pure Conversations and much more as well. If we just look at the Buddhist activity regarding the prajñāpāramitā literature from around the time that Bodhidharma was supposed to have visited China we can learn much.

The translation and retranslation of different sutras of this prajñāpāramitā genre were ongoing operations during this period. Kumārajīva (5th c.) translated the: *Pañcaviṃśati-*

sāhasrikā prajñāpāramitā Sūtra,[118] *Aṣṭasāhasrikā,*[119] *Diamond Sutra,*[120] and *Heart Sutra.*[121] Mandrasena (6th c.) translated the *Saptaśatikā.*[122] Saṅghabhara (6th c.) translated the *Saptaśatikā.*[123] Bodhiruci (6th c.) translated the *Diamond Sutra,*[124] and the *Adhyardhaśatikā prajñāpāramitā Sūtra.*[125] Paramārtha (6th c.) translated the *Diamond Sutra.*[126] Upaśūnya (6th c.) translated the *Devarāja pravara prajñāpāramitā Sūtra.*[127] Dharmagupta (7th c.) translated the *Diamond Sutra.*[128] Xuanzang (7th c.) translated the: *Śatasāhasrikā prajñāpāramitā Sūtra,*[129] *Pañcaviṃśatisāhasrikā prajñāpāramitā Sūtra,*[130] *Aṣṭādaśasāhasrikā prajñāpāramitā Sūtra,*[131] *Aṣṭasāhasrikā,*[132] *Suvikrāntvikrāmiparipṛcchā prajñāpāramitānirdeśa Sūtra,*[133] *Saptaśatikā,*[134] *Diamond Sutra,*[135] *Heart Sutra,*[136] *Pañcapāramitānirdeśa,*[137] and the *Adhyardhaśatikā prajñāpāramitā Sūtra,*[138] and more in this genre. Other individuals translated sutras from this genre as well. Further, there were about seventeen commentaries to various prajñāpāra-mitā sūtra translated or composed during this span of time.

All this activity testifies to the immense popularity of these teachings and the key ideas they present. From the fifth to the end of the seventh centuries China was inundated with the Mahayana concept of emptiness and the perfections. Thus, the inclusion of two courses in the *Two Ingresses and Four Courses* which are grounded on these concepts would have had significant appeal to the Chinese audience. The Chinese were impressed with this conceptual framework and continued their discussion regarding the mystery of mysteries.

Finally, we have to note that the use of particular expressions to describe various aspects of the Buddhist activities in the early Chan texts were a further enhancement in sinicizing these teachings. Tanlin's description of Bodhidharma's spirit being "gracious and clear," and his mind being "mysterious" not only helps make this South Indian seem Chinese like, but it also helps makes him familiar by meeting the qualifications of a Chinese sage. The *Two Ingresses and Four Courses* use of phrases like "true principle's mysterious state," "mysteriously in accord with the Dao" and "the ten thousand things are empty," irrefutably indicate a very Chinese manner of speaking. From the *Letters* we read such expressions as: "the bright pearl clearly discerns," "from the unnamed (people) create names" and "from the principle of true mystery," bring these teachings into line with familiar Chinese descriptions.

Chapter Seven

Buddhist Praxis in Light of Eschatology

Introduction

Basing itself on the combined heritage of the Indo-European cosmology along with the notions of karma, rebirth, and meditative states, the early Buddhists advanced a complex, systematic approach to explain the universe. Buddhist authors were not just conveyors of a received tradition but were actively involved in the growth and refinement of the system that has come down to us from more than two-thousand years ago. This chapter will present an explanation of the Buddhist trichiliocosm (*i.e.*, the three thousand great thousand world realms/*trisāhasra-mahāsāhasra-loka-dhātu*), and then view Indian Buddhist praxis in light of this world view. This will be followed by a look at Chinese Buddhist innovations to the trichiliocosm theory and an investigation into the tripartite time scheme that became prevalent and which acted as the justification for developments in praxis by one lineage of the Pure Land tradition. It will conclude by viewing the Chan approach to the same problems as the counter example.

The Buddhists hold that the knowable universe can be divided into the three major experiential spheres named the Desire realm (*kāmadhātu*), the Form realm (*rūpadhātu*), and the Formless realm (*ārūpadhātu*). Further, these spheres exist in time, although time is measured in kalpas which are immeasurable. Buddhist eschatology includes discussions of the end of world, the end of people, and the End of the Dharma. Before explaining Buddhist praxis in reference to their cosmological thought, I will begin with a presentation of the structural layout of the whole system and the duration of time.

The Trichiliocosm

The physical universe is found in the Desire realm in the Buddhist structure. The mandala of space supports all that is built above it. The next layers are the mandala of air, the mandala of fire, mandala of water, and finally the mandala of earth. On top of these mandalas is Mt. Sumeru (aka. Meru—similar to Mt. Olympus) surrounded by four major continents and various mountain ranges with seas interspersed. The outermost ring is the Adamantine (or Iron) Mountains (Cakravāḍa) which distinguishes the light from dark sectors. There are seven rings of mountains between the Adamantine Mountains and Sumeru. These mountain ranges are named: Nimindhara, Vinataka, Aśvakarṇa, Sudarśana, Khadiraka, Īṣādhāra, and Yugandhara is the closest to the center. These mountain ranges are thought of as concentric squares, according to the *Abhidharmakośa.*[1]

Mt. Sumeru is 160,000 yojanas (approx. 560,000 km) high with half of that height being under the waters of the first sea. The first sea is 80,000 yoganas wide. The Yugandhara Mountains are 40,000 yojanas high and the second sea is 40,000 yojanas wide. The Īṣādhāra Mountains are 20,000 yojanas high and the third sea is 20,000 yojanas wise. This pattern of each range being successively half of the previous height and each sea being half the previous width continues to the Nimindhara Mountains which are 1,250 yojanas high. Between the Nimindhara range and the Cakravāḍa range the only salt-water sea is 322,000 yojanas wide and therein is found the continents and sub-continents.

The Northern continent called Uttarakuru is square in shape and has two sub-continents off its coast. The eastern continent named Pūrvavideha is half-moon shaped has two sub-continents and the western continent named Apara-godānīya is circular and also has two sub-continents. Finally, the southern continent is called Jambudvīpa is a near pyramid trapezoid with the sub-continents of Cāmara and Avara-Cāmara off its coast.

Some people have argued that this arrangement (a tall mountain and four areas surrounding it) is a crude map of the Asian landmass. There is a similarity between Jambudvīpa's shape and the Indian sub-continent's shape and perhaps roughly some other areas as well. Support for such a view can be found in the *Abhidharmakośa* which does locate some of the geographic features of the Indian sub-continent on the idealized depiction of Jambudvīpa. The similarities are far from exact. According to the cosmological depiction, one would have to cross a sea to move out of Jumbudvīpa to any of the other landmass which simply is not the case in the real world when moving out of India. Further, Vasubandhu locating the mythic lake Anavatapta north of the Himalayas states that it is the source of the Ganges, Indus, Vakshu (= Oxus?) and Śitā rivers. This has been connected with Lake Mānasarovar in Tibet but four rivers do not issue from it. Whether the Mt. Sumeru map was inspired by the real geography of Asia seems undetermined at present.

Below the surface of Jambudvīpa are various layers of earth measuring one thousand yojanas in depth. Then, there are the hells (in descending order) of Saṃjīva, Kālasūtra,

Saṃghāta, Raurava, Mahāraurava, Tāpana and Pratāpana all of which are five thousand yojanas deep. The lowest is Avīci. Each of the hells has sub-hells and the combination equals 128 hells in total. Adjacent to these eight hot hells are eight cold hells called: Arbuda, Nirarbuda, Aṭaṭa, Hahava, Huhuva, Utpala, Padma, and Mahāpadma. Each of these abodes is peopled with those suffering the consequences of the karma they made. Five hundred yojanas below the surface of Jambudvīpa lies the realm of ghosts. On its surface, live humans and animals although the gods, titans and ghosts can visit the surface as well.

Near the peak (40,000 yojanas above the surface of Jambudvīpa) of Mt. Sumeru live the gods of the four directions, along with their armies: Vairśravaṇa and his *yakṣa* (nature-spirits) in the north, Dhṛtarāṣṭra and his *gandharva* (entertainers to the gods) in the east, Virūḍhaka and his *kumbhāṇḍa* (dwarf-spirits) in the south, and Virūpākṣa and his *nāga* (serpent/dragons, see: Chapt. 3) in the west. On the peak is the heaven of the Thirty-three (Trāyastriṃśa). This is the realm of the Vedic gods with Indra (similar to Jupiter) as their king. Above Sumeru by 80,000 yojanas height, is the realm of Yama (similar to Pluto), then Tuṣita heaven (where futures buddhas dwell teaching the gods before their final life on earth) is located at 160,000 yojanas above Yama's realm, Nirmāṇarati heaven is located at 320,000 yojanas above Tuṣita, and Paranirmitavaśavartin heaven appears 640,000 yojanas above Nirmāṇarati heaven or approximately 1,200,000 above the summit of Sumeru. This fills the Six Heavens of the Desire realm.

Ascending from the realm of desire is the realm of form with each of the heavens connected with meditative absorptions. First is Brahmakāyika at 2,560,000 yojanas above the surface, followed by Brahmapurohita and Mahābrahmā heavens, which concludes those associated with the first *dhyāna*. Starting with the lowest Parīttābha heaven then Apramāṇābha heaven and at the top Ābhāsvara heaven at 81,920,000 yojanas high are associated with the second *dhyāna*. The third *dhyāna* has associated with it the heavens: Parīttaśubha, Apramāṇaśubha and the top Śubhakṛtsna which is 655,360,000 yojanas above the surface. The fourth *dhyāna* has eight heavens associated with it: Anabhraka, Puṇyaprasava, Bṛhatphala, Abṛha, Atapa, Sudṛśa, Sudarśana and Akaniṣṭha being the highest at 167,772,160,000 yojanas high.

Finally, the formless realm has four abodes associated with it. These are not really physically locatable but they do exist in time. However, sometimes they are thought of as being above the heavens of the form realm as access is possible by further refinement in the *dhyāna* processes. The heavens are (from lowest to highest abodes): Ākāśa-ānantya-āyatana (infinite space), Vijñāna-ānantya-āyatana (infinite consciousness), Ākiṃcanya-āyatana (nothingness), and Naiva-saṃ-jñā-nāsaṃjñā-āyatana (neither thought/non-thought).

What is interesting about this map is that it has both a meditative and a moral dimension. That is, in order to be reborn as Indra, Yama, Brahma or any of the other gods, one must accumulate immense amounts of positive karma. Thus, entrance into at least some of these heavens is due to the positive karma one generated just like being reborn in the ghost realm or in one of the hells is a result of the negative karma one generated. However, entrance into the heavens associated with the absorptions can also be from achieving a refined meditative state. Refinement here means the dropping off or removing of different aspects of afflictions that keep us tied to desires or lower order mental states. Therefore, meditation in the Buddhist tradition has a moral aspect to it.

Secluded from sense desires, the attaining of the first *dhyāna* is accompanied by the abandoning of lust (Sk/Pali: *kāmachanda*), ill will, stiffness and torpor, agitation and worry, and uncertainty. It includes the arising of applied and sustained thought, and has happiness, bliss, and unification of the mind. The second *dhyāna* is entered when one moves from the applied and sustained thought yet retains happiness, bliss, and unification of the mind. Each successive *dhyāna* requires further refinement with entrance to the fourth taking place with the abandoning of the pleasure and pain.[2] The first of the formless realms is entered when after dwelling in the fourth *dhyāna* one notices that there still remains a subtle materiality and this, then, is abandoned. The highest of the formless realm's states is entered when one abandons perception of nothingness.[3] It is to be noted that nirvana is not located on this axis. According to the Pali *Mahāparinibbāna Sutta*, Śākyamuni takes a side step away from this axis at the fourth *dhyāna* to enter *parinirvāṇa* and thus it is not a linear progression above the formless realm.[4]

Time, in general, is measured in immeasurable units called kalpas. The largest unit is the Great *Kalpa* consisting of twenty Intermediate Kalpas. There are four Great Kalpas: Destruction (*Saṃvartakalpa*), Nothingness (*Saṃvartasthāyikalpa*), Origin (*Vivartakalpa*) and Duration (*Vivartasthāyikalpa*). The life span of people during the *kalpa* changes according to the general moral character of the society from an average of 80,000 years down to 10 years. Finally, according to the *Nirvana Sutra*, even the texts of the canon with the exception of the Vaipulya sutras will disappear along with morality.[5]

During the *kalpa* of Destruction, the realms from Avīci hell up to the highest heaven of the Desire realm become depopulated with some beings' mindstreams moving into the first *dhyāna* heaven but many simply being transferred to other trichiliocosms. The gods of the first *dhyāna* heaven enter the second *dhyāna* heaven. Then everything from the supporting elemental mandalas up to but not including the second *dhyāna* heaven is destroyed. Following its destruction there is nothing for the length of one Great *Kalpa*. This is followed by the beginning of the cycle of Origination and eventually the *kalpa* of Duration.

Different theories on the appearance of a buddha or of many buddhas during these time spans were put forward. At the lowest end of the spectrum of theories it is stipulated that one buddha will appear in a Great *Kalpa* and that appearance happens only during an Intermediate *Kalpa* of the Duration *Kalpa*. At the other end of the spectrum it is proposed that one thousand buddhas will appear in the present Great *Kalpa*. In addition, there will be arhats, bodhisattvas and other masters who accompany a buddha and continue to be available to help sentient beings in the absence of a buddha.

In general, Indian Buddhists accepted the idea of there being different time periods as to the duration of the Dharma. Jan Nattier has provided an in-depth study of the decline of the Dharma. In her study, she argues convincingly that the Indian Buddhist may not have had a three part division to their ideas regarding the duration of the Dharma. The Sanskrit terms that other scholars thought may indicate a third period (*i.e.*, *saddharmavipralopa*/ End of the Good Dharma) could refer to the second period and not a distinct period. She states that there are no unquestionable occurrences of each term for the three time periods found in a text of Indic origin.

She presents information that posits the influence of East Asian Buddhist notions being read back into the Indian Buddhist ideas in modern studies and translations. However, Nattier does not take up the question regarding the source of origin for the tripartite division of time in East Asian thought.[6] The two periods that all Indic texts agree upon are the period of the Good or True Dharma (*saddharma*) and the period of the Semblance Dharma (*saddharmapratirūpaka*). Different texts list various number of years for these periods from a few hundred (most common 500 years) to 10,000. These speculations are found in texts from the Nikāyas up to and including the *Kālacakra Tantra*.[7]

The True Dharma

The period of the Good or True Dharma is marked with many excellent qualities. These include the teachings on the thirty-seven dharmas that aid awakening (*bodhipākṣika-dharma*) which consists of the following:

- The four *smṛtyupasthānāni* (mindfulness of body, sensation, mind, and dharmas).

- The four *samyakprahāṇāni* (appropriate effort exerted towards preventing unarisen negativity, abandoning arisen negativity, producing the arising of positivity, and maintaining the arisen positivity).

- The four *ṛddhipāda* (spiritual power bases of will, thought, energy, and investigation each combined with concentration and effort).

- The five *indriya* (principles of confidence, energy, mindfulness, concentration, and wisdom).
- The five *bala* (power of confidence, energy, mindfulness, concentration, and wisdom).
- The seven *bodhyaṅga* (factors of mindfulness, investigating dharmas, energy, joy, calm, concentration, equanimity).
- The Eightfold Noble Path.[8]

The sutras, vinaya and abhidharma are all available during this time. People can more easily remove their hindrances (*kleśa*), apply the four-fold reasoning leading to realization (*pratisaṃvid*) and obtain the four fruits of arhat, non-returner (*anāgāmin*), once-returner (*sakṛdāgāmin*) and those entering the stream (*srotāpatti*). Monks and nuns will keep their vows purely. Bodhisattvas will perfect the pāramitās. Also, the average person will be moral and society will be generally moral as well. People will understand the teachings of the buddha as intended and liberation will be established. In some contexts, this period is limited to the life time of a complete perfect buddha.

The Semblance Dharma

The period of the Semblance Dharma in general is a degeneration from the pristine state of affairs delineated above. Even though this period is noted for its predominance of teaching, meditation, and recitation of sutras, the efficacy of the teachings has declined. Monks and nuns will still be able to keep their vows. Over the duration of this period, an easing in the rigor of seeking solitude and the application of logic to the teachings will set in. Toward the end of this period people become monks and nuns simply to obtain free room and board. They will have only a superficial approach to the Dharma. Also, the teachings, the community and the great masters will stop being respected and morality will decline.

Indian Approaches to the Problem

The Indian approach to addressing the possibility of the degeneration of the Dharma was not to emphasize a particular teaching in an effort to sidestep the issue as is found in East Asia, but to try to confront the problem at its root. This took several forms.

The first approach we can investigate is the actions of forestalling the inevitable. As noted by Nattier, the degeneration of the monastic sangha continues unabated until the last teacher of Dharma and the last arhat are murdered as found in the Kauśāmbī story. Much of the blame for the demise of the True Dharma falls on the shoulders of Buddhists themselves.[9] Within that four-fold group, it is the monks who have the greatest fault. The causes enumerated for the decline include: not reverencing the Buddha, Dharma, and

Sangha; lacking diligent meditation; being careless in transmitting and mastering the Dharma; the emergence of divisions in the sangha; monastics becoming increasingly associated with the secular world and the appearance of counterfeit Dharma.[10] However, the Aṅguttara Nikāya[11] and the Saṃyutta Nikāya [12] both claim that the True Dharma will last if these negative conditions are not met and their positive counterparts are embraced.

Paying respect to the Buddha in the post-*parinirvāṇa* state can continue with liturgical acts such as the famous Pali verse: "*Namo tassa bhagavato arhato sammāsambuddhassa.*" It is also possible to respect the Buddha by remembrance of the Buddha (*Buddha anusmṛti*), making offerings to the Buddha and by respecting stupas.

Both respecting the teachings and the careful transmission and learning of the Dharma are understood to be causes for the continuation of the Good or True Dharma. Here too, liturgical acts such as the second line in the Triple Refuge: "*Dharmaṁ śaraṇaṁ gacchāmi*" can be one form of expressing respect. The mastering and teaching in detail the Dharma allows for the teachings to be utilized and preserved. In the Aṅguttara Nikāya, the Buddha tells his disciples that the wrong arrangement of the words and letters of the teachings and the wrong interpretation of the meaning brings about the end of the True Dharma and their opposite maintains the True Dharma.[13] However, the preserving of the teachings also took on a physical form with the entombment of the Dharma. That is the preserving of the actual texts buried in stupas and at monastic sites. As proposed by Richard Salomon:

> Despite the uncertainties, it is interesting to learn that the practice of text burial in general, so widely and clearly attested in Tibet and East Asia is now shown to have also been common in ancient Gandhāra. Although the physical forms and visual manifestations of these early Gandhāran deposits are quite different from later *sūtra* burials in other parts of the Buddhist world, it is reasonable to suppose that the underlying theory and motivations were similar. So perhaps in this respect, as in so much of Buddhist tradition, there is a link between the traditions of Gandhāra and East Asia, and the Gandhāran text burials may well prefigure the later ones in East Asia. If this is correct, we can also look at the matter the other way round and read back at least tentatively, the well-documented motivations of later text burials in East Asia onto the older ones of Gandhāra. Since in the former a concern for the long-term preservation of the dharma stands out prominently, we may suspect that this was at least a part of the motivations of the Gandhāran Buddhist as well, despite the lack of direct testimony.[14]

Another form of forestalling the inevitable was the continuous revelations in both the sutric and tantric literature which testifies to the attempt to seriously mitigate or ameliorate the entire idea of the "End of the Dharma." This approach is sanctified by two sutras wherein the Buddha

Śākyamuni states that if he teaches men and gods, his teachings will last longer than if he only taught mankind as noted by Nattier.[15] As is well known, the epithet of a buddha "teacher of gods and men," is commonly encountered in Buddhist scriptures.

The acclaimed founder of Mahayana—Nāgārjuna brought back to the sphere of humans the profound prajñāpāramitā teachings which were held in the realm of the nagas, until humanity was ready for them. The extensive *Avataṃsaka* was kept by the gods in Akaniṣṭha heaven until people were more spiritually mature. The *Pratyutpanna* and other texts teach that new sutras can be obtained if one is adept at certain yogas.

> "Well done, well done, Bhadrapāla! You have done well, Bhadrapāla. So it is, Bhadrapāla, as you have said, because the forms are good and clear the reflections appear. In the same manner, when those bodhisattvas have cultivated this samādhi properly, those Tathāgatas are seen by the Bodhisattvas with little difficulty. Having seen them they ask questions, and are delighted by the answering of those questions."[16]

The Abhidharma master Asaṅga receives five books from the future Buddha, the Bodhisattva Maitreya. These efforts are encapsulated in the concept of the three turnings of the wheel of the Dharma (the early sutras and two divisions of the Mahayana sutras). This concept was first propagated by the Yogācāra School based on the *Saṃdhinirmocana Sūtra* but became useful throughout the Buddhist world and is clearly built on precedence long in place.[17] The *Saṃdhinirmocana Sūtra* was probably "published" in approximately the second century.

By the seventh century the Buddhist literary world was experiencing another creative phase with the "publication" of various tantras. These revelations would continue for several centuries radically changing Buddhism in India and became a major influence elsewhere as they are exported. Many of these texts begin in the realm of some buddha other than Śākyamuni and through the agency of a bodhisattva are brought into the realm of humans. Again Nāgārjuna is credited with revealing the *Mahāvairocana Sūtra* and *Sarvatathāgatatattvasaṃgraha Tantra* from an iron tower in south India after receiving initiation from Vajrasattva Bodhisattva who himself received the teachings from Vairocana Buddha.[18]

King Indrabodhi of Sahor received the texts of the Mahāyoga tantras which fell on the palace roof and the explanation of the teachings from Vajrapāṇi Bodhisattva.[19] The "biographical" literature from this period has numerous stories of different masters receiving teachings from bodhisattvas and other awakened beings.

Further, many Mahayana sutras, clearly state that even in the last period of the Dharma, there will still be people who gain realization. For example, after asking the Buddha Śākyamuni if the prajñāpāramitā teachings will be widespread in the final days, the Buddha answered Śāriputra:

> Yes, it will. In the last time, in the last period, there will be sons and daughters of good family who will hear this deep perfection of wisdom, will copy it out, take it up, bear it in

> mind, recite, and study it, wisely attend to it, and progress to its Thusness; and they will have set out for a long time in the vehicle, will have honoured many Buddhas, and will have planted wholesome roots under the Tathagatas.[20]

Texts such as the *Vimalakīrtinideśa* even claim that in the last days, these texts will not disappear and thus the teachings will still be available.

Finally, another method for dealing with the demise of the Dharma was to declare that the very source of reality, the source of the teachings, that which when realized is nirvana, *i.e.*, the *tathāgatagarbha*, is always accessible. Thus, the loss of Śākyamuni's transmitted teachings is not a complete loss. The *tathāgatagarbha* doctrine understands that each person manufactures his/her own samsara and if one ceases in the manufacturing awakening can take place. As buddhas and sentient beings are ultimately the same, no real distinction can be made. Logically, the End of the Dharma specifically refers to the end of Śākyamuni's teachings, not the inaccessibility of the awakened state.

In keeping with the above proposition, both the *Śrīmālādevī* and the *Mahāparinirvāṇa*, two of the main sutras teaching *tathāgatagarbha* doctrine, mention the End of the Dharma but only to say that bodhisattvas will uphold the Dharma at that time.

Chinese Innovations

Although the Chinese translated Buddhist works that presented the Indian picture of the trichiliocosm such as the

Abhidharmakośa, eventually they made a number of significant changes bringing the concept more in line with Chinese views of this worldly system. The vertical stacking of every realm, from the lowest hell to the highest heaven, became less emphasized with many native produced Buddhist texts speaking of heaven in a more general sense but without denying the Indic hierarchical structure. The Chinese had no mature idea of the underworld before the arrival of Buddhism and wed the Indian topography with the Chinese imperial juridical system. This is even noted in the translation of the Sanskrit term for hell, "*naraka*."[21] The Chinese not having a comparable fully developed concept translated this term as "earth prison" (*diyu* 地獄). Since the Indic sources locate the hells below the surface of the Jambudvīpa, "*di*" captures the idea of this place being in the ground. "*yu*" or prison was the closest concept the Chinese had to a place of torture for transgressions.

The Chinese system of hell has ten magistrates, along with bailiffs and other functionaries, each in their own hall or court. The Buddhist god of the dead, Yama (*Yanluo* 閻羅) is only one of the m/agistrates. The Chinese Buddhist hell system is far more complex than its Indic source. Each hall was associated with different offenses although some offenses like not being filial are transgressions evaluated in several halls. Further, the entire complex idea of the underworld filling an obvious lacuna in Chinese cosmology was accepted by all including the Daoists.

The halls are often simply numbered one through ten and the name of each magistrate (often called "kings") is as follows:

1st Hall: Qinguang Wang 秦廣王
2nd Hall: Chujiang Wang 楚江王
3rd Hall: Songdi Wang 宋帝王
4th Hall: Wuguan Wang 伍官王
5th Hall: Yanluo Wang 閻羅王
6th Hall: Biancheng Wang 卞城王
7th Hall: Taishan Wang 泰山王
8th Hall: Pingdeng Wang 平等王
9th Hall: Dushi Wang 都市王
10th Hall: Zhuanlun Wang 轉輪王[22]

Chinese Concepts of Time

Over the centuries the Chinese elaborated upon various systems of measuring time. Certainly the *Yi Jing's* (易經) hexagrams include both a line position and a temporal sequence.[23] These systems of measurement have been discussed by various scholars and include the four seasons, the heavenly stems and earthly branches individually and together, and various calendar formations.[24] One of the interesting systems for measuring time is termed *sanyuan* (三元) or "three phases" which demonstrates the penchant toward a three plus one division to time. Using the common place terminology for tripartite divisions, these three are: *shanyuan* (上元) "arising phase," *zhongyuan* (中元) "middle or flourishing phase," and *xiayuan* (下元) "declining phase."

The first thing to note is that the cycle does not immediately begin anew with the end of the declining phase but there is a period of non-production involved. This corresponds to the basic ideas as found in the *Yi Jing*. The three phases are the working out of the yin/yang principles with yang forces initiating movement in the arising phase. They are ascendant at the beginning of the flourishing phase and the yin forces gain during the flourishing phase becoming ascendant during the declining phase. Yin forces initiate the unmentioned rest period. The yearly cycle of crops can be seen as a demonstration of this system of time. The three phases equate to the life cycle of crops through spring, summer and autumn and the unmentioned repose of the earth during the winter. This period of rest, which followed production, (flourishing) and return (*i.e.*, decline), is connoted with the word "base," in this *Dao de jing* verse with its double entendre.

> Thoroughly apply yourself to vacating,
> Attend to quiet genuinely.
> The ten thousand things are together produced,
> I watch them cycle.
> Therefore all things,
> Each returns to the base.
> Return to the base is called quiet,
> This is called retuning to nature.
> Returning to nature is called eternity,
> Knowing eternity is called clarity.
> Not knowing eternity,
> Foolishness produces misfortune…[25]

The three phases are mentioned in the *Jin shu* (晋書)[26] and are sometimes understood to represent three ages of sixty years duration. Thus, it equals a total of one hundred and eighty years. However, this can easily be extended to great spans of time as noted by Richard Smith: "Cycles of sixty and their various sub-cycles were considered part of larger rhythmic cycles, culminating ultimately in Shao Yong's notion of recurrent and eternal periods of 129,000 years."[27] Yet, even before the Song dynasty, there were various durations proposed to the rise, flourishing, and decline of the ages. For example, the *Lao zi zhung jing* (老子中金), a Daoists text probably from the later part of the Han dynasty (25–220) provides a time scheme using the 180 year period that concludes a 360,000 year cycle. In addition, the text predicts that a "true person" will appear after 18,000 years and a great Immortal will appear after 36,000 years.[28] This time scheme, with variations on a theme, seems to be the most commonly encountered in ancient texts.

For the purposes of this study the time scheme in the *Ta ping jing* (太平經) is the most significant.[29] Therein, the theory of the "three antiquities" (*sangu* 三古) is presented. It too divides the three periods using the *shang*, *zhong* and *xia* terminology. However, unlike the "three phases" which posited a time trajectory of production, flourishing and decline, here *shang* can be understood as "upper or higher" indicating the golden age, *zhong* "middle" indicating the first phase of decline, and *xia* "lower or degenerate" indicating the last phase of decline.[30] Both sets of connotations for these three Chinese terms are normally found but the *Tai ping jing* seems original in applying the second group of connotations to a time scheme.

"Published" during the Eastern Han and used by various groups including the Yellow Turbans, the *Tai ping jing* was both influential and controversial.[31] The Yellow Turban rebellion taught the country an important lesson; that religion could be a viable base of power sufficient to bring down (or nearly bring down) a dynasty. In addition, there were other Daoist texts and Chinese generated Buddhist texts[32] in circulation at this time that held the idea of the degenerate age and the coming of a messiah. The continued use of the *Ta ping jing* and more importantly the idea that the "lower antiquity" or degenerate age was upon them, led to many Daoists inspired revolts even after the Yellow Turbans were subdued.[33]

From the first centuries of the Current Era, China was caught up in the idea of the declining age and the messianic vision of a new golden age. This is of little wonder considering the fall of the Han dynasty in 220, the period of disunity with the Wei (魏朝) and Shu Han (蜀漢朝) dynasties giving way to the Jin (晋朝) dynasty (266–316), then the short-lived kingdoms from 304 to 439 in the north and the Eastern Jin, Liu Song (刘宋朝), Southern Qi (南齐朝), Liang (梁朝), Eastern Wu (東吳朝) and Chen (陳朝) in the south. In general, various Chinese and non-Chinese militarily vied with each other to control as much of Chinese territory as possible. There were crop failures and famine. The suffering of the people compounded the situation giving rise to Daoist inspired rebellions in Zhejiang (suppressed in 324), Shandong (335–341), Hubei (345–356), Sichuan (suppressed in 370), Sun En's rebellion (399–402/411), Chang'an (407–417) and Gansu (424–427). The Northern Wei dynasty tried to deal with these conflicts by establishing a Daoist ecclesiastic structure that cooperated with the government somewhat similarly to how the Catholic Church acted as a powerful political force in the late Roman Empire.[34] Also there were the first two major persecutions against Buddhism in the north. The first by Emperor Taiwu (太武 408–452) of the Northern Wei dynasty beginning in 446 and lasting for seven years and the second by Emperor Wu (武 543–578) of the Northern Zhou dynasty first in 574 then again in 577. This last persecution extended to the Daoists as well. Thus, fears and the various attempts to mitigate them would play a role in many aspects of Chinese life for a few hundred years between the fall of the Han and the founding of the Sui dynasty.

While the Daoists held the hope for the coming of their messiah, the Buddhist countered with the hope for the birth of Maitreya here on earth. In this regard, Buddhists were far more advanced than the Daoists because the myth and cultic activities associated with Maitreya the future Buddha were already well advanced in India for hundreds of years.

That the Maitreya cult became vastly popular during the centuries between the fall of the Han dynasty and the final reunification of the country under the Sui dynasty is well attested to in a variety of sources. Tsukamoto Zenryū tabulated the inscriptions connected with Buddhist art at Yungang and Longmen and determined that the carving of Maitreya was the second most popular figure following Śākyamuni during the Northern Wei dynastic period.[35] In 370 Dao'an (道安) and his followers vow to be reborn in Maitreya's Tuṣita heaven: an act of far-reaching consequences.[36] Other famous monks associated with the Maitreya cult during this period are: Fayu (法遇), Zhusengfu (竺僧輔), Faxian (法顯), Dharmarakṣa, and Buddhabhadra to mention but a few. Works associated with Maitreya that were available during this period include: *Maitreyaparipṛcchādharmāṣṭa*,[37] *Maitreyaparipṛcchā*,[38] *Maitreyavyākaraṇa*,[39] *Maitreyābhisaṃbodhi Sūtra*,[40] *Maitreyavyākaraṇa*,[41] *Maitreyaparipṛcchopadeśa*,[42] as well as sections of the vastly popular *Lotus Sutra* and the *Avataṃsaka* and a large assortment of others texts that mention him. As noted by Arthur Wright, "Almost equally dangerous (to the theory of the End of the Dharma) were the worshipers of Maitreya, the future Buddha, who believed that the end of the world was at hand, that the descent of Maitreya would inaugurate a new heaven and a new earth."[43]

Tiantai

The great Tiantai systematizer Zhiyi's teacher was the Venerable Huisi (慧思) also known as Nanyue Huisi (515–576). He was from Shangcaixian in the Northern Wei kingdom. After becoming a monk and due to engaging in considerable yogic activities, he had a dream of joining Maitreya's entourage. His understanding of this event is noted by Leon Hurvitz:

> … the conviction of mo fa and the vision of Maitreya (not Amita) led to the belief that now if ever, when men are degenerate, is the time to strive not only for one's own salvation but for that of others as well.[44]

He was a strong advocate of the *Lotus Sutra*, a proponent of Mādhyamika and a master of meditation who twice survived poison attempts on his life.[45] Kumārajīva (344–413) seems to be the first translator to use the key term *mofa* (Final Dharma) in such works as *Lotus Sutra*[46] and *Si wei lue yao fa* (思惟略要法)[47] However, his understanding of *mofa*, a substitute for *moshi*, or "final age," may have been more in line with Indian thought. The creation of the term *mofa* allowed for a more stylistically systematic presentation of terms on the duration of the Dharma. That is *zhengfa* (正法 True/Good Dharma), *xiangfa* (像法 Semblance Dharma), and *mofa* read better than *zhengfa*, *xiangfa*, and *moshi* even given the possibility of understanding that the final age is not a separate time period

It is with Huisi that we find the periodization of the Dharma taking on the tripartite system that has now become popular and parallels the more rare tripartite system found in the *Tai ping jing*. In his *Nan yue si da chan shi li shi yuan wen* (南嶽思大禪師立誓願文)[48] he explains the whole system. Huisi even set the date for the beginning of the *mofa* (Final Dharma) period as 433.[49] Whether he is the innovator or he took this from one of the apocrypha sutras no longer extant we cannot determine but we can firmly note that his is the first presentation of this system we have so far been able to document. His solution to the problem of the limitations brought on by the age of the End of the Dharma was to be more diligent in one's activities.

Three Level (*Sanjie* 三階) Sect

In the period of time from the collapse of the Northern Wei dynasty (386–535) to the establishment of the Sui dynasty, master Xinxing (信行 540–594) was born in the area around present day Anyang in northern China. He founded his first community in the old capital of Ye and died in the new capital of Chang'an. A charismatic leader, his sect grew at a phenomenal rate. However, its doctrine could have logically led to outcomes that were unacceptable to both the Buddhist monastic establishment and the government, hence the sect was suppressed and its teachings proscribed from the official canon. A full treatment of this interesting sect's teachings is beyond the scope of the present chapter, but a look at their teachings on the end of the Dharma and the associated activities with this age will be presented below.

Xinxing divided humanity into three levels or grades of the wise, the ordinary and the foolish people. We note here the usual tripartite division used in China of upper/arising, middle/flourishing and lower/declining. The system of three levels of people does not match the three ages of Dharma as noted by Jamie Hubbard and in contrast with other scholars.[50] He believed that the majority of people living in the end age were foolish. Again as noted by Hubbard, his use of the concept End of the Dharma Age and its cognates was focused on the rhetoric of decline and not on specific time periods:

> In other words, I am not denying the connotative resonance of Hsin-hsing's usage of *mo fa* (or *mo shih*) as "latter dharma" with *mo fa* as the "final dharma" of three periods of the dharma vis-a-vis the destruction of the dharma, but more simply the presence of this latter scheme-and its sense of temporal periodization-within the texts of the Three Levels movement.[51]

To address the problem of having the majority of the people in the "latter days of the Dharma" belong to the lowest level, Xinxing recommends a number of activities. Because people in the last age could no longer distinguish the true from the false, then, one should indiscriminately reverence all beings' buddhahood. This also led the sect to be critical of other sects because the other sects maintained distinctions groundlessly. The inability of making correct determinations also invalidated Buddhist activities leaving only the Three Level's universalists approach. Self-denial and generosity to the poor were two main activities enjoined on members. The rejection of the distinction between monastic and lay and the rejection of the efficacy of the Buddhist scriptures were advocated.[52]

Pure Land

As noted in chapter one, the Pure Land lineage that runs from Tanluan to Shandao is more a listing of significant teachers than a lineage of master to disciple transmission. Daochuo is considered the fourth in this line of development (*i.e.*, Nāgārjuna, Vasubandhu, Tanluan, Daocho, Shandao). Daochuo was born in present Shanxi Province, then ruled by the Northern Qi (550–577), who had replaced the Eastern Wei, who themselves replaced the Northern Wei. Originally an advocate of the *Mahāparinirvāṇa*, Daochuo changed his focus to the Pure Land teachings of Tanluan after visiting the latter's home temple. Daocho was very much a man of his times and the many difficulties brought on by war, famine, pestilence, and the persecution of Buddhism weighed heavily on him. His only surviving work the *An le ji* (安樂集) reveals a very pessimistic view of life in this world.[53] Unlike many Chinese Buddhists who held a more naturalist view of human life, these pages reveal a person who is very sensitive to the suffering of the human condition. Reading through his compilation, one does not get the sense of someone who realizes the emptiness of all things but one who contemplates that life is suffering. This view provides motivation for one to go to some better place–the Pure Land.

His work mentions the Dharma Ending Age (*mofa/ moshi*) at a number of places.[54] According to his text, we have already entered the Dharma Ending Age[55] and this will last for 10,000 years.[56] Because of this there is no longer any real hope of gaining awakening in this world and thus we must rely on Amitābha and recite his name (*nianfo* 念佛) with the aim of gaining birth in the Pure Land and then awakening.[57] Yet, unlike the Three Level sect, there is no devaluing of the Buddhist establishment, the distinction between monastic and lay is maintained, and millennialism is not connected with Amitābha as it was with Maitreya. So there is only a shift from the ineffective activities in the Dharma Ending Age to the effective Dharmic activities.

Again, according to the study by Tsukamoto Zenryū, there were few statues carved during the Sui dynasty. With the Tang dynasty there was an increase of activity with carvings of Amitābha and Avalokiteśvara outnumbering by far the carving of either Śākyamuni or Maitreya.[58] With the unification of China under the Sui-Tang, the rhetoric of "End of the Dharma" and the advent of a new age under Maitreya began to lose its appeal. It does not altogether disappear as we know Empress Wu used the Maitreya myth to justify her usurpation and other groups throughout the years will appeal to this powerful myth.

From the above it can be determined that masters from Northern China, during the period of disunity, addressed the needs of the people by progressing ideas around the notion of the End of the Dharma and the coming of Maitreya. We have seen three examples above with each attempting to address the problems it envisioned with very different answers. Perhaps we can understand the Shandao line of Pure Land's approach to eschatological questions as an attempt at co-opting the energy behind much of the latter days of the Dharma rhetoric and direct it to the promise of a world to come once this suffering place is left behind. This changes the focus from the millenarian approach associated with Maitreya and the dangers it poses to the ruling elite. It also avoids the negative implications of devaluing Buddhist activities and the monastic institution and therefore avoids the proscription that the Sanjie sect had to face.

Chan

We find a different approach to the concept of the End of the Dharma taken by the early Chan teachings.[59] Overall little is made with regard to the End of the Dharma rhetoric. Bodhidharma's famous treatises on the *Two Ingresses and Four Courses* does not mention it nor does any of the letters referred to above in chapter six. This very early material only has two possible references to the notion of different ages of the Dharma and these references do not use standard terminology in a direct manner but only allude to the concept.

Tanlin's "Preface" to Bodhidharma's teachings states:

> (Bodhidharma's) virtue surpassed worldly degrees. Being compassionate and having remorse towards this extreme corner (of the world, *i.e.*, China) and because of the true teachings deterioration, he was consequently able to come from a distance over mountains and seas, traveling to transform the Han and Wei kingdoms …[60]

It also states:

> At that time, he only had Daoyu and Huike. These two śramaṇa although born of a later generation, had superior aspirations for the

lofty and far-ranging Dharma.[61]

Tanlin (506–574) was affiliated with the Eastern Wei court. Knowing Sanskrit, he was a participant in a number of translation projects. Because of this, he was probably familiar with the whole complex of ideas associated with the various ages of the Dharma and particularly the End of the Dharma rhetoric. However, in his "Preface" he only alludes to these ideas in passing and does not make any argument or even direct statement regarding the different ages or the End of the Dharma.

If we follow traditional accounts, then Jianzhi Sengcan's *Xin xin ming* (信心銘),[62] Daoxin's *Ru dao an xin* (入道安心),[63] Daman Hongren's (弘忍) *Xiu shang cheng lun* (㝡上乘論),[64] and Hui-neng's *The Platform Sutra of the Sixth Patriarch*[65] do not present teachings on the End of the Dharma. Although there are serious historic questions regarding these works, the authorship and date of composition of some have been challenged; they still represent a pre-classic formation in the growth of the emerging Chan tradition.

The *Fu fa zang yin yuan zhuan* (付法藏因緣傳),[66] *Xu gao seng zhun* (續高僧傳)[67] and *Leng qie shi zi ji* (楞伽i師資記),[68] are works significant in the formation of the authoritative lineage list of Chan and none have the term "*mofa*" nor "*moshi*." Although the *Xu gao seng zhun*[69] and the *Li dai fa bao ji*[70] mention the latter days or destruction of the Dharma for example, they do so outside of the Chinese created tripartite frame work of *zhengfa*, *xiangfa* and *mofa*.

Conclusion

It is interesting to note that the complex description of

the cosmos by Indian Buddhist authors presents both a horizontal structure of alternating mountains and seas surrounding the *axis mundi* with four major continents in each of the cardinal directions, and a vertical structure with ever more refined heavens stacked above the *axis mundi*, ever worsening hells descending into the depths below it and all six states of beings (*gati*) located somewhere on the vertical axis.

By the time Buddhism was entering China the whole theory of the cosmos, with its detailed composition including exactly what gets destroyed at the end of the world was widely accepted. The Chinese learned and generally accepted the system but, because of lacking an established notion of the underworld, remodeled the Indic description by adding both details and new elements primarily replicating the imperial judicial and penal system. In addition, in the Chinese system one finds emphasis being placed on Confucian values and the punishment in the next life for violating them. However, even given these alterations, the Chinese did not redefine what gets destroyed at the end of the world but accepted the position presented in the Buddhist scriptures.

As the idea of the degeneration of the ages leading to the end of the world was accepted by Hindu, Jain, and Buddhist authors through the ages, besides differences in some terminology and specific details, it can be understood as part of the general spiritual setting of India. For Buddhists, the end of the world and the generation of the new world were presented in different works but the emphasis was placed on the End of the Dharma of Śākyamuni—a precursor to the eventual end of the world. The Indic Buddhist material unquestionably presents two time periods: the time of the Good or True Dharma (*saddharma*) and the time of the Semblance of the Good or True Dharma (*saddharmapratirūpaka*). Nattier followed by others have argued that the Indian material probably did not contain a notion of a distinct third period. Although this idea is popular in modern studies according to these arguments, the notion was probably a reading back into the original materials a theory that originated in China.

This chapter has presented material on the origination and growth of the concept of a tripartite system of ever more degenerate ages in the decline and final destruction of the Dharma. The tripartite idea seems to be a coupling of Buddhist notions with a distinct development that was presented in the *Tai ping jing*. Distinct because it posited a more lineal decline instead of the common cyclic time sequence as manifested in the change and renewal of the seasons. The terminology used to denote the ages in the *Tai ping jing* was "three antiquities" with the final age being degenerate, immoral, and having a proliferation of suffering brought on by various causes.

Buddhists in the North of China, captured by the popularity of the notion of the degenerate age, experiencing the general uncertainty brought on by a few centuries of dynastic changes and warfare, and seriously affected by the persecution of Buddhism first in the fifth and later in the sixth centuries, also joined in the degenerate age rhetoric. The idea of a tripartite structure in Buddhism first being presented within the Tiantai tradition was rapidly taken up by other Buddhists.

I have presented above some case examples of how the teaching on the final age of the Dharma was fostered by different groups during the same historic period. This unambiguously demonstrates the popularity of this notion in China during those early centuries. This chapter focused on the use of the Final Dharma Age teachings in the Pure Land tradition that ran through Shandao and contrasted it with the early

Chan materials.

The outcome of this research is that whereas the Pure Land tradition under study utilized the motivating rhetoric of the Final Dharma Age to propagate its understanding of the teachings, unlike the Sanjie tradition it avoided directly challenging the Buddhist monastic institution and posing a threat to the political structure. It was able to do this by refocusing the cultic object of adherence from the messianic figure of Maitreya to the safer figure of Amitābha and maintaining the centrality of the monastic establishment.

This chapter also allows the reader to see sinicization in three areas: First, the remolding of the underworld to mimic Chinese judicial and penal systems would provide Chinese Buddhists a presentation of something radically new dressed within a garb that was familiar. Second, the co-opting of a declining periodization scheme presented in a very popular contemporaneous work and melding it to Buddhist ideas with only slight modification from the Indic model, allowed Buddhists to utilize the energy behind this popular idea to promote the Dharma in general and specific teachings in particular. Third, and perhaps most importantly, the idea of the decline of the Dharma, logically necessary in a doctrine that posits constant change, with ample unquestioned scriptural support, was understood as providing motivation for diligence in activities and study in the Indian cultural sphere. In the Tanluan lineage of Pure Land teachings, there are two forms of siniciziation as indicated above. Not only do we find the acceptance of the Chinese tripartite periodization scheme borrowed and modified from the *Tai ping jing*, but the declaration that in this final age the staples of Buddhist praxis are no longer efficacious and thus, people must rely on Amitābha to be reborn in his realm and achieve nirvana not here or in this life time, but in the future life in that purified land.

The doctrine of Buddha-nature was one of the scriptural elaborations in India that ameliorated the whole decline of the Dharma scenario by claiming that one has the same mind as a buddha albeit adventitiously covered up. Thus, it is never out of reach or unrealizable. Because the budding Chan tradition from its beginning was developed based on the Buddha-nature teachings at least in part, in its pre-classical phase there was little need to utilize the Final Dharma Age rhetoric. Finally, although the Pure Land tradition based its approach to Buddhism on the above innovations, the Chan tradition did not formulate its form of praxis using the Final Dharma Age teachings as a basis for its innovations.

Conclusion

> After circling around the ancient wood structure of Fo Guan Temple noticing the pagoda towards the rear, one enters and is awed by the presence of so many Tang works of art. Buddhas and bodhisattvas are displaying elements of Chinese and Indian artistic influences in their various poses. Here, in exquisite three dimensional colored refinements is sinicization of Buddhism.[1]

There are many topics that could have been explored that were not presented in this volume. The introduction of: the pagoda (stupa), the cult of the relics, pilgrimage, the keeping of private chapels within the palace, music and musical instruments, further philosophical ideas and other topics remain to be explored. All of these have been influenced by Buddhism and Buddhism in East Asian has been influenced by Chinese culture and thus worthy of being included in a study on sinicization.

We have seen from chapter one, that, overall, the Chinese did not critique history in a similar fashion to what we noted in some Indian materials. Their orientation toward history was based on native developments in historiography. We also noted similarities between the Indian Buddhist approach and that taken in China. The similarities discussed in that chapter included using history as a pedagogical tool (teaching cause/effect and how the awakened live in the world), the "golden age" mentality, and the idea of history being an account of great men and great events. Further, in our analysis of the Pure Land tradition's use of history, we noted that the Tanluan branch of the Pure Land teachings stayed within the parameters of contemporaneous Chinese expectations regarding historiography. However in the Sui and Tang periods, the Chan tradition broke new ground by not only incorporating the use of history for pedagogy, "golden age" mentality, and the idea of history being an account of great men and great events but by using the idea of an unbroken lineage within a ritual context. Finally, this was further developed in the Song dynasty when the assigning of the *gong'an/huatou* as a technique made meditation an encounter with ancient masters. Therefore, the uniting of Indic and Chinese thought regarding history, the Chinese rejecting the Indian critique and following their own traditions, and the bringing together of Chinese notion of lineage and ritual are some of the techniques of sinicization of Buddhism.

Buddhism showed itself unique within the Indian philosophical context by upholding a no-self position and yet accepting the idea of rebirth. These two positions created various philosophical problems which were addressed by different solutions spread across the multitude of Buddhist sects in India. One of these solutions was the development of the concept of *tathāgatagarbha* and of particular interest was its expression in the *Mahāparinirvāṇa* with its use of "great self" and "true self." The pre-Buddhist Chinese did not have an idea of a self trapped in an endless round of suffering lives and so their philosophy understood the "self" in very different terms than the Indian position. For the Chinese, a self was something that was a part of a great context of interrelated circles forming meaning. Of course, as with all people, suffering was recognized as a common human experience. The quest for nirvana was just as much a quest for wholeness as it was for release. In this regard, we demonstrated that in the early teachings of Chan, there is documentation of how the tradition was tapping into the Chinese ideas of self and not the Indian. It was also shown that the Chan tradition used the notion of a "true self" probably from the *Mahāparinirvāṇa* to connect its teachings with the native generated idea of a "true man/person" as found in Zhuangzi's writings and to the idea of the *junzi* (superior person) found in Confucianism. This demonstrates that while assimilating Buddhism from India, the Chinese kept to their own ideas of self, they amalgam the Indian notion of release with their own desire for wholeness, and by using native produced technical terms to discuss Chan ideas, they reassured the receptive audience that this profound teaching was in line with their own ancient sages' wisdom.

We have also seen how, in the performing arts, the Chinese blended native elements with Indic elements to create new aspects and meaning for ancient traditions. The inclusion of many aspects of the Indic *nāga* cult and the addition of the "pearl of wisdom" to the Dragon Dance expanded the symbolism of the dance and hence its meaning as well as enhancing the significance of the dragon. It is also worth noting that in the final formulation of this art, only Shaolin Buddhist monks could perform the five clawed golden Dragon Dance for the emperor. In this way, the dragon not only is the bringer of auspiciousness and fortune but reminds one that obtaining Buddhist wisdom is the real goal. The beginning of the Lion Dance in the Tang dynasty era demonstrates how Buddhists answered a popular need by creating a new form from blending various elements of Chinese culture and Indian Buddhism. The performance of a costume dance to bring about various benefits from the "other realm" (however conceived) is indeed an ancient Chinese idea. Leveraging the popularity of the Indian Bodhisattva Mañjuśrī by using his mount, which gets transformed into a playful Pekingese dog-like character, was a stroke of genius. It answered the need for auspiciousness, bringing the teachings alive, adding to the grandeur of the parade, and it had entertainment value. Thus, both adaptation and creation came to be tools used in the transitioning of Buddhism on Chinese soil.

Although play is a universal activity among all peoples and even in many other mammals to understand that the spiritual activities engaged in by a buddha and the accomplishing of profound meditational states are to him mere play, requires a particular view of how the universe is structured differently in the perceptions of ordinary people and those of a buddha. In both the Pali and Sanskrit Buddhist texts, "buddha play" is well documented. Pre-Buddhist China had some nonhuman celestial types that allowed for a merging of concepts with particular Indic Buddhist other worldly beings. The Indian gods could be identified with Chinese gods or at the least seated in heaven. Daoist immortals would act as the prototype for the arhats. Yet a Buddha was a being demanding a new category, one allowing for augustness, spiritual mastery, mystic powers, both present and not, defying all other categories, the very embodiment of microcosm and the macrocosm, nirvana manifest and more. The idea that such a unique being seeing the difficulties of spiritual advancement as mere play puzzled the Chinese translators sufficiently that over the centuries they continued to offer different attempts to translate the term, capture the Indic connotation and bring it into the Chinese spiritual dialogue. Spiritual play is then furthered in the Pure Land and Chan traditions as a regular feature as the centuries pass demonstrating how the notion had become part of the Chinese concept.

The reader has seen that the famous quotation "to see the Dharma is to see the Buddha" has its counterpoint in the phrase "to see the Buddha is to see the Dharma." Over time, the *śrāvaka* traditions allowed the importance of *darśana* (seeing the Buddha and entering into the nirvanic sphere of power) to diminish even though this approach to Buddhism is documented from the beginning of the tradition with the accounts of Vakkali and others. The Buddhist activities of *darśana* again gained significance in the Mahayana branch. It appears that the relationship that Indian Buddhists had with their icons was similar to what we know from ancient Greek culture and thus like with the ancient Greeks it is reasonable to speak of a ritual appreciation of the image and not simply the art-historic/aesthetic appreciation.

This Indian approach of a ritual appreciation of an image appears in China promoted by the Tiantai School and this becomes a significant aid in the growth of the Amitābha cult. Tanluan's line of Pure Land teachings does not follow this precedent but instead developed the use of art for devotional aids devoid of an association with the meditative tradition and as a means of inspiration to enhance one's longing for rebirth in the *Sukhāvatīvyūha.* This approach did not require the artist to attempt to render his vision from meditation into Pure Land art but to merely follow an academic prescription in art production.

The Chan tradition was very innovative in its production of Buddhist art in comparison to the Pure Land art of the Tanluan line. Not only is it often more down-to-earth in both subject selection and the subject's rendering, but the art studied also incorporates the awakened vision of the artists and can act as a visual *gong'an* (Jp. *koan*). Landscape paintings in particular bring together the artist's vision of both form and emptiness. This in turn, points to something outside the frame—to the emptinesses of emptinesses. It is the experience of this emptiness of emptiness that the art will hopefully trigger.

Here we see sinicization taking place in art with the Tiantai maintaining the Indic model, Tanluan's Pure Land line removing the meditative aspects and Chan innovating in such a way as to capture the core of the Perfection of Wisdom while originating a visual means to point to awakening. This is an interesting case where two different movements were developed based on doctrine and Buddhist activities.

Even when we examined the founding document of the Chan tradition, the *Two Ingresses and Four Courses*, along with other early materials, we have found different aspects of sinicization. First, the activities that are listed in the group of documents are locatable in various Buddhist texts all of which were translated from Indic texts before or contemporaneously with Bodhidharma's arrival. In addition, the technical terms too were locatable in various Buddhist texts with the exception of *biguan* (wall contemplation). In this regard, the term was not locatable but the state of meditation as defined in the Chan texts is documentable.

Sinicization in this case took place in the topic selection and in the organization of the information. Using the "principle/function" bi-polar analytic approach is a Chinese way of organizing knowledge and allows for harmonizing divergent positions on various difficult topics. This approach is generally not found in Indian Buddhist material but is found in the native Chinese intellectual tradition. Further topics included in the teachings were shown to have connections to Chinese sentiments, well within the parameters of the Chinese spiritual tradition and leveraging contemporaneously popular points.

Finally, the cosmology of Indian Buddhists was in general acceptable by the Chinese because they had no equivalent in details. However, they did not simply take over the entire system but made modifications to bring it in line with various Chinese notions. They amalgamated their idea of the penal system to the underworld creating interesting variations on the theme in particular. The Indian notion of different ages of the Dharma which may have only included two: the age of the Good Dharma and the age of the Semblance of the Good Dharma coupled with an age with no dharma available in the realm of humans was influenced by Chinese ideas of degeneration. The tripartite Buddhist system that is ubiquitous in China from the Sui dynasty, seems to have incorporated ideas from the *Tai ping jing* on a lineal degeneration which was different than the cyclic generation/degeneration found more popularly in multiple Chinese works. The idea of the degeneration of the Dharma was a motivating factor in developing Buddhist activities both in India and in China. In India, the idea was to hold off the advent of the decline in the Dharma by keeping cultivation strong and true, by the introductions of ultimately sanctioned new teachings, and by teachings that nullified the importance of the decline in the Semblance Dharma age. In China, the Tanluan line of Pure Land thought determined that in the final age of Dharma, Buddhist activities were meaningless and one could only rely on the Buddha Amitābha compassion to be reborn in his realm. This truly is a Chinese innovation which seems to have no precedent in India in terms of praxis. The Chan tradition based on Buddha-nature notions did not feel the need to innovate in a similar manner. Since beings and buddhas have the same nature, one only needs to uncover it and therefore nothing is actually lost. Therefore, the idea of the inefficiency of the activities due to having entered the age of the End of the Dharma did not provide impetus in the Chan tradition at its inception.

Robert Gimello in his "Random Reflections on the "Sinicization" of Buddhism,"[2] presents a delineation of the hermeneutical orientation taken on this topic by the eminent scholars Walter Liebenthal and Richard H. Robinson. He demonstrates that these different orientations produce very different "understandings" of Seng Chao (Sengzhao 384–414). Liebenthal accepting the idea that "world-interpretations are not transferable" finds Sengzhao not much of a Buddhist let alone a Mādhyamikin. Robinson however taking the middle ground on the possibility or lack of possibility of transferring ideas finds Sengzhao very much a Mādhyamikin. Gimello also expounds on how one's hermeneutical orientation is significant for undertaking the topic of sinicization. There are, of course, many arguments that may be advanced for and against the possibility of something like "sinicization" being considered a valid concept. Or, if considered somehow valid for intellectual reasons, one may ask what type of sinicization is one expounding upon? I would like to make my own position clear as a means of hopefully avoiding problems as we proceed to my final thoughts.

For me, as a scholar, the core of Buddhism is an inaccessible experience called "awakening." It is inaccessible to scholars as scholars because that experience is ineffable. According to tradition, accessing that experience is through yoga and the tools of a scholar fall far short. In brief, we can talk all around the topic but never once actually touch it. Yogis and yoginis can freely access it because they have a different box of tools than a scholar. As explained in the sutra entitled *A Discourse on Ready Eloquence*:

> Then Pure Giving said to Ānanda, "Virtuous one, the World-Honored One says that you stand first among the learned. Is your knowledge that of the real meaning of things, or that of words? If it is knowledge of the real meaning of things, consider that the real meaning is beyond speech. What is beyond speech cannot be known through the auditory consciousness. What cannot be known through the auditory consciousness cannot be expressed by speech. If your knowledge is that of words, [it is meaningless, for] the World-Honored One says that one should rely on the ultimate meaning of a discourse, not on mere words. Therefore, Virtuous Ānanda, you are no learned, nor do you understand the ultimate meaning."[3]

Given this, sinicization as a concept, for me, is not about making the real meaning or core of Buddhism Chinese. However, it also is not a statement about the core of Buddhism being immutable. Sinicization as a concept is simply not a statement about that core because with the tools scholars have at their disposal, they cannot evaluate, measure, gauge or even access the core of Buddhism. Sinicization is about the periphery for that is where the intellectual traditions of India and China have their field of activity within Buddhism. This does not mean that there are two inexplicably separate spheres; one the core and the other the peripheral intellectualization. In fact, there is a dynamic relationship between the two in many cases in that the intellectual expression often grows out of the core experience and can help in leading one to the core. That is, great masters who have gained insight have tried to articulate that insight to their disciples so that they could be lead to gain the insight for themselves.

When we look at current Tibetan Buddhism and compare it with Japanese Buddhism we can notice that they are very different although having similarities. Some of these differences can be attributed to sources internal to Buddhism such as texts emphasized, doctrines adapted, lineages, *et cetera*. However, some are clearly cultural. Because of this case, it is not difficult to imagine that differences existed between Indian Buddhism and Chinese Buddhism in various historic periods that were also cultural in origin. Here we are on far less firm ground than when comparing Tibetan and Japanese forms because we have to theoretically reconstruct Indian Buddhism. Although we have many excellent tools we are still severely handicapped in our efforts. One also has to reconstruct medieval Chinese Buddhism but this is a different task. Unlike in India where Buddhism was no longer a force for the past half millennium and the dynamics of medieval India allowed for considerable destruction and removal of Buddhist material culture and general cultural influences, China has a continuing Buddhist influenced culture. These undertakings of reconstructions are further exacerbated by my personal limitations being a person of the twenty-first century living in North America.

I also fully agree with Gimello in the same article that it would be just as reasonable to talk about the "Buddhacization" of China. Just as the Chinese made Buddhism a phenomenon in their culture, their culture was permanently altered by Buddhism. Viewing Buddhism in China as presenting some sort of parasitic relationship as some past scholars tried to argue would be to go too far. The Buddhacization type of study will have to wait for another time. The task here is to try to understand the methods employed in generating a Buddhism that is Chinese. In the introduction, I cautioned the reader to not see in the studies presented here the setting up of India as a measure of what is or what is not authentic Buddhism. To investigate Buddhism in China and to try to see how much the Chinese became "Indianized" in their adherence to the Dharma would be to set up false measures and expectations.

Buddhism is a living organism. It claims that there are universal truths that transcend cultural and historic barriers. First, this position seems to have been a natural outgrowth of the environment in India during the formative period of Buddhism. India is not a single monolithic culture and we could say there are a number of "Indias." Different groups settled in the South Asian land mass over the centuries and Buddhism had to be able to speak to each individual in those communities. Thus, it had to advance its ideological foundation with a more open stance. Further, the success of Buddhism to have flourished in India for 2,000 years regardless of the significant changes that took place demonstrates its truths are not those confined to a particular time. Also, the fact that it spread beyond the confines of the South Asian sub-continent and beyond spheres of various Indian cultures demonstrates that it can also transcend place. Given the above, setting up any one cultural form of Buddhism as a standard would be meaningless. Buddhism on Indian soil had its particular expression, Buddhism on Chinese soil had another, and so too with Buddhism in Japan, Korea, Vietnam, Tibet, and elsewhere, each had its unique expression.

Raising the question, "was Buddhism overwhelmed by

Chinese culture," would begin an inquiry on the wrong premises. It has been shown in this particular case of the original documents forming the foundation of the Chan tradition that the activities being promoted are all based on documented preexisting Indian forms. Although the Chan tradition is often thought to be the quintessential form of "Chinese Buddhism," its inception did not stray far from its mooring in the Indian heritage. Whatever outgrowth that would follow from this beginning was a marriage. Like with all healthy marriages there is a continuous renewal while growth is transpiring. In the case of the Chan tradition, even Linji quotes from the sutras.

It was the continual return to the Buddhist sources and inspirations in India that allowed for the growth to not become a cancer growing out of control and becoming dangerous to health. This too was the case in China. A case in point is in ancient times catalogers would classify some texts as suspicious and others were utterly rejected. Indubitably, some of those texts which were questioned were drawn from Chinese cultural inspiration and participated in the Chinese spiritual dialogue in one way or another. The reason for rejection was based on standards used in Buddhism. This questioning/rejecting process demonstrates that there were limits beyond which the Buddhist community would not accept a text as authentic Dharma. It also clearly shows that there was no overwhelming of Buddhism by Chinese culture but a dynamic accord of Indic and Chinese influences.

There are of course a hundred and one questions that can be raised making interested readers on such topics more sensitive to the problems. Gimello does an excellent job of isolating a number of questions for consideration in his "Random Reflections ..." However, when it is all said and done:

After circling around the ancient wood structure of Fo Guan Temple noticing the pagoda towards the rear, one enters and is awed by the presence of so many Tang works of art. Buddhas and bodhisattvas are displaying elements of Chinese and Indian artistic influences in their various poses. Here, in exquisite three dimensional colored refinements is sinicization of Buddhism.

Endnotes

Front Matter

1. Cited as requested.

Introduction

1. Needham, Joseph, *Science and Civilisation in China*. Taipei: Caves Books. Ltd. 1985, Vol. 1, pg. 156.
2. Derris, Karen, and Gummer, Natali. *Defining Buddhism(s)*. London: Equinox Publishing Ltd. 2007, pg. 2.
3. This is not to say that there were no educated women or that some women did not play a significant role in the literary life of China in classic times. However, the number of women who contributed was small in comparison.
4. Ideda, Daisaku. *The Flower of Chinese Buddhism* (trans. Burton Watson). Santa Monica: Middle Way Press, 2009, pg. 29.
5. Zurcher, Erik. "Perspectives in the Study of Chinese Buddhism," *Journal of the Royal Asiatic Society of Great Britain and Ireland*, No.1 (1982), pg. 164.
[captured 10/08/2010: http://www.jstor.org/stable/25211314].
6. Zurcher, Erik. "Buddhism and Education in T'ang Times," in de Bary, Wm. Theodore and Chaffee, John W. *Neo-Confucian Education: The Formative Stage*. Berkeley: University of California Press, 1989, pp. 19–56.
7. Zurcher, *"Perspectives…" ibid.* pg. 164.
8. See: Yü, Chün-fang, "The Chinese Transformation of Avalokiteshvara," in Weidner, Marsha (ed.) *Latter Days of the Law Images of Chinese Buddhism 850–1850*. Lawrence & Honolulu: Spencer Museum of Art, The University of Kansas in association with University of Hawaii Press, 1994.
9. Demiéville, Paul. "La penetration du Bouddhisme dans la tradition philosophique chinoise," *Cahiers d'histoire modiale*, III, No.1 (1956), pp. 19–38.
10. Zurcher, Erik. *The Buddhist Conquest of China: The Spread and Adaptation of Buddhism in Early Medieval China*. Leiden: E.J. Brill, 1959.
11. Gregory, Peter N. *Tsung-mi and the Sinification of Buddhism*. Princeton, Princeton University Press, 1991.
12. Ch'en, Kenneth K.S. *The Chinese Transformation of Buddhism*. Princeton: Princeton University Press, 1973.

13. Sharf, Robert H. *Coming to Terms with Chinese Buddhism: A Reading of the Treasure Store Treatise*. Honolulu: University of Hawaii Press, 2002.
14. Buswell, Robert E. Jr. (ed.) *Chinese Buddhist Apocrypha.* Honolulu: University of Hawaii Press, 1990.
15. Whitehead, James. *The Sinicization of Buddhism: A Study of the "Vimalakīrtinirdeśa Sūtra" and Its Interpretations in China from the Third Through the Sixth-Century*. [Harvard, Dissertation, ProQuest Dissertations Publishing, 1976].
16. Ch'en, Kenneth K.S. *Buddhism in China*. Princeton: Princeton University Press, 1964, pp. 68–69.
17. Tsukamoto, Zenryū. *A History of Early Chinese Buddhism* (trans. Leon Hurvitz). Tokyo: Kodansha International Ltd. 1979. pg. 248. Parenthesis added.
18. Ge Hong Zhuan, *Bao pu zi*. Taibei: 1965, https://openlibrary.org/books/OL18909433M/Bao_pu_zi
19. See: T.52 #2102; and Keenan, John P. *How Master Mou Removes Our Doubts*. Albany: State University of New York Press, 1994.
20. Fung, Yu-lan. *A History of Chinese Philosophy* (trans. Derk Bodde). Princeton: Princeton University Press, 1952, Vol.2, pg. 242.
21. Sharf, *ibid.*
22. Dante. *The Divine Comedy*, (Vol. I) *Inferno*, (trans. Musa, Mark). New York: Penguin Books, 2003, pg. 89.
23. For example, On Bai Juyi and the three religions see: Naismith, Earl George. *Bai Juyi (Bai Lo Tian) 易居白 (樂白天), 772–846 AD, Tang Dynasty Poet, Midst Everyday Life, Musings on the Ordinary, Influences of the Not So Obvious*. Vancouver: University of British Columbia Thesis (2003) [captured 2/4/2019: https://open.library.ubc.ca/media/download/pdf/24/1.0067082/1].
24. Mair, Victor H. "What is Geyi, After All?" in Chan, Alan K. L. and Lo, Yuet-Keung (eds.) *Philosophy and Religion in Early Medieval China.* Albany: State University of New York Press, 2010, pg. 227.

Chapter One

Buddhist Historiography in China

1. This is a considerably reworked version of my ideas on this topic first presented in "Memory and Chinese Buddhist Historical Writings," *Proceedings of the 8th Symposium of Confucianism, Buddhism, Communication and Philosophy of Culture*, (Taipei: 2005).
2. Gardner, W., Pickett, C., & Brewer, M. "Social Exclusion and Selective Memory: How the Need to Belong Influences Memory for Social Events." *Personality and Social Psychology Bulletin*, Vol. 26, No. 4,

April 2000, pp. 486–497.
[3.] Woike, B., Mcleod, S., & Goggin, M. "Implicit and Explicit Motives Influence Accessibility to Different Autobiographical Knowledge." *Personality and Social Psychology Bulletin*, Vol. 29, No. 8, Aug. 2003, pp. 1046–1055.
[4.] Rhys-Davids, T.W. *The Questions of King Milinda.* New York: Dower Publications, Inc. 1963, Part I, pp. 122–23, (see note on numbering).
[5.] Botella, Luis. "Personal Construct Psychology, Constructivism, and Postmodern Thought." [captured 10/16/04: www.massey.ac.nz/~alock/virtual/Construc.htm], pg. 6.
[6.] *E.g.*, Poussin, Louise de La Valle, *Abhidharmakośabhāṣyam.* (trans. Pruden, Leo M.) Berkeley: Asian Humanities Press, 1990, pg. 194.
[7.] Rhys-Davids, Caroline. (trans.) *A Buddhist Manual of Psychological Ethics (Dhamma-saṅgaṇī).* London: The Pali Text Society, 1974, pg. 14.
[8.] Jaini, Padmanabh S. "*Smṛti* in the Abhidharma Literature and the Development of Buddhist Accounts of Memory of the Past," in Gyatso, Janet. *In the Mirror of Memory: Reflections on Mindfulness and Remembrance in Indian and Tibetan Buddhism.* Delhi: Sri Satguru Publications, 1992, pp. 49–50. See also: Poussin, Louis de La Vallee. *ibid.* pg. 1339; for the original Sanskrit see: Shastri, Swami Dwarikadas (ed.) *Abhidharmakośam & Bhāṣya of Acharya Vasubandhu with Sputārthā Commentary of Ācārya Yaśomitra* (*sic.*). Varanasi: Bauddha Bharati, 1973, pp. 1215–1216. Jaini's reading is closer to the original Sanskrit than Pruden's rendering and thus my selection.
[9.] Wayman, Alex. "Buddhist Terms for Recollection and Other Types of Memory," in Gyatso, *ibid.* pp. 139–141.
[10.] Rhys-Davids, T.W. *Dialogues of the Buddha.* London: Pali Text Society, 1977, pp. 13–14.
[11.] Gokhale, Valkrishna G. "On Buddhist Historiography," in Narain, A.K. (ed.) *Studies in Pali and Buddhism.* Delhi: B.R. Publishing Corporation, 1979, pp. 99 *ff.*
[12.] Gokhale, *ibid.* pg. 99.
[13.] For an interesting discussion of Buddhist use of different concepts of time see: Wayman, Alex, "No time, Great Time, and Profane Time in Buddhism," in his *Buddhist Insight.* Delhi Motilal Banarsidass, 1984, pp. 269 *ff.*
[14.] Kulasurya, Ananda S. "The Jatakas and their Ethical Foundation," in Dhammajoti, K. Tilakaratne, A. Abhayawansa, K. (eds.) *Recent Research in Buddhist Studies.* Colombo: Y. Karunada Felicitation Committee, 1997, pp. 403 *ff.;* Winternitz, Maurice. *History of Indian Literature.* Delhi: Motilal Banarsidass, 1988, pp. 109 *ff.*
[15.] Winternitz, *ibid.* pg. 263.
[16.] See: Thomas, Edward. *The Life of Buddha as Legend and History.* London: Routledge & Kegan Paul, 1975.

17. Lamotte, Etienne. *History of Indian Buddhism.* (trans. Webb-Boin, S.) Louvain: Petters Press, 1988, pg. 574.
18. Lamotte, *ibid.* pp. 275–277.
19. Lamotte, *ibid.* pp. 277–281.
20. Bhāvaviveka, *Madhyamakahṛdayavṛttitarkajvāl.* TP. 5256 and Lamotte, *ibid.* pp. 281–282.
21. Norman, K.R. *Pali Literature.* Wiesbaden: Otto Harrassowitz, 1983, pg. 26.
22. Lamotte, *ibid.* pg. 206; and: Strong, John. *The Legend of King Aśoka.* Princeton: Princeton University Press, 1983, pg. 78 n.18.
23. Lamotte, *ibid.* pp. 205–206. Lamotte notes that this lineage has no historic value.
24. On the critical stance in the Song dynasty see: "The Historian as Critic: Li Hsin-ch'uan and the Dilemmas of Statecraft in Southern Sung China," in Hymes, Robert P. and Schirokauer, Conrad. (eds.) *Ordering the World Approaches to State and Society in Sung Dynasty China.* Berkeley: University of California Press, 1993, pp. 310–335.
25. Watson, Burton., Nivison, David., & Bloom, Irene. "Classical Sources of Chinese Tradition," in de Bary, Wm. Theodore & Bloom, Irene. *Sources of Chinese Traditions* (Vol. 1. 2nd ed.) New York: Columbia University Press, 1999, pg. 26.
26. See: *Ziporun, Brook. Evil and/or/as The Good.* Cambridge, Mass.: Harvard University Press, 2000, pg. 87, for a discussion of Chinese fusion of fact/value.
27. Watson, Burton. "The Great Han Historians," in de Bary, Wm. Theodore and Bloom, Irene. *ibid.* pg. 368.
28. Watson, Burton. "Han Views of the Universal Order," in *ibid.* pp. 346 *ff.*
29. Watson, Burton. *Ssu-Ma Ch'ien Grand Historian of China.* New York: Columbia University Press, 1963, pg. 8.
30. Meskill, John. *The Pattern of Chinese History.* Boston: D.C. Heath and Company, 1965, pg. vii.
31. Watson, *Ssu-Ma Ch'ien Grand Historian of China. ibid.* pg. 183.
32. Watson, *Ssu-Ma Ch'ien Grand Historian of China ibid.* pg. 183.
33. On the necessity of rituals for one's ancestors see: The *Analects of Confucius* [2.5.2–3] "…The master replied, 'I meant to serve one's parents with ritual when they are alive, to bury them with ritual when they die, and thereafter to sacrifice to them with ritual.' " in Sommer, Deborah. (ed.) *Chinese Religion an Anthology of Sources.* Oxford: Oxford University Press, 1995, pg. 46. On the rituals associated with the funeral see dated by still worthy: de Groot, J.J. M. *The Religious System of China.* Vol. II. Leyden: E.J. Brill, 1894, *passim*; also Loewe, Michael. *Faith, Myth and Reason in Han China.* Indianapolis: Hackett Publishing Company, Inc, 2005, pp. 114 *ff.*

[34] For a study of Zhuxi's (Chiu Hsi) notions of history see: Schirokauer, Conrad. "Chu Hsi's Sense of History," in Hymes, Robert P. and Schirokauer, Conrad. *ibid.* pp. 193–220.
[35] *Liang gao seng zhuan (Liang kao seng chuan)*: T.50, #2059.
[36] T.50, #2059 . pg. 418c.
[37] This literature is often referred to as "hagiographies." However I find this term to be a poor choice for the material it supposes to describe. Both the *Oxford English Reference Dictionary* (2nd ed. / Pearsall, Judy & Trumble, Bill. Oxford: Oxford University Press, 2001, pg. 632 and the *Merriam Webster Collegiate Dictionary* (10th ed. Mish, Frederic C. ed.-in-chief. Springfiled, Mass.: Merriam-Webster, Inc., 1995) pg. 522, associate this literature with the lives of saints. However, Buddhism does not have an internal category "saint." The internal categories are: buddhas, bodhisattvas, arhats, and various types of masters. None of these are canonized or generally reside in the creator's heaven. Yet, this genre of literature is clearly not biographies. As they have been called biographies, I place this term in quotations to indicate these problems.
[38] *Xu gao seng zhuan* (*Hsu kao seng chuan*). T.50, #2060. and see: Kieschnick, John. *The Eminent Monk: Buddhist Ideas in Medieval Chinese Hagiography.* Honolulu: University of Hawaii Press, 1997, pg. 10
[39] *Song gao seng zhuan (Sung koa seng chuan*) T.50, #2061.
[40] For several excellent studies see: Adamek, Wendi L. *The Mystique of Transmission On an Early Chan History and its Contexts.* New York: Columbia University Press, 2007, *passim*; Foulk, T. Griffith, "Myth, Ritual, and Monastic Practice in Sung Ch'an Buddhism," in Ebrey, Patricia B. & Gregory, Peter N. *Religion and Society in T'ang and Sung China.* Honolulu: University of Hawaii Press,1993; Foulk, T. Griffith, "Sung Controversies Concerning the "Separate Transmission" of Ch'an," in Gregory, Peter N. and Daniel A. Getz, Jr. *Buddhism in the Sung.* Honolulu: University of Hawai'i Press, 1999; Welter, Albert. "Lineage and Context in the *Patriarch's Hall Collection* and the *Transmission of the Lamp*," in Heine, Steven & Wright, Dale S. *The Zen Canon: Understanding the Classic Texts. Oxford: Oxford University Press,* 2004.; and for the use of lineage in Tiantai histories, see: Shinohara, Koichi. "From Local History to Universal History: The Construction of the Sung T'ien-T'ai Lineage," in Gregory, Peter N. and Getz, Jr. Daniel A. *ibid.* pp. 524–576.
[41] See: T.50, #2059, pg. 422c.
[42] Foulk, "Myth, Ritual, and Monastic Practice," *ibid.* pp. 149 *ff.* Foulk's position on Zen historic material is defensible, whereas Alan Cole's position in *Fathering Your Father The Zen Fabrication of Tang Buddhism*. Berkeley: University of California Press, 2009, finds little history in the documents but considerable questionable motivations in fabricating accounts.
[43] Yanagida Seizan, *Shoki zenshū shisho no kenkyū*. Kyoto: Hōzōkan,

1967.

44. Yanagida S. *ibid.* pg. 155.

45. For an in depth reviews of Chan historiography see: Faure, Bernard. *Chan Insight and Oversight An Epistemological Critique of the Chan tradition.* Princeton: Princeton University Press, 1993, pp. 89–125.

46. Poceski, Mario. "Monastic Innovator, Iconoclast, and Teacher of Doctrine: The Varied Images of Chan Master Baizhang," in Heine, Steven and Wright, Dale S. *Zen Masters.* New York: Oxford University Press, 2010.

47. Kieschnick, *ibid.* pg.4. The following section is based on Keischnick's explanation of the use of the models and draws on the material he presented.

48. For accounts of tantric yogins see: Robins, James. *Buddha's Lions.* Berkeley: Dharma Publishing, 1979. On unkeptness see pp. 103–105.

49. To his credit, Foulk does discuss aspects of this in his article, see: "Myth, Ritual, and Monastic Practice," *ibid.* pg. 155.

50. See: Getz, Daniel A. Jr. "T'ien-t'ai Pure Land Societies and the Creation of the Pure Land Patriarchate," in Gregory, Peter N. & Getz, Daniel A. Jr. *ibid.*

51. *An le ji (An le chi).* T.47, #1958.

52. T.46, #1956, pp. 14b*ff.* and Inagaki, Hisao. *T'an Luan's Commentary on Vasubandhu's Discourse on the Pure Land*, Kyoto: Nagata Bunshodo, 1998, pp. 30.

53. Shinko Mochizuki, "Pure Land Buddhism in China: A Doctrinal History," (Pruden, Leo M. trans.), ebook: *Journal of the Institute of Buddhist Studies*: http://elibrary.ibc.ac.th/files/public/HistoryOfPureLand_ibc2010v1.pdf and *Chugoku jodokyorishi, Hozokan, Kyoto*, 1942 &1964, pp. 64–7, as cited in Inagaki, *ibid.* pg. 109 n84.

54. *Jodosangoku-bussodenshu by Shogei*, see: Inagaki, *ibid.* pg. 109.

55. Chinese sources: *An le ji (An le chi)* T.47, #1958; *Xu gao seng zhuan (Hsü kao-seng ch'uan)* T.50, #2060; *Wang sheng xi fang jing tu rui ying zhuan (Wang-sheng hsi-fang ching-t'u jui-ying chuan)* T.47, #2070.

56. *Jing tu lun (Ching-t'u lun).* T.26, #1524.

57. Corless, Roger J. "T'an-luan: The First Systematizer of Pure Land Buddhism," in Foard, James, Solomon, Michael, and Payne, Richard K. (eds.) *The Pure Land Tradition: History and Development.* Berkeley: Berkeley Buddhist Studies Series, 1996; Corless, Roger J. *T'an-luan's Commentary On The Pure Land Discourse: An Annotated Translation and Soteriological Analysis of the Wang-Sheng-Lun Chu (T.1819).* Ann Arbor: University Microfilms, 1975; Inagaki, *ibid.* pp. 17–25; Unno, Tetsuo. *An Introduction to the Jodoronchu with Translation and Footnotes.* Kyoto: Ryukoku University, (Master Thesis) 1958.

58. Inagaki, Hisao. *The Three Pure Land Sutras.* Kyoto: Nagata Bunshodo, 1994, pp. 90–93.

[59] On Daochuo and Shandao see: Chappell, David. "The Formation of the Pure Land Movement in China: Tao-ch'o and Shan-tao" in Foard, James, Solomon, Michael, and Payne, Richard K (eds.) *ibid;* on Shandao see: Fujiwara, Ryosetsu. *The Way to Nirvana.* Tokyo: The Kyoiku Shincho Sha, 1974; Pas, Julian. *Visions of Sukhāvatī: Shan-Tao's Commentary on the Kuan Wu-Liang-Shou-Fo Ching*. Albany: State University of New York Press, 1995.
[60] T.51, #2070.
[61] For a study of Chan lineage formation see: Adamek, *ibid.* and Faure, Bernard. *The Will to Orthodoxy.* Stanford: Stanford University Press, 1997; further see: Heine, Steven and Wright, Dale S. *Zen Canon. ibid. passim.*
[62] See: Yanagida S. *Shoki no zenshi 1 —Ryōgo shiji ki —Denhōbō ki,* in *Zen no goroku,* no.2. (Tokyo: Chikuma Shobō, 1971); McRae, John. *The Northern School and the Formation of Early Ch'an Buddhism.* Honolulu: University of Hawaii Press, 1986, *passim*; Yampolsky, Philip. "New Japanese Studies in Early Ch'an History," in Lai, W. & Lancaster, L. *Early Ch'an in China and Tibet.* Berkeley: University of California Press, 1983,; Yanagida S. "The Li-Tai Fa-Pao Chi and the Ch'an Doctrine of Sudden Awakening," in Lai, W. & Lancaster, L. *ibid.*; Chappell, David. "The Teachings of the Fourth Ch'an Patriarch Tao-hsin (580–651)" *ibid.*; and Faure, Will. *ibid.*; Adamek, *ibid.*; and Heine and Wright, *Zen Canon. ibid.*
[63] T.15, #618.
[64] T.50, #2060.
[65] See: Yampolsky, Philip. *The Platform Sutra of the Sixth Patriarch.* New York: Columbia University Press, 1967, pp. 5–16.
[66] T.85, #2837, See: Yampolsky, Philip. "New Japanese Studies in Early Ch'an History," *ibid.*: Yanagida S. "The Li-Tai Fa-Pao Chi and the Ch'an Doctrine of Sudden Awakening," *ibid.*; Chappell, David. "The Teachings of the Fourth Ch'an Patriarch Tao-hsin (580–651)," *ibid.*; Ueyama, Daishun. "The Study of Tibetan Ch'an Manuscripts Recovered from Tun-huang: A Review of the Field and its Prospects," in Lai, W. & Lancaster, L. *ibid.*; and Faure, Will. *ibid* ; Adamek, *ibid.*; and Heine and Wright, *Zen Canon. ibid.*
[67] T.51, #2075. See: Yampolsky, Philip. "New Japanese Studies in Early Ch'an History," *ibid.*; Yanagida S. "The 'Recorded Sayings' Texts of Chinese Ch'an Buddhism," in Lai, W. & Lancaster, L. *ibid.*; Ueyama, Daishun. "The Study of Tibetan Ch'an Manuscripts…," *ibid.*; and Faure, Will. *ibid.*
[68] See: Yamplosky, Philip. "New Japanese Studies in Early Ch'an History," *ibid.;* Yanagid S. "The 'Recorded Sayings' texts in Chinese Ch'an Buddhism," *ibid.;* Lai, Whalen W, "The Pure and the Impure: The Mencian Problematic in Chinese Buddhism," in Lai, W. & Lancasater, L.; *ibid.*; Yamploski, Philip, *The Platform. ibid.* pp. 47–52,; and

Faure, *Will. ibid;* Adamek, *ibid;* and Heine and Wright, *Zen Canon. ibid.*

69. Many of the names of the Patriarchs from the different Chinese lists mentioned above are also mentioned in Tibetan sources not associated with Chan. However, the Tibetans knew of at least some of these masters in association with the *Laṅkāvatāra.* see: Chimpa, Lama and Chattopadhyaya, Alaka. *Tāranātha's History of Buddhism in India.* Simla: Indian Institute of Advanced Study, 1970, pp. 20–78. Obermiller, E. *History of Buddhism in India and Tibet by Bu-ston.* Heidelberg, 1931. pp. 86–95. Roerich, George. *The Blue Annals.* Delhi: Motilal Banarsiddas Publishers, 1979, pp. 22–25. For early portions of this lineage see: Strong, John. *The Legend and Cult of Upagupta.* Delhi: Motilal Banarsidass Publishers, 1994, pp. 60 *ff.* and Hirakawa, Akira. *A History of Indian Buddhism.* (trans. Groner, Paul), Delhi: Motilal Banarsidass Publishers, 1993, pp. 76–94.

70. See: Padma, Sree. and Barber, A.W. *Buddhism in the Krishna River Valley of Andhra.* Albany: State University of New York Press, 2008; throughout and in particular, Dessein, Bart. "Of Tempted *Arhats* and Supermundane Buddhas: Abhidharma in the Krishna Region," and Barber, A.W. "Two Mahāyāna Developments Along the Krishna River"; and Wayman, Alex. "The Mahāsāṃghika and the Tathāgatagarbha," (Buddhist Doctrinal History, Study 1), *Journal of the International Association of Buddhist Studies* 1 (1978) pp. 35–52.

71. On mourning for teachers see: de Groot, *ibid.* pp. 638–640. For rituals dedicated to the Patriarchs, and Chan abbots see: "The Differences and Agreements between the Vinaya and the Po-ching Ch'ing-kuei," in Tzo, Sze-bong. *The Transformation of Buddhist Vinaya in China.* Dissertation, Canberra: Australian National University, 1982. pg. 331.

72. See: Buswell, Robert E. "The 'Short-cut' Approach of *K'an-hua* meditation: The Evolution of a Practical Subitism in Chinese Chan Buddhism," in Gregory, Peter N. (ed.) *Sudden and Gradual Approaches to Enlightenment in Chinese Thought.* Honolulu: University of Hawaii Press, 1987 and McRae, John R. *Seeing Through Zen Encounter, Transformation, and Genealogy in Chinese Chan Buddhism.* Berkeley: University of California Press, 2003, pp. 126 *ff.*

Chapter Two
What Self?

1. Although I would argue that in the Buddhist context this is better understood as "unawareness" or "lack of clarity."

2. Basham, A.L. *The Wonder That was India.* Calcutta: Rupa and Co., 1991, pg. 138.

3. Olivelle, Patrick. *The Early Upanisads Annotated Text and Translation.* Oxford: Oxford University Press, 1998, *sītā, tejas, amṛita, Brahman* pg. 72 (14); *antarya – retas* pp. 88–9; *aśanāya – sañj* pg. 85 (5), translations mine.
4. Rahula, Walpoa Sri. *What the Buddha Taught.* London: The Gordon Fraser Gallery Ltd., 1978, pg. 56, [from the Majjhima Nikāya].
5. Conze, Edward. *Buddhist Thought In India.* Ann Arbor: The University of Michigan Press, 1973, pg. 37.
6. Rhys-Davids, T.W. *The Questions of King Milinda (part i). ibid.* pp. 40 *ff.*
7. Kashyap, Bhikkhu J. (ed.) *The Saṃyutta Nikāya.* Vol II. Nalanda: Pāli Publication Board, 1959, pp. 261–262.
8. Conze, *Buddhist Thought. ibid.* pp. 125 *ff.*
9. Chau, Thich Thien Bhikshu. *The Literature of the Personalists of Early Buddhism* (trans. *Boin-Webb Sara).* Delhi: Motilal Banarsidass Publishers Private Limited. 1999, pp. 139–140.
10. Priestley, Leonard C.D.C. *Pudgalavāda Buddhism The Reality of the Indeterminate Self.* Toronto: University of Toronto Centre for South Asian Studies, 1999, pp. 2 *ff.* provides a listing of scholarly works on the topic.
11. Chau, *ibid.* pg. 5.
12. T.24, #1506.
13. T.24, #1505.
14. T.32, #1649.
15. T.24, #1461; see: Chau, *ibid.* pg. 19; and Priestley, *ibid.* pg. 44.
16. Priestley, *ibid.* pg. 54.
17. Priestley, *ibid.* pg. 194.
18. Barber. "Two Mahāyāna Developments Along the Krishna River," *ibid.* pp. 151 *ff.*
19. T.16, #666. pg. 457b. Others have translated the passage as "having a *tathāgatagarbha*". Since in the wilted flowers there is a buddha then the parallel case would be in the polluted body there is a tathāgata. The important line is a statement affirming the identity. Because within the pollutants there is the *tathāgata's* wisdom and *tathāgatakāya* then beings are *tathāgatagarbha*. TP #258, pg. 71 plt. 496 is not much help here. The Tibetan uses "*can du*" which can be read as "with *tathāgatagarbha*," "*tathāgatagarbha –y*," "*tathāgatagarbha –ful*," *etc.* The Chinese uses the verb "*yu*". In certain settings this may mean "to have" but in others it comes closer to "occurs". In English it is often translated as "is" or another rendering of the "to be" verb although this is not technically accurate. See: Graham, A.C. *Disputers of the Tao.* LaSalle: Open Court, 1989, pp. 406 *ff.*
20. See: Wayman, Alex, and Wayman, Hideko. *The Lion's Roar of Queen Śrīmālā. New* York: Columbia University Press, 1974, pp. 34 *ff.*
21. Wayman and Wayman. *ibid.* pg. 106.

[22] T.16, #670, pg. 489b.
[23] T.12, #374, pg. 379a.
[24] T.12, #374, pg. 502c.
[25] T.2, #120, pg. 523b.
[26] T.25, #1509, pg. 94b.
[27] T.31, #1610, pg. 799b.
[28] T.31, #1604, pg. 603c.
[29] Suzuki, Daisetz Teitaro. *An Index to the Lankavatara Sutra.* Kyoto: The Sanskrit Buddhist Texts Publishing Society, 1934, pg. 329 only shows the use of "true *ātman*" in the phrase "without true *ātman.*" An online search of the CBETA files produced no results. "True *ātman*" as an independent technical term is found in T.16, #375, pg. 653c l.11. Here the text explains that the true *ātman* is the Buddha-nature.
[30] On this concentric arrangement of relationships see: Ames, Roger T. "The Focus-Field Self in Classical Confucianism," in *Self as Person in Asian Theory and Practice.* Delhi: Sri Satguru Publications, 1997, pp. 204 *ff.* Also see: de Bary, Wm. Theodore. "Individualism and Humanitarianism in Late Ming Thought," in de Bary, Wm. Theodore (and the Conference on Ming Thought). *Self and Society in Ming Thought.* New York: Columbia University Press, 1970, pg. 149. An excellent explanation of the various centers and the relativity inherent in this system is found in: Ziporyn, Brook. *ibid.* pp. 30 *ff.*
[31] Ames, Roger T. "The Classical Chinese Self and Hypocrisy" in *Self and Deception a Cross-Cultural Philosophical Inquiry.* Albany: State University of New York Press, 1996, pg. 220.
[32] I use the term *śrāvakayāna* or *śrāvaka* tradition as an alternative to Hīnayāna. The term is employed in ancient texts and is descriptive instead of pejorative.
[33] Watson Burton. *The Complete Works of Chuang Tzu.* New York: Columbia University Press, 1968, pg. 278. Chinese added from: *Zhuangzi.* Taipei: San-Ming Publishing, 1974, pg. 150.
[34] *Ibid.* pp. 276–277.
[35] Parentheses mine.
[36] Maspero, Henri. *Taoism and Chinese Religion*, Amherst: The University of Massachusetts Press, 1981, pg. 48.
[37] Wu, Teresa L. *The Origin and Dissemination of Chinese Characters.* Taipei: Cave Books, Ltd., 1990, pg. 140; and Mathews, R. H. *Mathews' Chinese – English Dictionary.* Cambridge: Harvard University Press, (13th printing), 1975, pg. 280.
[38] Wu, *ibid.* pg. 140.
[39] Wu, *ibid.* pg. 224.
[40] Wu, *ibid.* pg. 174; Mathews, *ibid.* pg. 1026.
[41] Ames, Self. *ibid.* pg. 227.
[42] Watson, *Chuang Tzu. ibid.* pp. 36–38; Chinese added from *Zhuangzi. ibid.* pg. 6.

43. Watson, *Chuang Tzu. ibid.* pp. 132–133. Parenthesis mine. Chinese added from *Zhuangzi. ibid.* pg. 68.
44. Yanagida S. *Daruma no goroku–Zen no goroku* 1. Tokyo: Chikuma shobō, 1969, pp. 125–128.
45. T.16, #669, pg. 471c.
46. T.9, #270, pg. 297b.
47. T.1, #1, pg. 15b.
48. The idea of meditation and wisdom in the *Platform Sutra* comes from the *Mahāparinirvāṇa*, see: Yampolsky, Philip B. *Platform. ibid.* pg. 135 n.54. This sutra is referred to in the Fourth Patriarch's teachings, see: Chappell David W. "The Teachings of the Fourth Ch'an Patriarch Tao-hsin (580–651)," *ibid.* pg. 111. It is paraphrased by Mazu, see: Jia, Jinhua. *The Hangzhou School of Chan Buddhism in Eighth-through Tenth-Century China.* Albany: State University of New York Press, 2006, pp. 122 n.28 & 123 n.48. One final example is the teachings of Tung-shan, see: Powell, William P. *The Record of Tung-shan.* Honolulu: University of Hawaii Press, 1986, p. 23–24 n13 & n15. There is also a connection here with the teachings of Zhuangzi.
49. X.63, #1225, pg. 35b.
50. T.48, #2015, pg. 406b.
51. T.48, #2016, pg. 564c.
52. T.47, #1995, pg. 666b.
53. T.48, #2015, pg. 406b.
54. X.01, #14, pg. 366b.
55. *Zhuangzi. ibid.* pg. 3.
56. *Zhuangzi. ibid.* pp. 35 *ff.*
57. *Zhuangzi. ibid.* pg. 77.
58. See: Watson, *Chuang Tzu. ibid.* pp. 149–150. His translation does not permit one to gain insight into the technical terms being employed in this passage. I have followed his suggestion for textual emendation.

Chapter Three
Dragons, Lions and Buddhas

1. Lee, Sherman E. *A History of Far Eastern Art.* Englewood Cliffs: Prentice-Hall and New York: Harry N. Abrams, Inc. 1973, see the example on pg. 49.
2. Zhao, Qiguang. *A Study of Dragons, East and West.* New York: Perter Lang, 1992, pg. 18.
3. Visser, Marinus. W. *Dragons in China and Japan.* [https://archive.org/details/cu31924021444728/page/n5].
4. Bates, Roy. *Chinese Dragons.* Oxford: Oxford University Press,

2002, pg. 31. This distinction seems to have ceased after the Qing dynasty. Although there are different opinions as to when the numbers of claws were differentiated.
5. Although in the Song dynasty the four clawed dragon became most popular. One cannot know the number of claws of a dragon puppet by observation; one has to ask the master about his dragon tradition.
6. Basham, *ibid.* pg. 319.
7. Visser, *ibid.* prt. Â§ i.
8. Abridged from: Rhys-Davids, T.W. and Oldenberg, Herman. *Vinaya Texts*. (Sacred Books of the East Series: vol. 13) Delhi: Motilal Banarsidass, 1974, pp. 80–81; also see: Woodward, F.L. *The Minor Anthologies of the Pali Canon* (prt. II. Udāna: Verses of Uplift and Itivuttaka: As It Was Said). London: Routledge and Kegan Paul PLC., 1985, pp. 12–13.
9. Woodward, F. L. *The Book of the Kindred Sayings*. Part III, London: Routledge and Kegan Paul Ltd., 1980, pp. 192–194.
10. Hare, E.M. *The Book of the Gradual Sayings*. (Vol. IV) London: Routledge and Kegan Paul Ltd., 1973, pg. 137.
11. Rhys-Davids, T.W. and Rhys-Davids, C.A.F. *Dialogues of the Buddha.* Pt. III, Oxford: Oxford University Press, 1977, pg. 142.
12. Nāgā [www.palikanon.com/english/pali_names/n/nagaa.htm].
13. Hare, E.M. *The Book of the Gradual Sayings.* (vol. III), London: Routledge and Kegan Paul Ltd., 1973, pp. 243–246.
14. Rhys-Davids, Mrs. *Psalms of the Early Buddhist (I-Psalms of the Sisters).* London: Routledge and Kegan Paul. Ltd., 1980, pg. 79.
15. Ichimura, Shohei. *Buddhist Critical Spirituality Prajñā and Śūnyatā*. Delhi: Motilal Banarsidass Publishers, 2001, pg. 62.
16. Ingersoll, Ernest. *Dragons and Dragon Lore*: 1928, [captured 9/6/2010: http://www.sacred-texts.com/etc/ddl/ddl12.htm.]
17. Lee. *ibid.* pg. 51.
18. Marcus, Margaret F. "Sculptures from Bihar and Bengal," *The Bulletin of the Cleveland Museum of Art*, Vol. 54, No. 8 (Oct., 1967) pp. 240–262.
19. Münsterberg, Hugo. "Buddhist Bronzes of the Six Dynasties Period," *Artibus Asiae*. Vol. 9, No. 4, 1946, pp. 275–315.
20. Wenjie, Duan (ed.) *Mural Paintings of the Dunhuang Mogao Grotto*. Osaka?: Kenbun-sha, Inc. 1994.
21. Wogihara, Unrai and Tsuji Naoshirō. *Bonwa daijiten.* Suzuki Research Foundation; Taipei: Hsin Won Fang Publishing, 1979, pg. 474.
22. A buddha and universal emperor have to be male because one of their characteristics is they have a penis.
23. Hurvitz, Leon. *Lotus Blossom of the Fine Dharma.* New York: Columbia University Press, 2009. pg. 184.; Hurvitz simply translated *baozhu* as "precious gem." This does not indicate the magical wish-granting gem about which the original Chinese text is very clear. See:

T.9, #262, pp. 35b–c.
24. Du, Feiban and Hong Su. *Things Chinese and Their Stories*. Beijing: China Travel and Tourism Press, 1994. pg. 65.
25. Hu, William C. *The Lion Dance Explained*. Ann Arbor: Ars Ceramica, Ltd., 1995, pg. 30.
26. Hu, *ibid.* pg. 33. There is no evidence for lions inhabiting south-east Asia.
27. Hu, *ibid.* pg. 43.
28. Hu, *ibid.* pp. 5–33, calls each story a "theory" on the origin of the Lion Dance. The Exorcism Theory is simply another version of the year-end "*nien*" monster story, the Martial Arts Cooperation Theory is purely a local story, the Chivalrous Theory is from the 14th century, The Patriot's Theory is from the 17th century, the Emperor Ch'ien-lung's Dream Theory is from the 18th century, the Emperor's Pet Lion Theory mixes elements from the Story of the Foreign Tribute of a Lion. The Story of the Foreign Tribute of a Lion Theory although containing some historical facts, also contains a very disrespectful challenge by the Kushan ambassador to the Han emperor and thus very unlikely to have occurred. The Buddhist Theory and the *Ta-Ch'ing-shih* or the Black Lion Dance story both have Buddhist elements. This is certainly not to say that any of these stories actually inform us of the origins of the dance.
29. Hu, *ibid.* pp. 7–8.
30. Hu, *ibid.* pp. 13–16.
31. Yang Hsüan-chih. *A Record of Buddhist Monasteries in Lo-Yang*. Princeton: Princeton University Press, 1984, pp. 45–46.
32. Yang, *ibid.* pp. 45 *ff.* and 124 *ff.*
33. Hu, *ibid.* pg. 71.
34. Hu, *ibid.* pg. 69, from the *Jiu tang shu (Chiu-tang-shu).*
35. Carpenter, J. Estlin. (ed.) *The Dīgha Nikāya.* London: for the Pali Text Society by Messrs. Luzac, and Company, Ltd. 1960, vol. III, pp. 36–57.
36. Carpenter, *ibid.* pp. 58–79.
37. Trenckner, V. (ed.) *Majjhima Nikāya.* London: for the Pali Text Society by Messrs. Luzac, and Company, Ltd. 1964. Vol I, pp. 63–68.
38. Trenckner, *ibid.* pp. 68–83.
39. Trenckner, *ibid.* pg. 354; in the *Sekhasuttaṁ.*
40. Andersen, Dines, and Smith Helmer. *Sutta-Nipāta.* London: for the Pali Text Society by Routledge & Kegan Paul, 1984, pg. 107.
41. Frederic, Louis. *Buddhism Flammarion Iconographic Guides.* Paris: Flammarion, 1995, pg. 60.
42. T.20, #1185a.
43. T.51, #2098.
44. T.51, #2099.
45. T.51, #2100.

[46] See: Fazang's *Hua yan jing chuan ji* (華嚴經傳記), T.51, #2073; Chengguan's *Da fang guan fo hua yan jing shu* (大方廣佛華嚴經疏), T.35, #1735.
[47] Birnbaum, Raoul. "The Manifestation of a Monastery: Shen-Ying's Experiences on Mount Wu-t'ai in T'ang Context," in *Journal of the American Oriental Society*. Vo 106, No.1. Jan–Mar. pp. 124–125.
[48] Cartelli, Mary Anne. "On a Five-colored Cloud: the songs of Mount Wutai," *Journal of the American Oriental Society*, 124.4 (2004) pg. 736.
[49] Tribe, Anthony. Manjusri: Origins, Role and Significance, (Part 3. The Cult of Mañjuśrī). *Western Buddhist Review*, Dec. 1994, [captured: 8/22/2010], pg. 10.
[50] Adamek, *ibid.* pg. 119. Part of the reason for the governmental expenditures has to do with the challenges facing the court with the growing tension crystallizing in the An Lushan rebellion (755–763) and the growing threat of the Tibetan Empire which finally sacks the capital of Chang'an in 763.
[51] Bhattacharyya, Benoytosh. *The Indian Buddhist Iconography*. Calcutta: Firma K.L. Muchopadhyay, 1987, pp. 100–123.
[52] Frederic, *ibid.* pg. 195.
[53] Ding, Guanpeng. *A Long Roll of Buddhist Images*. Hong Kong: Commercial Press, 1994.

Chapter Four
Buddha's Play

[1] From Hardy, E. *The Netti Prakaraṇa*, London: Pali Text Society, 1902, pg. 124.
[2] Other groups of four are found.
[3] Perhaps the four are: cutoff impediment (*papañca*), cutoff {cyclic existence} way (*vaṭuma*), exhausting the rolling on {of karma} (*pariyādinnavaṭṭa*), all suffering overcome (*sabbadukkhavītivatta*). The *Acchariyabbhutadhamma Sutta* lists many marvels associated with the Buddha. See: Chalmers, Robert. *Majjhima Nikāya* (Vol. III) London: Pali Text Society, 1960, #123.
[4] See: Hardy, *Netti Prakaraṇa, ibid.*
[5] Trenckner, V. (ed.) *The Majjhima-Nikāya*. London: Pali Text Society, 1964, pg. 229.
[6] Rhys Davids, T.W. and Carpenter, J. Estlin (eds.) *The Dīgha Nikāya.* (vol. II), London: Pali Text Society, 1947, pg. 196.
[7] Rhys Davids and Carpenter. The *Dīgha Nikāya, ibid.* pg. 19.
[8] Hardy, Edmund. *Aṅguttara-Nikāya.* (Vol. V), London: Pali Text Society, 1900, pp. 202–203. [captured 2/27/2015:

http://www.scribd.com/doc/133801046/Aṅguttara-Nikaya-Part-5-Roman-Script].
9. Dhammapālatthera, *Vimānavatthu Aṭṭhakathā*. Yangon: Buddhasāsana Society, 2008, pg. 8. [captured 2/27/2015: https://vignette.wikia.nocookie.net/tipitaka/images/2/23/Vimanavatthu-atthakatha.pdf/revision/latest?cb=20151128035544] .
10. Marks-Tarlow, Terry. "From Emergency to Emergence: The Deep Structure of Play in Psychotherapy." In *Psychoanalytic Dialogues: The International Journal of Relational Perspectives*. 09 Feb 2015, pg. 109.
11. Marks-Tarlow, *ibid.* pg. 110.
12. Merk, Laura E., Mann, Trish D., and Ogan, Amy T. "Make-Believe Play: Wellspring for Development of Self-Regulation." in Singer, Dorothy G., Hirsh-Pasek, Kathy. Golinkoff, Roberta Michnick. *Play = Learning: How Play Motivates and Enhances Children's Cognitive and Social-Emotional Growth*. Oxford: Oxford University Press, 2006, pg. 74.
13. Singer, Dorothy G., and Singer, Jerome L. *House of Make-Believe: Children's Play and the Developing Imagination*. Cambridge: Harvard University Press, 1990, pg. 270.
14. Marks-Tarlow, *ibid.* pg. 111.
15. Schwartzman, Helen B. *Transformations The Anthropology of Children's Play*. New York: Plenum Press, 1978, pp. 326–27. She argues against including "unproductive" in this generally agreed upon characteristics.
16. Schwartzman, *ibid.* pg. 327.
17. Schwartzman, *ibid.* pg. 328.
18. Pellegrini, A.D. and Bjorklund, David F. "The Ontogeny and Phylogeny of Children's Object and Fantasy Play," *Human Nature*, Vol 15, No. 1, 2004, pp. 23–43.
19. Pellegrini, A.D. and Bjorklund, *ibid.*
20. Padilla, Elaine. *Divine Enjoyment A theology of Passion and Exuberance*. New York: Fordham University Press, 2015, pg. 42.
21. *Saddharmapundarīkasūtram*, #82 [captured 5/5/2015: http://www.dsbcproject.org/canon-text/content/54/459].
22. *Sukhāvatīvyūhaḥ (vistaramātṛkā)* [captured 5/4/2015: http://www.dsbcproject.org/canon-text/content/59/528].
23. *Aṣṭasāhasrikā prajñāpāramitā Sūtra*. [captured 5/1/2015: http://gretil. sub.uni-goettingen.de/gretil/1_sanskr/4_rellit/buddh/bsu049_u.htm].
24. T.1, #26, pg. 522a.
25. T.1, #1, pg. 6c.
26. T.9, #263, pg. 76b.
27. T.9, #263, pg. 121a.
28. T.1, #44, pg. 829c.
29. *The Analects*, Ruan Yuan (ed.) *Shi san jing gu zhu*. Taipei: Xin Wen

Feng Chu Ban, 1977, pg. 2375b.
30. *The Classic of Poetry, Shi san jing ... ibid.* pg. 191a.
31. *Zhuangzi. ibid.* pg. 181.
32. *Ibid.* pg. 183.
33. T.26, #1524.
34. T.8, #236.
35. T.16, #671.
36. T.26, #1522.
37. T.40, #1819, pg. 843a.
38. T.40, #1819, pg. 843b.
39. See: Monier-Williams, Monier. Sir. *A Sanskrit-English Dictionary*. Oxford: The Clarendon Press, 1951, pg. 620.
40. T.47, #1958, pg. 14a.
41. T.47, #1979.
42. *Ibid.* pg. 429b.
43. T.12, #365.
44. T.47, #1960.
45. *Ibid.* pg. 56b.
46. Sasaki, Ruth Fuller. Iriya, Yoshitaka and Fraser, Dana R. *The Recorded Sayings of Layman P'ang*. New York: Weatherhill, 1971. [captured 7/17 /2015: http://terebess.hu/zen/pang.html].
47. T.50, #2060.
48. T.85, #2838.
49. T.85, #2838.
50. T.51, #2075, pg. 182a (13). Adamek, *ibid.* pg. 319 translates the term "joked."
51. *Ibid.* pg. 184b (20).
52. *Ibid.* pg. 194a (8). Adamek, *ibid.* translates this passage as … "idle theories."
53. T.48, #2008 pg. 358c–359a.
54. See: T.48, #2003 pp. 152b, 191a, 199a, 201c, 210c, *etc.*
55. T.2, #100, pg. 470b.
56. T.12, #339, pg. 104b.

Chapter Five

A Comparison of Ritual Creation and Use of Chan and Pure Land Art in China

1. Some of the ideas contained in this chapter were first presented at the *Arts in Society Conference*, Venice, 2009. However, this is a thorough reworking of this earlier presentation.
2. Schopen, Gregory. "Archaeology and Protestant Presuppositions in the Study of Indian Buddhism," *Bones, Stones, and Buddhist Monks.*

Honolulu: University of Hawaii Press, 1997.
3. Cort, John, E. "Art, Religion, and Material Culture. Some Reflections on Method," *Journal of the American Academy of Religion*, LXIV/3, Fall, 1996, pp. 613–632.
4. Elsner, John. "Image and Ritual: Reflections on the Religious Appreciation of Classic Art." *Classical Quarterly*, Oxford, 1996, [captured 2/7 /2019: https://www-jstor-org.ezproxy.lib.ucalgary.ca/stable/pdf/639805.pdf?refreqid=excelsior%3A63317c021b4387cd3a3cb1161e1c37ec].
5. Elsner. *ibid.* pg. 6.
6. See: Mitchiner, John, E. *Traditions of the Seven Ṛṣis.* Delhi: Motilal Banarsidass, 1982.
7. See: Olderberg, Hermann. *Sacred Books of the East: Vedic Hymns*, part II. Vol. X–LVI (Muller, Max. Ed.) Delhi: Motilal Banarsidass, 1973, where in (Mandala III, Hymn 43, vrs. 5) speaks of becoming a *ṛṣi* by drinking *soma.*
8. Eck, Diana L. *Darśan.* (3rd ed.*)* New York: Columbia University Press, 1998, pg. 3.
9. The "feet of one's teacher" is an enduring theme in Indian spirituality. We see it iconographically on many Buddhist monuments as well as elsewhere in Indian culture. Even today, many on the spiritual path have an image of their teachers feet on cloth which they pay respect to daily.
10. For a complete analysis see: Barber, A.W. "Darshanic Buddhism: The Origins of Pure Land Practice." In *The Pure Land*, New Series Nos. 18–19, Dec. 2002.
11. Accounts state that he is the head of Buddhism after the *parinirvāṇa* of Śākyamuni. See for example: Strong, *The Legend.* pg. 11.
12. Accounts of this story are found in the *Theragāthā* and the Saṃyutta Nikāya. Vakkali is considered foremost in applying himself to *śrāddhā* and *śrāddhā* is part of the matrix of ideas associated with *darśana.*
13. See: Andersen, Dines. and Smith, Helmer. (eds.) *Sutta Nipāta.* London: The Pali Text Society, 1965, vrs. 976–1149; and Saddhatissa, H. *The Sutta Nipata.* Richmond: Curzon Press, 1985.
14. Strong, *ibid.* pp. *93 ff.* Although I disagree with Strong's explanation of this referring to *bhakti.*
15. For example, the *Lotus Sutra,* T.9, #262 pp. 32b–34b; the *Pratyutpanna*, T.13, #416 pp. 877c (verses) & 877c–878b; the *Avataṃsaka*, T.10, #279 pp. 115a–124a; the *Aṣṭasāhasrikā*, T.8, #228 pp. 668a–673c; and the *Sukhāvatīvyūha Sūtra*, T.12, #366.
16. Chen, Kenneth. *Buddhism in China. ibid.* pp. 28–30.
17. See: [http://www.chinaknowledge.de/Art/Grottoes/grottoes.html]
18. Wenjie, Duan. *Mural Paintings of the Dunhuang Mogao Grotto.* Np.: Kenbun-Sha Inc. 1994, pg. 38.
19. Rhie, Marylin M. *The Fo-kuang ssu: Literary Evidence and Buddhist*

Images. New York: Garland Publishing, 1977.
[20] Gimello, Robert M. "Chang Shang-ying on Wu-t'ai Shan," in Naquin, Susan. and Yu, Chun-gang. *Pilgrims and Sacred Sites in China.* Berkeley: University of California Press, 1992. pp. 89 *ff.*
[21] Yu, Chun-gang. "P'u-t'o Shan," Naquin and Yu, *ibid.* pp. 190 *ff.*
[22] Teiser, Stephen F. *The Scripture on the Ten Kings and the Making of Purgatory in Medieval Chinese Buddhism.* Honolulu: University of Hawaii Press, 1994, pp. 166 & 197; and Inagaki, *Pure Land. ibid.* pp. 44–46.
[23] See: Corless, Roger J. "T'an-luan: The First Systematize …", *ibid.* pp. 107 *ff.*
[24] See: Chappell, David. "The Formation of the Pure Land Movement in China: Tao-ch'o and Shan-tao," *ibid.* pp. 139 *ff.*
[25] T.51, #2070, pg. 105, C6–7, and Pas, *ibid.* pg. 370, n. 148 and pp. 94 *ff.*
[26] Pas. *ibid.* pg. 83.
[27] Inagaki, *Pure Land. ibid.* pp. 106 *ff.* and Fujiwara, Ryosetsu. *The Way to Nirvana. ibid.*
[28] Stevenson, Daniel B. "Protocols of Power: Ts'u-yun Tsun-shir (964–1032) and T'ien-t'ai Lay Buddhist Ritual in the Song." in Gregory, Peter N. and Getz, Daniel A. *Buddhism in the Sung. ibid.* pp. 362–363.
[29] Stevenson "Protocols…" *ibid.* pp. 360–361.
[30] T.12 #365.
[31] T.37, #1753. *Guan wu liang shou fo ching shu.*
[32] T.27, #1524. There are questions regarding authorship of this text.
[33] The experience of things as they are free of machinations. See: Conze. *Buddhist Thought. ibid.* pg. 225.
[34] Inagaki, *T'an-luan. ibid.* pp. 212–214. For an explanation of both calm abiding and insight also see: "Selections from the Commentary to Vasubandhu's Essay on Rebirth," in Olson, Carl (ed.) *Buddhist Sources.* New Brunswick: Rutger University press, 2005, pp. 279 *ff.*
[35] Pas. *ibid.* pp. 153 *ff.* and Inagaki, *Pure Land. ibid.* pp. 108–109.
[36] Hisamatsu, Shin'ichi. *Zen and the Fine Arts.* Tokyo: Kodansha International Ltd. 1971, pg. 17.
[37] For example, regarding portraits see: Foulk, Griffith. and Sharf, Robert H. "On the Ritual use of Ch'an Portraiture in Medieval China," in *Cashiers d'Extreme-Asia,* (Special Issue Ch'an/Zen Studies en l'honneur de Yanagida Seizan) 1993–1994, pp. 149 *ff.*
[38] Munsterbert, Hugo. *Zen & Oriental Art.* Rutland: Charles E. Tuttle Company, 1993, pg. 33; (paradise scenes = Pure Land depictions).
[39] Fuller, Winston. "Zen and the Practice of an Art as a Spiritual Discipline," *Studia Mystica*, Sacramento: California State University, 1987, Vol. X, No. 4, pg. 40.
[40] See: Hisamatsu. *ibid.* pg. 18.
[41] Cheng, Francois. *Empty and Full.* Boston: Shambhala. 1994, pg. 64.

42. Cheng. *ibid.* pp. 96–97.
43. Hisamatsu. *ibid.* pp. 52–59.
44. Wan, Ven. Hiu. *Revelation From Ch'an Practice Ch'an Paintings.* Taipei: Yuan Ch'uan Press, 1992, pp. 81–82.
45. Bol, Peter K. "Government, Society, and State: On the Political Visions of Ssu-ma-Kuang and Wang An-shih." in Hymes, Robert P. and Schirokauer, Conrad. *ibid.* pg. 139.
46. Parker, Joseph D. *Zen Landscape Arts of Early Muromachi Japan (1336–1573).* Albany: State University of New York Press, 1999. pg. 24.
47. Nienhauser, Willaim H. Jr. (ed.) *The Indiana Companion to Traditional Chinese Literature.* Bloomington: Indiana University Press, 1986, pg. 95.
48. Parker. *ibid.* pg. 31.
49. Parker. *ibid.* pg. 32.
50. Bush, Susan & Shih, Hsio-yen. (eds.) *Early Chinese Texts on Painting.* Cambridge: Harvard University Press, 1985, pp. 207–211.
51. Bush & Hsio. *ibid.* pp. 209–211.
52. Cheng. *ibid.* pg. 88.
53. Conze, Edward. *Buddhist Thought. ibid.* pp. 226–227.
54. Williams, Lynn. "Spirituality and Gestalt: A Gestalt-Transpersonal Perspective," *Gestalt Review.* 10(1): 6–21, 2006, pg.7.
55. Adams, Will W. "The Interpermeation of Self and World: Empirical Research, Existential Phenomenology, and Transpersonal Psychology," *Journal of Phenomenological Psychology.* Fall 99, Vol. 30, pg. 40.

Chapter Six
Early Chan Buddhist Activities

1. McRae. *Northern. ibid.*
2. McRae presents the *Second Letter* as possibly being one letter having two parts with only the second part identified as penned by Hsiang. These however, may be different letters. Huike's *Reply* may be limited to only part B. see: McRae. *Northern. ibid.* pp. 105–106.; However, Broughton, *ibid.* pp. 12–13 makes McRae's *Second Letter* part A the concluding section of the *First Letter* and part B the *Second Letter.* For the purposes of this study these differences in structuring the materials are not germane. McRae's arrangement is based on Yanagida's study (see below). This is my main source for the material and thus I follow Yanagida/McRae for convenience.
3. McRae. *Northern. ibid.* pp. 107–108.
4. McRae. *Northern. ibid.* pp. 110–115.
5. Bopp, Francisco. *Glossarium Sanscritum.* 1896 [captured 6/26/2012:

http://books.google.ca/books?id=xaMIAAAAQAAJ&printsec=frontcover&redir_esc=yv=onepage&q&f=false].

6. The Sanskrit term "*samyak*" usually translated "right" is derived from *sami* plus *añc*. *Samyañc* means "to go along with or together," from this other meaning are derived. "Appropriate" has the meaning of being compatible, fitting, suitable. "*Samyak*" is that which is compatible (goes along) with nirvana. It is not a question of right or wrong. See: Monier-Williams *ibid.* pg. 1181; Mish, Frederick C. (Ed.-in-Chief) *Merriam-Webster's Collegiate Dictionary* (10th ed.) Springfield, Mass., Merriam-Webster Inc. 1995, pg. 57.

7. T.16, #666.

8. T.12, #353.

9. On this interpretation see: Barber. "Two Mahāyāna Developments Along the Krishna River," *ibid.* pp. 151 *ff.*

10. *The Two Ingresses and Four Courses*. T.85, #2837, pg. 1285a.

11. *Two Ingresses and Four Courses, ibid.*

12. T.12, #374 pg. 574c.

13. T.32, #1667 pp. 586a, 586b, 586c, 587a, 587b, 588a (6, 20, 28), *etc.* This work is considered non-Indic but it is canonical within the East Asian tradition.

14. Other possibilities are: *citta dhāraṇa* and *hṛidi sthāpya.*

15. T.8, #223, pg. 236a.

16. T.24, #1462, pp. 748c, 762c.

17. Although as noted by McRae, Paul Swanson thinks this is a mixed binome with one element a transliteration and the other a translation. See: McRae, *Seeing. ibid.* pg. 160, n. 18. In the same section McRae also mentions "wall samādhi" used by Tiantai Zhiyi.

18. For example T.12, #353 pg. 217a.

19. For example T.12, #374 pg. 365a.

20. For example T.16, #670 pg. 484c.

21. For example T.32, #1667 pg. 584b.

22. The re-Sanskritization of this name is problematic. See my article: "The Identification of dGa' rab rdo rje," in *The Journal of the International Association of Buddhist Studies*, Vol. 9 No. 2, 1986. Also see: Reynolds, John Myrdhin. *The Golden Letters.* Ithaca: Snow Lion, 1996. A number of authors have dated dGa' rab rdo rje to the first century CE. However, he is listed as the author of tantric texts and there is no proof of the tantras existing in the first century. More probable dating would be in the 6th century or maybe even later.

23. Mathes, Klaus-Dieter. "Can *sutra mahāmudrā* be justified on the basis of Maitrīpa's Apratiṣṭhānavāda?" in Kellner, B., Krasser, H., Lasic, H., Much, M.T., and Tauscher, H. (eds.) Pramāṇakīrtiḥ. *Papers Dedicated to Ernst Steinkellner on the Occasion of his 70th Birthday.* Part 2, Wien: Wiener Studien zur Tibetologie und Buddhismuskunde, 2007. [captured 1/30/2019:

https://www.scribd.com/document/255575915/Can-Sutra-Mahamudra-Be-Justified-on-the-Basis-of-Maitripa-s-Apratisthanavada].

24. Hookham, S.K. *The Buddha Within. ibid.* pg. 62. Hookham translates *śraddhā* (Tb. Dad pa) as "faith."

25. Yanagida, S. *Zen no goroku 1. ibid.* "Preface"; pg. 25.

26. For example T.12, #353 pg. 217a.

27. Broughton, *ibid.* pp. 68–69 and 144 n.26.

28. T.12, #352, pg. 222c; Wayman, and Wayman. *ibid.* pp. 108–109 in part reads: "…those who now and, after my passing, in future times are my disciples possessed of confidence and [then] are controlled by confidence, they by depending on the light of confidence have a knowledge in the precincts of the Dharma, by which they reach certainty in the intrinsic purity and in the defilement of consciousness.

29. *Da cheng qi xin lun*. Taipei: 1992, pg. 142. Hakeda. *ibid.* translates this passage: "Briefly, there are four kinds of faith. The first is the faith in the *Ultimate Source*. Because [of this faith] a man comes to meditate with joy on the principle of Suchness." pg. 92.

30. T.12, #374 pg. 575c. The other major sutra the term appears in is the *Gaṇḍhavyūha Sūtra,* T.10, #293 pg. 817a. This later text was translated by Prajñā in 798, well after the earliest Chan documents.

31. T.16, #666.

32. T.12, #374 pg. 408b.

33. T.32, #1667 pg. 583c.

34. T.9, #278 pg. 482c.

35. T.10, #279 pg. 300b; translated into Chinese by Śikṣānanda roughly contemporaneous with *Two Ingresses and Four Courses.*

36. T.32, #1666, pg. 580b ln.12–14.

37. T.32, #1666 pg. 580c 18.

38. T.32, #1666 pg. 575a 15.

39. T.6, #220 pg. 919b; T.7, #220 pp. 708c, 860b.

40. T.10, #279 pg. 225b; roughly contemporaneous with *Two Ingresses and Four Courses.*

41. T.12, #374 pg. 603b.

42. T.12, #390, 1113c 22; Levi, Sylvain and Takakusu, J. *Hōbōgirin.* Tokyo: Maison Fransco-Japonaise, 1931, pg. 24; Hirakawa, Akira. *Buddhist Chinese-Sanskrit Dictionary.* Tokyo: The Reiyukai, 1997, pg. 119 identify this as the *Mahāparinirvāṇa.* Hirakawa indicates this identification is based on the fact that this is a transliteration of the Sanskrit sounds. However, even given Tang dynasty pronunciations, the Chinese does not approximate the supposed Sanskrit. The Chinese translates to something like: "The Buddha Approaching Nirvana Explanatory Dharma Stability Sutra". "Explanatory" (*vyākaraṇa)*, is one of the divisions of *Buddhavacana.* The Sanskrit title given in modern Chinese based sources seems likely to be derived from the Tibetan title which does agree.

[43.] T.12, #353, pg. 222b.
[44.] T.16, #670 pg. 489b.
[45.] T.12, #374 pg. 569c.
[46.] T.32, #1666, pg. 579b; T.32, #1667, pp. 585a & 589b.
[47.] T.12, #374 pg. 393b.
[48.] T.10, #279 pg. 110c.
[49.] T.16, #670 pg. 486b.
[50.] T.12, #374 pg. 443a.
[51.] T.16, #1667 pg. 586b.
[52.] T.5, #220 pp 71a, 202a; T.6, #220 pp. 557c, 1042b; T.7, #220 pp. 926a, 987c.
[53.] T.9, #278 pp. 399b, 558a, 582b. Also see: T.10, #279 pp. 1c, 289a.
[54.] T.12, #353 pg. 222a.
[55.] T.12, #374 pp. 409c, 422c, 555b.
[56.] *Two Ingresses and Four Courses, ibid.*
[57.] Although not always with the same connotation, for example: T.14, #492 pg. 753b the context is different.
[58.] T.3, #190, pp. 666b, 779c.
[59.] T.7, #220 pp. 891c, 1045a.
[60.] T.15, #606 pg. 209a.
[61.] Conze, Edward. *Buddhist Meditation*. New York: Harper Torchbooks, 1956, pg. 122.
[62.] *Two Ingresses and Four Courses*, *ibid.*
[63.] The *Mahāprajñā Sūtra* also speaks of the mind not increasing or decreasing; T.5, #220 pg. 911b.
[64.] T.9, #278 pp. 416b, 451b; T.10, #279 pg. 352a - Śikṣānanda's translation.
[65.] T.16, #670 pg. 491b.
[66.] T.31, #1585 pp. 1a, 29c, 37a, *etc*; translation roughly contemporaneous with *Two Ingresses and Four Courses*.
[67.] Nagarjuna. *Suhṛllekha.* (ed. By Padma Tendzin), Varanasi: Central Institute of High Tibetan Studies, 2002, [captured 1/30/19: http://gretil.sub.uni-goettingen.de/gretil/1_sanskr/6_sastra/3_phil/buddh/bsa015_u.htm].
[68.] *Two Ingresses and Four Courses, ibid.*
[69.] T.1, #26 pp. 422b, 682b, 746b, 773a.
[70.] T.1, #49 pg. 839a.
[71.] T.5, #220 pp. 1b, 293c.
[72.] Conze, Edward. *The Perfection of Wisdom in Eight Thousand Lines and its Verse Summary*. Bolinas: Four Seasons Foundation, 1973, pg. 296; Conze translates *anapekṣa* with "disregards," I have inserted "indifferent" for consistency.
[73.] *Two Ingresses and Four Courses*, *ibid.*
[74.] T.39, #1783 pg. 1a.
[75.] T.39, #1785 pg. 59a.

76. T.2, #100 pg. 421b.
77. T.26, #1537 pg. 496c; translation roughly contemporaneous with *Two Ingresses and Four Courses*.
78. Yanagida, S. *Zen no goroku I. ibid.* "Preface"; pg. 25.
79. T.10, #279 pg. 68a- Śikṣānanda's translation.
80. For example see: the *Mahāparinirvāṇa* T.12, #374 pg. 443a; the *Laṅkāvatāra* T.16, #670 pg. 486b; the *Avataṃsaka* T.10, #279 pg. 193b.
81. T.39, #1787 pg. 160a.
82. Broughton. *ibid.* pg. 12.
83. Sakaki, R. (ed.) *Mahāvyutpatti*. Kyoto: Shingonshu Kyoto Daigaku, 1916–1925, #581.
84. T.10, #279 pg. 204b- Śikṣānanda's translation.
85. T.32, #1647 pg. 375b.
86. T.12, #387 pg. 1087b.
87. T.3, #159 pg. 327c.
88. T.32, #1668 pg. 625c, attributed to Nāgārjuna.
89. For example: T.46, #1911 pg. 51c.
90. T.12, #374 pg. 367b.
91. For "mind king" T.12, #374 pg. 367b; for "self-king" T.12, #374 pg. 541c.
92. For example: T.9, #278 pp. 586a, 694c and T.10, #279 pg. 237b.
93. For example: The *Mahāparinirvāṇa* T.12, #374 pg. 365a; the *Laṅkāvatāra* T.16, #670 pg. 489b.
94. Conze. *Eight Thousand Lines. ibid.* pg. 83.
95. For examples of "true suchness" see: the *Avataṃsaka*, T.9, #278 pg. 503b and T.10, #279 pg. 161c and the *Awakening of Confidence,* T.32, #1667 pg. 584b; for example of "*dharmatā*" see: the *Mahāprajñā Sūtra* T.5, #220 pp. 473c, 541c, 704b; T.7, #220 pp. 144c, 936c; The *Avataṃsaka* T.9, #278 pp. 435b, 748a and T.10, #279 pp. 101b, 151a.
96. It is also found in *Mahāprajñā Sūtra:* T.7, #220, pg. 44b.
97. For example, Dīrghāgama: T.1 #1 pg. 55a; (*Mahā)parinirvāṇa*: T.1 #7 pg. 202b; and *Mahāvaipulyamahāsannipāta Sūtra*: T.13, #397 pp. 294c, 254a.
98. T.25, #1509 pg. 78b.
99. T.11, #310 1b.
100. T.31, #1597 pg. 321b.
101. McRae. *Northern. ibid.* used for convenience*; pp.* 105–106.
102. T.12, #374 pp. 450a–451a; from Broughton. *ibid.* pg. 123.
103. T.14, #456 pg. 430b; from Broughton. *ibid.* pg. 123.
104. T.8, #233 pg. 733b.
105. T.32, #1666 pg. 579c.
106. T.12, #374 pg. 466a.
107. T.13, #397 pg. 380a.
108. T.9, #278 pp. 709c, 713b; T.10, #279 pg. 444a.
109. T.12, #374 pg. 371c.

[110.] T.5, #220 pp. 19a, 236b, 425a; T.7, #220 pp. 12c, 790c, 969c for example.
[111.] T.12, #374 pg. 430a.
[112.] T.9, #278 pp. 399b, 431b, and T.10, #279 pp. 7b, 33a, 103a, for example.
[113.] From, "The Definitive Vinaya," in Chang, Garma C.C. (ed.) *A Treasure of Mahāyāna Sūtras*. University Park: The Pennsylvania State University Press, 1983, pg. 270.
[114.] Conze, *Eight Thousand Line. ibid.* pg. 199.
[115.] Watson, *Chuang Tzu. ibid.* pg. 192.
[116.] Zurcher, E. *Conquest. ibid.* pg. 73.
[117.] Watson, *Chuang Tzu. ibid.* pp. 231–232.
[118.] T.8, #223.
[119.] T.8, #227.
[120.] T.8, #235.
[121.] T.8, #250.
[122.] T.8, #232.
[123.] T.8, #233.
[124.] T.8, #236.
[125.] T.8, #240.
[126.] T.8, #237.
[127.] T.8, #231.
[128.] T.8, #238.
[129.] T.5, #220 (1).
[130.] T.7, #220 (2).
[131.] T.7, #220 (3).
[132.] T.7, #220 (4).
[133.] T.7, #220 (6).
[134.] T.7, #220 (7).
[135.] T.7, #220 (9).
[136.] T.8, #251.
[137.] T7, #220 (11).
[138.] T.7, #220 (10).

Chapter Seven

Buddhist Praxis in Light of Eschatology

[1.] Shastri. *ibid.* Chapt. 3: Lokanirdeśaḥ. Information also taken from Sadakata, Akira. Buddhist Cosmology Philosophy and Origins. Tokyo: Kōsei Publishing Co. 1999.
[2.] Buddhaghosa, Bhadantācariya. *The Path of Purification (Visuddhimagga)*. (trans. Nyāṇamoli, Bhikkhu), Colombo, A. Semage, 1964, pp. 144–177.

[3] Buddhaghosa. *ibid*, pp. 355–371. "Nothingness" here is not to be confused with the Mahayana notion of "emptiness."
[4] Rhys-Davids, T.W. and Carpenter, J. Estlin. *The Dīgha Nikāya. ibid.* pg. 156. Rhys-Davids, T.W. and Rhys-Davids, Caroline.A.F. *Dialogues of the Buddha,* part II, London: Pali Text Society, 1977, #16, pp. 173–175.
[5] T.12, #374, 472b.
[6] Nattier, Jan. *Once Upon A Future Time Studies in a Buddhist Prophecy of Decline.* Berkeley: Asian Humanities Press, 1991. Neither the Sanskrit-Chinese dictionary (Wogihara, Unrai and Tsuji, Naoshirō. *Konyaku Taisho: ibid.* pg. 1230 or Hirakawa, Akira. *Buddhist Chinese-Sanskrit Dictionary. ibid.* pg. 642 list *vipralopa* as a translation of/for *mofa* (末法).
[7] Nattier. *ibid.* pp. 59–61
[8] Dayal, Har. *The Bodhisattva Doctrine in Buddhist Sanskrit Literature.* Delhi: Motilal Banarsidass, 1970, pp. 80 *ff.* Similar lists can be found in whole or part in the Nikāyas.
[9] Nattier. *ibid.* pp. 120 *ff.*
[10] Nattier. *ibid.* pg. 120.
[11] Woodward, F.L. *The Book of the Gradual Sayings.* Vol.I, London: The Pali Text Society, 1979, text I, 69: #11. Also see: text iii, 5.
[12] Woodward, F.L. *The Book of the Kindred Sayings.* Part V, London: The Pali Text Society, 1980, text v, 173.
[13] Woodward. *Gradual Sayings. ibid.* text 1, 58 #10.
[14] Solomon, Richard. "Why did the Gandhāran Buddhist Bury Their Manuscripts?", in Berkwitz, Stephen. Schober, Juliane. And Brown, Claudia. *Buddhist Manuscript Cultures Knowledge, Ritual, and Art.* London: Routledge, 2009, pp. 31–32.
[15] Nattier. *ibid.* pg. 44n.
[16] Harrison, Paul. *ibid.* pg. 42.
[17] T.16, #676, pg. 697b; and Keenan, John. *The Scripture on the Explication of Underlying Meaning.* Berkeley: Numata Center for Translation and Research, 2000, pg. 49.
[18] Yamasaki, Taiko. *Shingon Japanese Esoteric Buddhism.* Boston: Shambhala, 1988, pg. 8.
[19] Dorje, Gyurme. *The Guhyagarbhatantra and its XIVth Century Commentary phyogs-bcu mun-sel.* School of Oriental and African Studies, University of London dissertation, 1987, pg. 73.
[20] Conze, Edward. *The Larger Sutra of Perfect Wisdom with the divisions of the Abhisamayālaṅkāra.* Delhi: Motilal Banarsidass Publishers Pvt. Ltd. 1990, pg. 328.
[21] The etymology of *naraka* is problematic as noted by Rhys-Davids, T.W. and Stede, William. *The Pali Text Society's Pali-English Dictionary.* London: Routledge & Kegan Paul Ltd. 1972, pg. 347. Monier-Williams, *ibid.* pg. 529 indicates that it is a name for or possibly derived

from *niraya* ("without happiness"/see: pg. 553) the *Pali-English Dictionary* agrees.

[22]. Vidor, Paul. *Ten Kings of Hades*. Taipei: The National Museum of History, 1984.

[23]. Lin, Li-Chen. "The Notion of Time and Position in the Book of Change and Their Development," in Huang, Chun-Dhieh and Zurcher, Erik. *Time and Space in Chinese Culture*. Leiden: E.J. Brill, 1995.

[24]. See: Huang and Zurcher, *ibid.* throughout.

[25]. Muller, Charles. *Dao de Jing*. 2016; No.16. [captured 7/25/2018: http://www.acmuller.net/con-dao/daodejing.html#div-17].

[26]. The *Jin shu* covers the years 265 to 420 CE, was written in the Tang dynasty and completed in 648 CE.

[27]. Smith, Richard J. *Fortune-Tellers and Philosophers Divination in Traditional Chinese Society*. Taipei: SMC Publishing Inc. 1991, pg. 59. Shao Yung was a neo-Confucian writer in the Song dynasty.

[28]. Schipper, Kristofer. "The Inner World of the Lao-Tzu Chung-Ching," in Huang and Zurcher *ibid.* pp. 114 *ff.*

[29]. The relationship between the different texts that incorporated the name "*Tai ping jing*" is problematic. However, as noted by Kandel, "The cosmological world view presented in the TPJ is not much developed beyond that of the Eastern Han Taiping faction…" Hence, because of this point and because of the fact that the three antiquities time scheme is integral to the conception of *Tai ping*, I take it that this aspect cannot be missing from the Han texts. See: Kandel, Barbara. *Tai ping Jing The Origin and Transmission of the 'Scripture on General Welfare' The History of an Unofficial Text*. Hamburg: 1979, Gesellschaft für Natur-und Völkerkunde Ostasiens e. V., pp. 83 *ff*; and Welch, H. and Seidel, *A. Facets of Taoism Essays in Chinese Religion*. New Haven: Yale University Press, 1979, "Discussion of Kaltenmark Paper," pp. 46–52.

[30]. See: Zhang, Qiyun *et al,* (eds.) *Zhong wen da ci dian*. Taipei: 1962–1968, Chinese Culture University, pg. 201c; Yoshioka Yoshitoyo. *Gugangyifeng, Dōkyō to Bukkyō II, Do kyō to bukyō*. Tokyo: 1970. as cited in Kaltenmark, Max. "The Ideology of the T'ai-p'ing ching," in Welch, H. and Seidel, A. *ibid.* pp. 19 *ff.*

[31]. Kandel. *ibid.*

[32]. These texts are usually called "apocrypha" in scholarly literature. The use of the term with Buddhist material indicates doubtful Indic origins. However, there is no requirement stated in the sutras that a text has to be of Indic origin to be authentic teachings.

[33]. On the nature of each "antiquity" see: Wang Mingbian. *Tai ping jing he jiao*. Shanghai: Zhonghua shuju, 1960, pp. 46 *ff.*, also see: Hendrischke, Barbara. *The Scripture of Great Peace the Taipingjing and the Beginnings of Daoism*. Berkeley, University of California Press, 2006, pp. 107–8 and 358 n14.

34. Mather, Richard B. "K'ou Ch'ien-chih and the Taoist Theocracy at the Northern Wei Court, 425–451," in Welch and Seidel *ibid.* pp. 103 *ff.*
35. As reported by Ch'en, *Buddhism in China. ibid.* pg. 173.
36. Zurcher, E. *Conquest. ibid.* pg. 128.
37. T.12, #348, translated 2nd century CE.
38. T.12, #349, translated 3rd century CE.
39. T.14, #454, translated 4th century CE.
40. T.14, #456, translated 4th century CE.
41. T.14, #457, translated 4th century CE.
42. T.26, #1525, translated 6th century CE.
43. Wright, Arthur F. *Buddhism in Chinese History*. Taipei: SMC Publishing Inc., 1990, pg. 69.
44. Hurvitz, Leon. *Chih-I (538–597) An Introduction to the life and Ideas of a Chinese Buddhist Monk*. Bruxelles: Institut Belge Des Hautes Etudes Chinoises, 1980.
45. T.46, #1933 pg. 787b.
46. T.9, #262. pg. 37c.
47. T.15, #617 pg. 299a. These are noted by Nattier. *ibid.* pg. 101n who also notes the possibility of an earlier work (T.17, #748) containing the term by an anonymous translator in the 4th century about the same time.
48. T.46, #1933 786c; also noted by Nattier. *ibid.* pg. 111n.
49. T.46, #1933, pg. 786c.
50. Hubbard, Jamie. *Absolute Delusion, Perfect Buddhahood*. Honolulu: University of Hawaii Press, 2001, pp. 77 *ff.*
51. Hubbard. *ibid.* pg. 79.
52. See: Lewis, Mark Edward. "The Suppression o the Three Stages Sect: Apocrypha as a Political Issue," in Buswell, Robert E. (ed.) *Chinese Buddhist Apocrypha. ibid.*
53. T.47, #1958 pg. 20a.
54. For example see: *moshi* T.47, #1958 pg. 4b: *mofa* T.47, #1958 pp. 5c; 13c; 18b.
55. T.47, #1958 pg. 13c.
56. T.47, #1958 pg. 18b.
57. T.47, #1958 pg. 4b.
58. Ch'en. *Buddhism in China. ibid.* pp. 172–173.
59. For an overview of early Chan, see Part I of Adamek. *ibid.*
60. Yanagida S. *Zen no goroku I. ibid.* "Preface"; pg.25.
61. Yanagida. S. *Zen no goroku I. ibid.* "Preface"; pg. 25.
62. T.48, #2010.
63. T.85, #2837 pg. 1286c.
64. T.48, #2011 also known as *Hsiu-hsin yao lun*, see: McRae. *Northern. ibid.* Chapt. VI.
65. T.48, #2007 and #2008 and see: Yamposky. *Platform. ibid.*
66. T.50, #2058.
67. T.50, #2060.

[68] T.85, #2837.
[69] T.50, #2060, pg. 525b.
[70] T.51, #2075, pg. 180a.

Conclusion

[1] My reflections after a visit.
[2] Gimello, Robert M. "Random Reflections on the "Sinicization" of Buddhism." *Society for the Study of Chinese Religions Bulletin* 5 (1978), pp. 52–89.
[3] Chang, Garma C.C. (ed.) *A Treasury of Mahāyāna Sūtras. ibid.* pg. 83.

Selected Bibliography

Tripiṭakas:

TP Barber, A.W. (ed.) *The Tibetan Tripitaka: Taipei Edition*. Taipei: Southern Materials Center, 1991.

T Takakusa Junjirō (ed.) *Taishō shinshū daizōkyō*. Tokyo: Daizō shuppan kai, 1922–33.

Chinese, Japanese Collections/Publications:

Da cheng qi xin lun. Taipei: 1992.

Ge Hong Zhuan, *Bao pu zi*. Taibei: 1965.

Lao zi du ben. Taipei: San Ming Publishing, 1974.

Ruan Yuan (ed.) *Shi san jing gu zhu*. Taipei: Xin Wen Feng Chu Ban, 1977.

Zhuangzi ji jiei. Taipei: San-Ming Publishing, 1974.

General:

Adam, Martin. "Two Concepts of Meditation and Three Kinds of Wisdom in Kamalaśīla's Bhāvanākramas: A Problem of Translation," *Buddhist Studies Review* 23(1) 2006.

---"Some Notes on Kamalaśīla's Understanding of Insight Considered as the Discernment of Reality (bhūta-pratyavekṣā)," *Buddhist Studies Review* 25(2) 2008.

Adams, Will W. "The Interpremeation of Self and World: Empirical Research, Existential Phenomenology, and Transpersonal Psychology," *Journal of Phenomenological Psychology*. Fall 99, vol. 30.

Adamek, Wendi L. *The Mystique of Transmission On an Early Chan History and its Contexts*. New York: Columbia University Press, 2007.

Ames, Roger T. "The Classical Chinese Self and Hypocrisy," in *Self and Deception a Cross-Cultural Philosophical Inquiry*. Albany: State

University of New York Press, 1996.

---"The Focus-Field Self in Classical Confucianism," in his *Self as Person in Asian Theory and Practice.* Delhi: Sri Satguru Publications, 1997.

---*Self as Person in Asian Theory and Practice.* Delhi: Sri Satguru Publications, 1997.

Andersen, Dines, and Smith Helmer. *Sutta-Nipāta.* London: for the Pali Text Society by Routledge & Kegan Paul. 1984.

Barber, A.W. "Darshanic Buddhism: The Origins of Pure Land Practice," in *The Pure Land*, New Series Nos. 18–19, Dec. 2002.

---"The Identification of dGa' rab rdo rje," in *The Journal of the International Association of Buddhist Studies*, vol.9 No. 2, 1986.

---"Memory and Chinese Buddhist Historical Writings," *Proceedings of the 8th Symposium of Confucianism, Buddhism, Communication and Philosophy of Culture*. Taipei: 2005.

---"Re-Viewing Chinese 'Religion'," *International Review of Chinese Religion and Philosophy.* Hawaii: International Advanced Institute, Inc. vol. 7, March 2002.

---"Two Mahāyāna Developments Along the Krishna River" in Padma, Sree and Barber, A.W. *Buddhism in the Krishna River Valley of Andhra.* Albany: State University of New York Press, 2008.

Basham, A.L. *The Wonder that was India*. Calcutta: Rupa & Co. 1991.

Bates, Roy. *Chinese Dragons.* Oxford: Oxford University Press, 2002.

Bhattacharyya, Benoytosh. *The Indian Buddhist Iconography*. Calcutta: Firma K.L. Muchopadhyay, 1987.

Birnbaum, Raoul. "The Manifestation of a Monastery: Shen-Ying's Experiences on Mount Wu-t'ai in T'ang Context," in *Journal of the American Oriental Society*. vol. 106, No.1. Jan–Mar. 1986.

Bol, Peter K. "Government, Society, and State: On the Political Visions of Ssu-ma-Kuang and Wang An-shih," in Hymes, Robert P. and Schirokauer, Conrad. (eds.) *Ordering the World Approaches to State and Society in Sung Dynasty China*. Berkeley: University of California

Press, 1993.

Botella, Luis. "Personal Construct Psychology, Constructivism, and Postmodern Thought." [captured 10/16/04: www.massey.ac.nz/~alock/virtual/Construc.htm].

Broughton, Jeffrey L. *The Bodhidharma Anthology The Earliest Records of Zen.* Berkeley: University of California Press, 1999.

Brown Brian Edward. *The Buddha Nature A Study of the Tathāgatagarbha and Ālyavijñāna.* Delhi: Motilal Banarsidass Publishers Private Limited, 1991.

Buddhaghosa, Bhadantācariya. *The Path of Purification* (*Visuddhimagga*). (trans. Nyāṇamoli, Bhikkhu), Colombo: A. Semage, 1964.

Bush, Susan & Shih, Hsio-yen. (eds.) *Early Chinese Texts on Painting.* Cambridge: Harvard University Press, 1985.

Buswell, Robert E. Jr. (ed.) *Chinese Buddhist Apocrypha.* Honolulu: University of Hawaii Press, 1991.

---"The 'Short-cut' Approach of *K'an-hua* meditation: The Evolution of a Practical Subitism in Chinese Chan Buddhism," in Gregory, Peter N. (ed.) *Sudden and Gradual Approaches to Enlightenment in Chinese Thought.* Honolulu: University of Hawaii Press, 1987.

Cartelli, Mary Anne. "On a Five-colored Cloud: the Songs of Mount Wutai," *Journal of the American Oriental Society*, 124.4 (2004).

Chaffee, John W. "The Historian as Critic: Li Hsin-ch'uan and the Dilemmas of Statecraft in Southern Sung China," in Hymes, Robert P. and Schirokauer, Conrad. (eds.) *Ordering the World Approaches to State and Society in Sung Dynasty China*. Berkeley: University of California Press, 1993.

Chalmers, Robert. *Majjhima Nikāya.* (vol. III) London: Pali Text Society, 1960.

Chang, Garma C.C. (ed.) *A Treasure of Mahāyāna Sūtras*. University Park: The Pennsylvania State University Press, 1983.

Chappell, David. "The Formation of the Pure Land Movement in China: Tao-ch'o and Shan-tao," in Foard, James, Solomon, Michael, and Payne, Richard K. (eds.) *The Pure Land Tradition: History and Development.* Berkeley: Berkeley Buddhist Studies Series, 1996.

---"From Dispute to Dual Cultivation: Pure Land Responses to Ch'an Critics," in Gregory, Peter N. (ed.) *Traditions of Meditation in Chinese Buddhism.* Honolulu: University of Hawaii Press, 1986.

---"The Teachings of the Fourth Ch'an Patriarch Tao-hsin in Lai, W. & Lancaster, L. *Early Ch'an in China and Tibet.* Berkeley: The Regents of the University of California, 1984.

Chau, Thich Thien Bhikshu. *The Literature of the Personalists of Early Buddhism.* (trans. Boin-Webb Sara) Delhi: Motilal Banarsidass Publishers Private Limited. 1999.

Ch'en, Kenneth K.S. *Buddhism in China*. Princeton: Princeton University Press, 1964.

---*The Chinese Transformation of Buddhism.* Princeton: Princeton University Press, 1973.

Cheng, Francois. *Empty and Full.* Boston: Shambhala. 1994.

Chimpa, Lama and Chattopadhyaya, Alaka. *Tāranātha's History of Buddhism in India*. Simla: Indian Institute of Advanced Study, 1970.

Conze, Edward. *Buddhist Meditation.* New York: Harper Torchbooks, 1956.

---*Buddhist Thought In India*. Ann Arbor: The University of Michigan Press, 1973.

---*The Larger Sutra of Perfect Wisdom with the divisions of the Abhisamayālaṅkāra*. Delhi: Motilal Banarsidass Publishers Pvt. Ltd. 1990.

---*The Perfection of Wisdom in Eight Thousand Lines and its Verse Summary*. Bolinas: Four Seasons Foundation, 1973.

---*The Prajñāpāramitā Literature*. Tokyo: The Reiyukai, 1978.

---*The Shorter Prajñāpāramitā Texts*. London: Luzac and Co., 1973.

Corless, Roger J. Corless, Roger J. *T'an-luan's Commentary On The Pure Land Discourse: An Annotated Translation and Sotereological*

Analysis of the Wang-Sheng-Lun Chu (T. 1819). Ann Arbor: University Microfilms, 1975.

---"T'an-luan: The First Systematizer of Pure Land Buddhism," in Foard, James, Solomon, Michael, and Payne, Richard K. (eds.) *The Pure Land Tradition: History and Development.* Berkeley: Berkeley Buddhist Studies Series, 1996.

Cort, Joh, E. "Art, Religion, and Material Culture. Some Reflections on Method," *Journal of the American Academy of Religion,* LXIV/3, Fall, 1996.

Dante (degli Alighieri, Durante). *The Divine Comedy*, (vol. I) *Inferno.*, (trans. Musa, Mark.) New York: Penguin Books, 2003.

Dayal, Har. *The Bodhisattva Doctrine in Buddhist Sanskrit Literature.* Delhi: Motilal Banarsidass, 1970.

de Bary, Wm. Theodore. "Individualism and Humanitarianism in Late Ming Thought," in de Bary, Wm. Theodore (and the Conference on Ming Thought*). Self and Society in Ming Thought.* New York: Columbia University Press, 1970.

---*Self and Society in Ming Thought.* New York: Columbia University, 1970.

de Bary, Wm. Theodore. and Bloom, Irene. *Sources of Chinese Tradition from Earliest Times to 1600.* New York: Columbia University Press, 1990.

de Groot, J.J. M. *The Religious System of China.* vol. II. Leyden: E.J. Brill, 1894.

Demiéville, Paul. *Le Concile de Lhasa*, Paris: Presses Universitaires de France, 1952.

---"La pénétration du Bouddhisme dans la tradition philosophique chinoise," *Cahiers d'histoire modiale*, III, No.1 UNESCO, Neuchâtel, 1956.

Derris, Karen, and Gummer, Natali. *Defining Buddhism(s).* London: Equinox Publishing Ltd. 2007.

Dessein, Bart. "Of Tempted *Arhats* and Supermundane Buddhas: Abhidharma in the Krishna Region," in Padma, Sree and Barber, A.W. *Buddhism in the Krishna River Valley of Andhra.* Albany: State University of New York Press, 2008.

Dhammapālatthera. *Vimānavatthu Aṭṭhakathā.* Yangon: Buddhasāsana Society, 2008.

Ding, Guanpeng. *A Long Roll of Buddhist Images*. Hong Kong: Commercial Press, 1994.

Donner, Neal. and Stevenson, Daniel B. *The Great Calming and Contemplation A Study and Annotated Translation of the First Chapter of Chih-I's Mo-Ho Chih-Kuan.* Honolulu: University of Hawaii Press, 1993.

Dumoulin, Heinrich. *A History of Zen Buddhism.* Boston: Beacon Press, 1963.

Dorje, Gyurme. *The Guhyagarbhatantra and its XIVth Century Commentary phyogs-bcu mun-sel.* School of Oriental and African Studies, University of London dissertation, 1987.

Eck, Diana L. *Darśan.*(3rd ed.) New York: Columbia University Press, 1998.

Elsner, John. "Image and Ritual: Reflections on the Religious Appreciation of Classic Art." *Classical Quarterly,* Oxford, 1996.

Faure, Bernard. *Chan Insight and Oversight An Epistemological Critique of the Chan tradition.* Princeton: Princeton University Press, 1993.

---"The Concept of One-Practice Samādhi in Early Chan," in Gregory, Peter N. (ed.) *Traditions of Meditation in Chinese Buddhism.* Honolulu: University of Hawaii Press, 1986.

---*The Will to Orthodoxy.* Stanford: Stanford University Press, 1997.

Feng, Gia-Fu and English, Jane. *Tao Te Ching: Lao Tsu.* New York: Vintage Books, 1989.

Foulk, T. Griffith, "Myth, Ritual, and Monastic Practice in Sung Ch'an Buddhism," in Ebrey, Patricia B. & Gregory, Peter N. *Religion and Society in T'ang and Sung China.* Honolulu: University of Hawaii Press, 1993.

---"Sung Controversies Concerning the "Separate Transmission" of Ch'an," in Gregory, Peter N. and Daniel A. Getz, Jr. *Buddhism in the Sung*. Honolulu: University of Hawai'i Press, 1999.

Foulk, Griffith. and Sharf, Robert H. "On the Ritual use of Ch'an Portraiture in Medieval China," in *Cashiers d'Extreme-Asia*, (Special Issue Ch'an/Zen Studies en l'honneur de Yanagida Seizan) 1993–1994.

Frederic, Louis. *Buddhism Flammarion Iconographic Guides*. Paris: Flammarion, 1995.

Fujiwara, Ryosetsu. *The Way to Nirvana*. Tokyo: The Kyoiku Shincho Sha, 1974.

Fuller, Winston. "Zen and the Practice of an Art as a Spiritual Discipline," *Studia Mystica*, Sacramento: California State University, 1987.

Fung, Yu-lan. *A History of Chinese Philosophy* (trans. Derk Bodde). Princeton: Princeton University Press, 1952.

Gardner, W., Pickett, C., and Brewer, M. "Social Exclusion and Selective Memory: How the Need to Belong Influences Memory for Social Events," *Personality and Social Psychology Bulletin,* vol. 26, No. 4, April 2000.

Getz, Daniel A. Jr. "T'ien-t'ai Pure Land Societies and the Creation of the Pure Land Patriarchate," in Gregory, Peter N. & Getz, Daniel A. Jr. *Buddhism in the Sung*. Honolulu: University of Hawai'i Press, 1999.

Gimello, Robert M. "Chang Shang-ying on Wu-t'ai Shan," in Naquin, Susan. and Yu, Chun-gang. *Pilgrims and Sacred Sites in China.* Berkeley: University of California Press, 1992.

---"Random Reflections on the "Sinicization" of Buddhism." *Society for the Study of Chinese Religions Bulletin* 5 (1978).

Gokhale, Valkrishna G. "On Buddhist Historiography," in Narain, A.K. (ed.) *Studies in Pali and Buddhism*. Delhi: B.R. Publishing Corporation, 1979.

Gomez, Luis. O. "Indian Materials on the Doctrine of Sudden Enlightenment," in Lai, Whalen and Lancaster, Lewis R. (eds.) *Early Ch'an in China and Tibet.* Berkeley: the Regents of the University of California, 1983.

Graham, A.C. *Disputers of the Tao.* LaSalle: Open Court, 1989.

Gregory, Peter N. (ed.) *Sudden and Gradual Approaches to Enlightenment in Chinese Thought.* Honolulu: University of Hawaii Press, 1987.

---*Tsung-mi and the Sinification of Buddhism*. Princeton: Princeton University Press, 1991.

Gregory, Peter N. and Getz, Daniel A.Jr. (eds.) *Buddhism in the Sung.* Honolulu: University of Hawai'i Press, 1999.

Guenther, Herbert V. *Buddhist Philosophy in Theory and Practice.* Boulder: Shambhala, 1976.

Gyatso, Janet. *In the Mirror of Memory: Reflections on Mindfulness and Remembrance in Indian and Tibetan Buddhism.* Delhi: Sri Satguru Publications, 1992.

Hakeda, Yoshito S. *The Awakening of Faith in the Mahayana.* New York: Columbia University Press, 1967.

Hardy, Edmund. *Anguttare-Nikāya.* (vol. V) London: Pali Text Society, 1900.

---*The Netti Prakarana*, London: Pali Text Society, 1902.

Hare, E.M. *The Book of the Gradual Sayings*. (vol. IV) London: Routledge and Kegan Paul Ltd. 1973.

Heine, Steven and Wright, Dale S. *The Zen Canon Understanding the Classic Texts*. New York: Oxford University Press, Inc. 2004.

---*Zen Masters*. New York: Oxford University Press, 2010.

Hirakawa, Akira. *A History of Indian Buddhism.* (trans. Groner, Paul), Delhi: Motilal Banarsidass Publishers, 1993.

Hisamatsu, Shin'ichi. *Zen and the Fine Arts.* Tokyo: Kodansha International Ltd. 1971.

Hookham S.K. *The Buddha Within.* Albany: State University of New York Press, 1991.

Hu, William C. *The Lion Dance Explained.* Ann Arbor: Ars Ceramica, Ltd., 1995.

Huang, Chun-Dhieh and Zurcher, Erik. *Time and Space in Chinese Culture*. Leiden: E.J. Brill, 1995.

Hubbard, Jamie. *Absolute Delusion, Perfect Buddhahood*. Honolulu: University of Hawaii Press, 2001.

Hurvitz, Leon. *Chih-I (538–597) An Introduction to the Life and Ideas of a Chinese Buddhist Monk*. Bruxelles: Institut Belge Des Hautes Études Chinoises, 1980.

---*Lotus Blossom of the Fine Dharma*. New York: Columbia University Press, 2009.

---"Selections from the Commentary to Vasubandhu's Essay on Rebirth," in de Bary, Wm. Theodore. and Bloom, Irene. *Sources of Chinese Tradition from Earliest Times to 1600*. New York: Columbia University Press, 1990.

Hymes, Robert P. and Schirokauer, Conrad. (eds.) *Ordering the World Approaches to State and Society in Sung Dynasty China*. Berkeley: University of California Press, 1993.

Ichimura, Shohei. *Buddhist Critical Spirituality Prajñā and Śūnyatā*. Delhi: Motilal Banarsidass Publishers, 2001.

Ideda, Daisaku. *The Flower of Chinese Buddhism*. (trans. Watson, Burton) Santa Monica: Middle Way Press, 2009.

Inagaki, Hisao. *T'an Luan's Commentary on Vasubandhu's Discourse on the Pure Land*, Kyoto: Nagata Bunshodo, 1998.

---*The Three Pure Land Sutras*. Kyoto: Nagata Bunshodo, 1994.

Jaini, Padmanabh S. "*Smṛti* in the Abhidharma Literature and the Development of Buddhist Accounts of Memory of the Past." in Gyatso, Janet. *In the Mirror of Memory: Reflections on Mindfulness and Remembrance in Indian and Tibetan Buddhism*. Delhi: Sri Satguru Publications, 1992.

Jia, Jinhua. *The Hangzhou School of Chan Buddhism in Eighth-through Tenth-Century China*. Albany: State University of New York Press, 2006.

Kaltenmark, Max. "The Ideology of the T'ai-p'ing ching," in Welch, H.

and Seidel, *A. Facets of Taoism Essays in Chinese Religion*. New Haven: Yale University Press, 1979.

Kandel, Barbara. *Taiping Jing The Origin and Transmission of the 'Scripture on General Welfare' The History of an Unofficial Text*. Hamburg: Gesellschaft für Natur-und Völkerkunde Ostasiens e. V., 1979.

Kashyap, Bhikkhu J. (ed.) *The Saṃyutta Nikāya.* vol. II. Nalanda: Pāli Publication Board, 1959.

Keenan, John P. *How Master Mou Removes Our Doubts*. Albany: State University of New York Press, 1994.

---*The Scripture on the Explication of Underlying Meaning.* Berkeley: Numata Center for Translation and Research, 2000.

Kieschnick, John. *The Eminent Monk: Buddhist Ideas in Medieval Chinese Hagiography.* Honolulu: University of Hawaii Press, 1997.

Kulasurya, Ananda S. "The Jātakas and their Ethical Foundation," in Dhammajoti, K. Tilakaratne, A. Abhayawansa, K. (eds.) *Recent Research in Buddhist Studies.* Colombo: Y. Karunada Felicitation Committee, 1997.

Lai, Whalen and Lancaster, Lewis R. (eds.) *Early Ch'an in China and Tibet.* Berkeley: the Regents of the University of California, 1983.

---"The Pure and the Impure: The Mencian Problematic in Chinese Buddhism," in Lai, Whalen and Lancaster, Lewis R. (eds.) *Early Ch'an in China and Tibet.* Berkeley: the Regents of the University of California, 1983.

Lamotte, Etienne. *History of Indian Buddhism*. (trans. Webb-Boin, S.) Louvain: Petters Press, 1988.

Lee, Sherman E. *A History of Far Eastern Art.* Englewood Cliffs: Prentice-Hall and New York: Harry N. Abrams, Inc. 1973.

Lewis, Mark Edward. "The Suppression o the Three Stages Sect: Apocrypha as a Political Issue," in Buswell, Robert E. Jr. (ed.) *Chinese Buddhist Apocrypha.* Honolulu: University of Hawaii Press, 1991.

Lin, Li-Chen. "The Notion of Time and Position in the Book of Change and Their Development," in Huang, Chun-Dhieh and Zurcher, Erik. *Time and Space in Chinese Culture*. Leiden: E.J. Brill, 1995.

Loewe, Michael. *Faith, Myth and Reason in Han China.* Indianapolis: Hackett Publishing Company, Inc., 2005.

Mair, Victor H. "What is Geyi, After All?" in Chan, Alan K. L. and Lo, Yuet-Keung (eds.) *Philosophy and Religion in Early Medieval China.* Albany: State University of New York Press, 2010.

Marcus, Margaret F. "Sculptures from Bihar and Bengal". *The Bulletin of the Cleveland Museum of Art*, vol. 54, No. 8 (Oct., 1967).

Marks-Tarlow, Terry. "From Emergency to Emergence: The Deep Structure of Play in Psychotherapy," in *Psychoanalytic Dialogues: The International Journal of Relational Perspective*. (09 Feb 2015).

Maspero, Henri. *Taoism and Chinese Religion*, Amherst: The University of Massachusetts Press, 1981.

Mather, Richard B. "K'ou Ch'ien-chih and the Taoist Theocracy at the Northern Wei Court, 425–451," in Welch and Seidel *Facets of Taoism Essays in Chinese Religion*. New Haven: Yale University Press, 1979.

Matthes, Klaus-Dieter. "Can *sutra mahāmudrā* be justified on the basis of Maitrīpa's Apratiṣṭhānavāda?" in Kellner, B., Krasser, H., Lasic, H., Much, M.T., and Tauscher, H. (eds.) Pramāṇakīrtiḥ. *Papers Dedicated to Ernst Steinkellner on the Occasion of his 70th Birthday*. Part 2, Wien: Wiener Studien zur Tibetologie und Buddhismuskunde, 2007.

McRae, John. *The Northern School and the Formation of Early Ch'an Buddhism.* Honolulu: University of Hawaii Press, 1986.

---*Seeing Through Zen Encounter, Transformation, and Genealogy in Chinese Chan Buddhism*. Berkeley: University of California Press, 2003.

Merk, Laura E., Mann, Trish D. and Ogan, Amy T. "Make-Believe Play: Wellspring for Development of Self-Regulations," in Singer, Dorothy G., Hirsh-Pasek, Kathy. Golinkoff, Roberta Michnick. *Play = Learning: How Play Motivates and Enhances Children's Cognitive and Social-Emotional Growth*. Oxford: Oxford University Press, 2006.

Meskill, John. *The Pattern of Chinese History.* Boston: D.C. Heath and Company, 1965.

Mitchiner, Joh, E. *Traditions of the Seven Riṣis.* Delhi: Motilal Banarsidass, 1982.

Muller, A. Charles. Muller, Charles. *Dao de Jing*. 2016; No.16. [captured 7/25/2018: http://www.acmuller.net/con-dao/daodejing.html#div-17].

---*The Sutra of Perfect Enlightenment.* Albany: State University of New York Press, 1999.

Münsterberg, Hugo. "Buddhist Bronzes of the Six Dynasties Period," *Artibus Asiae*. vol. 9, No. 4, 1946.

---*Zen & Oriental Art.* Rutland: Charles E. Tuttle Company, 1993.

Nagao, Gadjin *Mādhyamika and Yogācāra A study of Mahāyāna Philosophies.* Albany: State University of New York Press, 1991.

Naismith, Earl George. *Bai Juyu (Bai Lo Tian) 772–846 AD, Tang Dynasty Poet, Midst Everyday Life, Musings on the Ordinary, Influences of the Not So Obvious*. Vancouver: University of British Columbia Thesis, 2003.

Nattier, Jan. *Once Upon A Future Time Studies in a Buddhist Prophecy of Decline*. Berkeley: Asian Humanities Press, 1991.

Naquin, Susan. and Yu, Chun-gang. *Pilgrims and Sacred Sites in China.* Berkeley: University of California Press, 1992.

Needham, Joseph. *Science and Civilisation in China*. Taipei: Caves Books. Ltd. 1985.

Nienhauser, Willaim H. Jr. (ed.) *The Indiana Companion to Traditional Chinese Literature.* Bloomington: Indiana University Press, 1986.

Norman, K.R. *Pali Literature*. Wiesbaden: Otto Harrassowitz, 1983.

Obermiller, E. "A Study of the Twenty Aspects of Śūnyatā," in the *Indian Historical Quarterly*, March 1933.

Olderberg, Hermann. *Sacred Books of the East: Vedic Hymns*, part II. vol. X–LVI (ed. Muller, Max.) Delhi: Motilal Banarsidass, 1973.

Olivelle, Patrick. *The Early Upanisads Annotated Text and Translation.* Oxford: Oxford University Press, 1998.

Olson, Carl (ed.) *Original Buddhist Sources.* New Brunswick: Rutgers University Press, 2005.

Padilla, Elaine. *Divine Enjoyment A Theology of Passion and Exuberance.* New York: Fordham University Press. 2015.

Padma, Sree and Barber, A.W. *Buddhism in the Krishna River Valley of Andhra.* Albany: State University of New York Press, 2008.

Parker, Joseph D. *Zen Landscape Arts of Early Muromachi Japan (1336–1573).* Albany: State University of New York Press, 1999.

Pas, Julian. *Visions of Sukhāvatī: Shan-Tao's Commentary on the Kuan Wu-Liang-Shou-Fo Ching.* Albany: State University of New York Press, 1995.

Pellegrini, A.D. and Bjorklund, David F. "The Ontogeny and Phylogeny of Children's object and Fantasy Play," in *Human Nature* (vol. 15, NO.1) 2004.

Poceski, Mario. "Monastic Innovator, Iconoclast, and Teacher of Doctrine: The Varied Images of Chan Master Baizhang," in Heine, Steven and Wright, Dale S. *Zen Masters.* New York: Oxford University Press, 2010.

Poussin, Louise de La Valle, *Abhidharmakośabhāṣyam.* (trans. Pruden, Leo M.) Berkeley: Asian Humanities Press, 1990.

Powell, William P. *The Record of Tung-shan.* Honolulu: University of Hawaii Press, 1986.

Priestley, Leonard C.D.C. *Pudgalavāda Buddhism The Reality of the Indeterminate Self.* Toronto: University of Toronto Centre for South Asian Studies, 1999.

Rahula, Walpoa Sri. *What the Buddha Taught.* London: The Gordon Fraser Gallery Ltd., 1978.

Ren, Jiyu *Book of Lao Zi.* (trans. He, Guanghu, Gao, Shining, Song, Lidao, and Xu Junyao), Beijing: Foreign Languages Press, 1993.

Reynolds, John Myrdhin. *The Golden Letters.* Ithaca: Snow Lion, 1996.

Rhie, Marylin M. *The Fo-kuang ssu: Literary Evidence and Buddhist Images.* New York: Garland Publishing, 1977.

Rhys-Davids, Caroline. (trans.) *A Buddhist Manual of Psychological Ethics* (*Dhamma-saṅgaṇī*). London: The Pali Text Society, 1974.

---*Psalms of the Early Buddhist* (*I-Psalms of the Sisters*). London: Routledge and Kegan Paul. Ltd., 1980.

Rhys-Davids, T.W. *Dialogues of the Buddha.* London: Pali Text Society, 1977.

---*The Questions of King Milinda.* New York: Dower Publications, Inc. 1963.

Rhys-Davids, T.W. and Carpenter, J. Estlin. (ed.) *The Dīgha Nikāya.* London: for the Pali Text Society by Messrs. Luzac, and Company, Ltd. 1960.

Rhys-Davids, T.W. and Oldenberg, Herman. *Vinaya Texts*. Delhi: Motilal Banarsidass, 1974.

Robins, James. *Buddha's Lions.* Berkeley: Dharma Publishing, 1979.

Robinson, Richard H. *Early Mādhyamika in India and China.* New York: Samuel Weiser, Inc. 1978.

Roccasalvo, Joseph F. "The debate at bsam yas: Religious Contrast and Correspondence" *Philosophy East and West.* Honolulu: The University of Hawaii Press, 30:4 (Oct. 1980).

Roerich, George. *The Blue Annals.* Delhi: Motilal Banarsiddas Publishers, 1979.

Ruegg, David Seyfort. *La Théorie du Tathāgatagarbha et du Gotra: etudes su la sotéologie du bouddhisme.* Paris: École Française d' Extrême-Orient, 1969.

---*The Literature of the Madhyamaka School of Philosophy in India.* Wiesbaden: Otto Harrassowitz, 1981.

Rump, Ariane. *Commentary on the Lao Tzu by Wang Pi.* Honolulu: The University Press of Hawaii, 1979.

Sadakata, Akira. *Buddhist Cosmology Philosophy and Origins*. Tokyo: Kōsei Publishing Co. 1999.

Saddhatissa, H. *The Sutta Nipāta.* Richmond: Curzon Press, 1985.

Sasaki, Ruth Fuller. Iriya, Yoshitaka. And Fraser, Danna R. *The Recorded Saying of Layman P'ang.* New York: Weatherhill. 1971.

Schipper, Kristofer. "The Inner World of the Lao-Tzu Chung-Ching", in Huang, Chun-Dhieh and Zurcher, Erik. *Time and Space in Chinese Culture*. Leiden: E.J. Brill, 1995.

Schirokauer, Conrad. "Chu Hsi's Sense of History," in Hymes, Robert P. and Schirokauer, Conrad (eds.) *Ordering the World Approaches to State and Society in Sung Dynasty China*. Berkeley: University of California Press, 1993.

Schopen, Gregory. "Archaeology and Protestant Presuppositions in the Study of Indian Buddhism," *Bones, Stones, and Buddhist Monks*. Honolulu: University of Hawaii Press, 1997.

Schwartzman, Helen B. *Transformations The Anthropology of Children's Play*. New York: Plenum Press, 1978.

Sharf, Robert H. *Coming to Terms with Chinese Buddhism: A Reading of the Treasure Store Treatise*. Honolulu: University of Hawaii Press, 2002.

Shinko Mochizuki, "Pure Land Buddhism in China: A Doctrinal History," (trans. Pruden, Leo M.), ebook: *Journal of the Institute of Buddhist Studies*:
http://elibrary.ibc.ac.th/files/public/HistoryOfPureLand_ibc2010v1.pdf and *Chugoku jodokyorishi, Hozokan, Kyoto*, 1942 &1964.

Shinohara, Koichi. "From Local History to Universal History: The Construction of the Sung T'ien-T'ai Lineage," in Gregory, Peter N. and Getz, Jr. Daniel A. *Buddhism in the Sung*. Honolulu: University of Hawai'i Press, 1999.

Singer, Dorothy G. and Singer. Jerome L. *House of Make-Believe: Children's Play and the Developing Imagination*. Cambridge: Harvard University Press, 1990.

Smith, Richard J. *Fortune-Tellers and Philosophers Divination in Traditional Chinese Society*. Taipei: SMC Publishing Inc. 1991.

Solomon, Richard. "Why did the Gandhāran Buddhist Bury Their Manuscripts?" in Berkwitz, Stephen. Schober, Juliane. and Brown, Claudia. *Buddhist Manuscript Cultures Knowledge, Ritual, and Art*. London: Routledge, 2009.

Sommer, Deboray (ed.) *Chinese Religion an Anthology of Sources*. Oxford: Oxford University Press, 1995.

Sopa, Geshe Lhundup and Hopkins, Jeffrey. *Practice and Theory of Tibetan Buddhism.* New York: Grove Press, Inc. 1976.

Stcherbatsky, Th. *The Conception of Buddhist Nirvana.* Delhi: Motilal Banarsidass, 1977.

Stein, R.A. "Sudden Illumination or Simultaneous Comprehension: Remarks on Chinese and Tibetan Terminology," in Gregory, Peter N. (ed.) *Sudden and Gradual Approaches to Enlightenment in Chinese Thought.* Honolulu: University of Hawaii Press, 1987.

Stevenson, Daniel B. "The Four Kinds of Samādhi in Early T'ien-t'ai Buddhim," in Gregory, Peter N. (ed.) *Traditions of Meditation in Chinese Buddhism.* Honolulu: University of Hawaii Press, 1986.

---"Protocols of Power: Ts'u-yun Tsun-shir (964–1032) and T'ien-t'ai Lay Buddhist Ritual in the Song." in Gregory, Peter N. and Getz, Daniel A. *Buddhism in the Sung.* Honolulu: University of Hawai'i Press, 1999.

Strong, John. *The Legend and Cult of Upagupta.* Delhi: Motilal Banarsidass Publishers, 1994.

---*The Legend of King Aśoka.* Princeton: Princeton University Press, 1983.

Suzuki, Daisetz Teitaro. *An Index to the Lankavatara Sutra.* Kyoto: The Sanskrit Buddhist Texts Publishing Society, 1934.

Swami Dwarikadas (ed.) *Abhidharmakośam & Bhāṣya of Acharya Vasubandhu with Sputārthā Commentary of Ācārya Yaśomitra* (*sic.*). Varanasi: Bauddha Bharati, 1973.

Teiser, Stephen F. *The Scripture on the Ten Kings and the Making of Purgatory in Medieval Chinese Buddhism.* Honolulu: University of Hawaii Press, 1994.

Tendzin, Padma. (ed.) Nāgārjuna. *Suhṛllekha.* Varanasi: Central Institute of High Tibetan Studies, 2002.

Thomas, Edward. *The Life of Buddha as Legend and History.* London: Routledge & Kegan Paul, 1975.

Trenckner, V. (ed.) *Majjhima Nikāya.* London: for the Pali Text Society by Messrs. Luzac, and Company, Ltd. 1964.

Tribe, Anthony. "Manjusri: Origins, Role and Significance", (Part 3. The Cult of Mañjuśrī). *Western Buddhist Review*, Dec. 1994.

Tsukamoto, Zenryū. *A History of Early Chinese Buddhism* (trans. Leon Hurvitz). Tokyo: Kodansha International Ltd. 1979.

Tzo, Sze-bong. T*he Transformation of Buddhist Vinaya in China*. Dissertation, Canberra: Australian National University, 1982.

Ueyama, Daishun. "The Study of Tibetan Ch'an Manuscripts Recovered from Tun-huang: A Review of the Field and its Prospects," in Lai, Whalen and Lancaster, Lewis R. (eds.) *Early Ch'an in China and Tibet*. Berkeley: the Regents of the University of California, 1983.

Unno, Tetsuo. *An Introduction to the Jodoronchu with Translation and Footnotes*. Kyoto: Ryukoku University, (Master Thesis) 1958.

Vidor, Paul. *Ten Kings of Hades*. Taipei: The National Museum of History, 1984.

Visser, Marinus. W. *The Dragon in China and Japan*. Amsterdam: J. Muller. 1913, [https://archive.org/details/cu31924021444728/page/n5].

Wan, Ven. Hiu. *Revelation From Ch'an Practice Ch'an Paintings*.Taipei: Yuan Ch'uan Press, 1992.

Watson, Burton. *The Complete Works of Chuang Tzu*. New York: Columbia University Press, 1968.

---"The Great Han Historians," in de Bary, Wm. Theodore and Bloom, Irene. Irene. *Sources of Chinese Traditions* (vol. 1. 2nd ed.) New York: Columbia University Press, 1999.

---*Ssu-Ma Ch'ien Grand Historian of China*. New York: Columbia University Press, 1963.

Watson, Burton., Nivison, David., & Bloom, Irene. "Classical Sources of Chinese Tradition," in de Bary, Wm. Theodore & Bloom, Irene. *Sources of Chinese Traditions* (vol. 1. 2nd ed.) New York: Columbia University Press, 1999.

Wayman, Alex. "Buddhist Terms for Recollection and Other Types of Memory," in Gyatso, Janet. *In the Mirror of Memory: Reflections on Mindfulness and Remembrance in Indian and Tibetan Buddhism*. Delhi: Sri Satguru Publications, 1992.

---"The Mahāsāṃghika and the Tathāgatagarbha," (Buddhist Doctrinal History, Study 1), *Journal of the International Association of Buddhist Studies* 1 (1978).

---"No time, Great Time, and Profane Time in Buddhism," in his *Buddhist Insight.* Delhi: Motilal Banarsidass, 1984.

Wayman, Alex, and Wayman, Hideko. *The Lion's Roar of Queen Śrīmālā. New* York: Columbia University Press, 1974.

Welch, H. and Seidel, *A. Facets of Taoism Essays in Chinese Religion.* New Haven: Yale University Press, 1979.

Welter, Albert. "Lineage and Context in the *Patriarch's Hall Collection* and the *Transmission of the Lamp*," in Heine, Steven & Wright, Dale S. *The Zen Canon: Understanding the Classic Texts.* Oxford: Oxford University Press, 2004.

Wenjie, Duan (ed.) *Mural Paintings of the Dunhuang Mogao Grotto.* Osaka?: Kenbun-sha, Inc. 1994.

Whitehead, James D. "The Sinicization of the Vimalakīrtinirdeśa Sūtra," *Society for the Study of Chinese Religions Bulletin*, 5.01 Spr. 1978.

Williams, Lynn. "Spirituality and Gestalt: A Gestalt-Transpersonal Perspective," *Gestalt Review.* 10(1):6–21, 2006.

Williams, Paul. *Mahāyāna Buddhism the Doctrinal Foundations.* London: Routledge, 1991.

Winternitz, Maurice. *History of Indian Literature.* Delhi: Motilal Banarsidass, 1988.

Wogihara, Unrai and Tsuji Naoshirō. *Bonwa daijiten.* Suzuki research Foundation; Taipei: Hsin Won Fang Publishing, 1979.

Woike, B., Mcleod, S., and Goggin, M. "Implicit and Explicit Motives Influence Accessibility to Different Autobiographical Knowledge," *Personality and Social Psychology Bulletin*, vol. 29, No. 8, Aug. 2003.

Woodward, F.L. Woodward, F.L. *The Book of the Gradual Sayings.* vol. I, London: The Pali Text Society, 1979.

---*The Book of the Kindred Sayings.* Part III, London: Routledge and

Kegan Paul Ltd., 1980.

---*The Minor Anthologies of the Pali Canon* (prt. II.). London: Routledge and Kegan Paul PLC, 1985.

Wu, Teresa L. *The Origin and Dissemination of Chinese Characters.* Taipei: Cave Books, Ltd., 1990.

Yamasaki, Taiko. *Shingon Japanese Esoteric Buddhism.* Boston: Shambhala, 1988.

Yampolsky, Philip. "New Japanese Studies in Early Ch'an History," in Lai, W. & Lancaster, L. *Early Ch'an in China and Tibet.* Berkeley: University of California Press, 1983.

---*The Platform Sutra of the Sixth Patriarch.* New York: Columbia University Press, 1967.

Yanagida Seizan. *Daruma no goroku—Zen no goroku 1.* Tokyo: Chikuma shobō, 1969.

---"The Li-Tai Fa-Pao Chi and the Ch'an Doctrine of Sudden Awakening," in Lai, W. & Lancaster, L. *Early Ch'an in China and Tibet.* Berkeley: The Regents of the University of California, 1984.

---"The 'Recorded Sayings' Texts of Chinese Ch'an Buddhism," Lai, Whalen and Lancaster, Lewis R. (eds.) *Early Ch'an in China and Tibet.* Berkeley: the Regents of the University of California, 1983.

---*Shoki no zenshi 1 —Ryōgo shiji ki —Den'hōbōki,* in *Zen no goroku,* no.2. Tokyo: Chikuma Shobo, 1971.

---*Shoki Zenshū shisho no kenkyū.* Kyoto: Hōzōkan, 1967.

Yang Hsüan-chih. *A Record of Buddhist Monasteries in Lo-Yang.* Princeton: Princeton University Press, 1984.

Yin shun. *Chungou chanzong shi.* (3rd. ed.) Jayi: Yin Hsun Publishing, 1978.

Yū, Chün-fang, "The Chinese Transformation of Avalokiteshvara," in Weidener, Marsha (ed.) *Latter Days of the Law Images of Chinese Buddhism 850–1850.* Lawrence & Honolulu: Spencer Museum of Art, The University of Kansas in Association with the University of Hawaii Press, 1994.

Yu, Chun-gang. "P'u-t'o Shan," in Naquin, Susan. and Yu, Chun-gang. *Pilgrims and Sacred Sites in China.* Berkeley: University of California Press, 1992.

Zhao, Qiguang. *A Study of Dragons, East and West.* New York: Perter Lang, 1992.

Ziporun, Brook. *Evil and/or/as The Good.* Cambridge, Mass.: Harvard University Press, 2000.

Zurcher, Erik. "Buddhism and Education in T'ang Times," in de Bary, Wm. Theodore and Chaffee, John W. *Neo-Confucian Education: The Formative Stage*. Berkeley: University of California Press, 1989.

---*The Buddhist Conquest of China: The Spread and Adaptation of Buddhism in Early Medieval China*. Leiden: E.J. Brill, 1959.

---"Perspectives in the Study of Chinese Buddhism," *Journal of the Royal Asiatic Society of Great Britain and Ireland*, No.1 (1982).

Index

A

Amitābha Meditation Sutra, 113

Amogavajra, 96

Analects, 109, 120, 232(33), 244(29)

Angulimālīya Sūtra, 57

Aṅguttara Nikāya, 50, 103, 162, 193

An le ji, 207

Annals of the Transmission of the Dharma Jewel, 116

Anshiguo, 109

Anthologie raisonnee de la literature chinoise, 139

Anuttarāśraya Sūtra, 68

Asaṅga, 23, 195

Aśoka (Emperor), 27, 92, 95, 125, 232(22)

Aśoka-Avadāna, 28

Aṣṭasāhasrikā, 108, 120, 164, 173, 181, 243(23), 245(15)

ātman, 13, 46, 47, 48, 50, 51, 55–57, 59–62, 66, 70, 71, 238(29)

Avadānaśataka, 26

Avalokiteśvara (see Guanyin)

Avataṃsaka, 54, 80, 92, 94, 95, 97, 100, 129, 143, 157–159, 162, 166, 167, 169, 171, 195, 203, 245(15), 251(80, 95)

avidyā, 44, 51

awakening, 25, 26, 38, 41, 77, 99, 107, 108, 111, 112, 115, 118, 129, 134, 141, 142, 149, 153, 169, 190, 197, 207, 220, 222, 235(62, 66),

Awakening of Confidence, 152, 153, 156, 157, 158, 159, 160, 169, 171, 172, 251(95)

B

Bao lin chuan, 39

Bao pu zi, 10, 230(18)

Basham, A.L., iii, 44, 237(2), 240(6)

Bearer Sutra, 50

Berk, Mann, and Ogan, 104

Bhadrayānīyas, 52

bhavanga, 51

Bhāvaviveka, 27, 232(20)

bhikṣu, 5, 6, 48

bhikṣunī, 5

Biographies of Eminent Monks, 31, 41, 116

Blue Cliff Records, 118

Bodhidharma, 39, 64–68, 72, 116, 147, 150–153, 155, 159, 162, 170, 174–176, 180, 181, 209, 220

Bodhidharma Anthology, 64

Bodhiruci, 36, 94, 111, 181

Bodhisattva, 7, 26, 82, 85, 93–97, 99, 100, 108, 109, 111, 112, 114, 115, 121, 129, 131, 132, 135, 137, 143, 155, 157, 164, 167, 168, 172–174, 176, 189, 191, 195–197, 215, 218, 227, 233(37), 253(8)

Bol, Peter, 138, 247(45)

Brahmajāla Sūtra, 24, 103

Brahman, 47, 237(3)

Buddha Nature Treaties, 57

Buddhabhadra, 94, 157, 203

buddhadhātu, 53, 54, 157

Buddhaghoṣa, 28, 101, 103, 253(2, 3)

Buddhayaśas, 109

C

Cakkavatti Sīhanāda Suttanta, 92

calm abiding, 134, 135, 141, 144, 246(34)

Catuḥsatyaśāstra, 167

Chan yuan zhu quan ji du xu, 68

Chau, Thich Thien Bhikshu, 237

Ch'en, Kenneth, 7, 8, 9, 10, 229(12), 130(16), 254(35), 255(58)

Cheng, Francois, 137, 141, 241(41, 42, 52)

Chinese Buddhist Apocrypha, 7, 230(14), 255(52)

Chuan fa bao ji, 38, 116

Chuji, 39

cintāmani, 78, 83, 84, 99

Ci yun zun shi, 132

Collection (of Passages Concerning Birth in the Land of) Peace and Bliss, 36

Collection of Biographies of Buddhist Masters in the Pure Land Tradition in the Three Countries, 36

confidence, 69, 150, 151, 154–156, 165, 172, 191, 249(28)

Confidence in Mind Inscription, 116

Confucian classics, 9

Confucius, 29, 61, 63, 64, 66, 67, 69–71, 110, 122

Continued Biographies of Eminent Monks, 116

Conze, Edward, 49, 142, 161, 162, 237(5, 8), 246(33), 247(53), 250(61, 72), 251(94), 252(114), 253(20)

Cort, John E., 125, 245(3)

Cūḷa Sīhanāda Suttanta, 92

D

Da cheng ben sheng xin di guan jing, 167

Da fa gu jing, 68

Dahai, 36

Da mo duo luo chan jing, 38

Dante, 11, 230(22)

Dao, 29, 65, 67, 71, 72, 112, 114, 115, 121, 137, 151, 152, 157, 160, 162, 175–179, 182

Dao'an, 203

Daochang, 36

Daochuo, 36, 37, 112, 131, 207, 235(59)

Dao de jing, 9, 10, 11, 200, 254

Daoxin, 210

Daoxuan, 31, 34, 116,

darśana, 127, 128, 129, 130, 133, 143, 219, 245(8, 12)

Demiéville, Paul, 7, (229(9)

Derris and Gummer, 3, 4, 229(2)

Description of Greece, 125

Devarāja pravara prajñāpāramitā Sūtra, 181

dGa' rab rdo rje, 154, 248(22)

Dhammapada, 163, 173

Dhammapālatthera, 103, 243(9)

Dharma Ending Age, 137, 207, 208

Dharmagupta, 93, 181

Dharmakāya, 135, 136, 141, 145, 152

Dharmakīrti, 23

Dharmarakṣa, 109, 203

Dhammasaṅgaṇī, 20

Dharmottarīyas, 52

Diamond Sutra, 111, 169, 181

Dīgha Nikāya, 103, 241(35),

242(6)253(4)

Dīrghāgama, 68, 109, 251(95)

Dignāga, 23

Dilun, 36

Discourse on Ready Eloquence, 222

Discourse on the Pure Land, 36, 234(52)

dragon, 73–77, 80–86, 93, 98–100, 186, 217, 239(2, 3), 240(4, 5, 16)

Dufei, 38, 116,

E

Eck, Diana, 127, 245(8)

Elsner, John, 125, 133, 143, 245(4, 5)

emptiness, 137, 138, 141, 142, 144, 145, 148, 165, 169, 173, 179, 181, 207, 220, 253(3)

empty, 25, 63, 141, 163, 164, 165, 182, 241(41)

Er ru si xing lun, 15

Essay on the Golden Lion, 94

F

Fashang, 36

Fa yan chan shi yu lu, 68

Fazang, 94–96, 241(46)

Fo lin nie pan ji fa zhu jing, 158

Foshuo guan wu liangshou jing, 133

Fo shuo wu shang yi jing, 68

Foulk, T. Griffith, 233(40)

Fu fazang yin yuan zhuan, 210

Fuller, Winston, 137, 246(39)

Fung Yu-Lan, 10

G

Gaṇḍavyūha Sūtra, 94, 249(30)

Gardner, W., Pickett, C. and Brewer, M., 18, 230(2)

Gautama Sanghadeva, 109

geyi, 9, 11, 230(24)

Gimello, Robert, 222, 224, 226, 247(20), 256(2)

golden age, 26, 30, 31, 34, 40, 41, 44, 201, 202, 215, 216

gong'an, 15, 34, 35, 41, 140, 141, 142, 145, 216

Gregory, Peter, 7, 229(11), 233(40), 234(50), 236(72), 246(28)

Gregory Schopen, 125, 244(2)

Gu qing liang zhuan, 95

Guan wu liang shou fo jing, 113, 246(31)

Guang qing liang zhuan, 95

Guanyin, 7, 82, 93, 97, 208, 229(8)

Gu lai shi shi jing, 109

Guṇabhadra, 57

guwen, 139

H

Han, 3, 9, 75, 80, 87, 88, 91, 95, 98, 130, 201–203, 209, 232(27, 28, 30), 233(40), 241(28), 254(29)

Heart Sutra, 141, 142, 181

Hindu, 43, 44, 46–48, 89, 127, 211

Hisamatsu Shin'ichi, 136, 137, 246(36, 40), 247(43)

historiography, 13, 17, 25, 28, 29, 31, 40, 215, 216, 230, 231(11), 234(45)

Hiu Wan, 137

Hongren, 117, 210

Hookham, S.K., 154, 249(24)

Hou ha shu, 87

Hu, William, 87, 88, 241(25–30, 33, 34)

Huaigan, 37, 113–115, 121

Huayan, 68, 94, 95, 241–2(46)

Hubbard, Jamie, 206, 255(50, 51)

Huichong, 36

Huijiao, 31

Huineng, 38

Huisi, 204, 205

hun, 60

Hurvitz, Leon, 204, 230(17), 240(23), 255(43)

I

Ichimura Shohei, 79, 240(15)

Inagaki, Hsiao, 234, 246

insight, 58, 65, 79, 102, 119, 123, 134, 135, 140–142, 144, 145, 155, 157, 169, 173, 175, 177, 224, 231(13), 234(45), 239(58), 246(34)

J

Jātakas, iv, 25, 231(14)

Jianzhi Sengcan, 116, 210

Jingjue, 116

Jin guang ming jing wen ju, 165

Jin guang ming jing xuan yi, 165

Jin guang ming shu, 167

Jin shu, 200, 254(26)

Jiu tang shu, 91, 241(34)

K

Kālacakra Tantra, 190

Kauśāmbī, 192

Kṣitigarbha, 82

Kuiji, 52

Kumārajīva, 3, 180, 204

Kushans, 87, 241(28)

L

Laṅkāvatāra, 54–57, 61, 111, 116, 153, 157, 159, 162, 170, 171, 236(69), 238(29), 251(80, 93)

Laozi, 10, 63, 66, 67, 70, 110, 117, 169, 177

Lao zi zhung jing, 201

Layman Pang, 116, 244(46)

Leng qie shi zi ji, 116, 210

Li dai fa bao ji, 38, 39, 116, 121, 210

Liebenthal, Walter, 222

literati, 2, 6, 60, 98, 138

Lokottaravādin, 26

Long Roll of Buddhist Images, 97, 242(53)

Long Scroll, 64, 72

Lotus Sutra, 80, 84, 86, 107, 109, 120, 129, 143, 203, 204, 245(15)

Lu er shier ming liao lun, 52

M

Madhyamāgama, 109, 232(20)

Madhyamika, 79, 204

Mahā Sīhanāda Suttanta, 92

Mahābherīhārakaparivarta Sūtra, 68

Mahākassapa, 128

Mahāmegha Sūtra, 167

Mahāparinibbāna Sutta, 127, 188

Mahāparinirvāṇa, 14, 54, 56, 61, 68, 69, 71, 72, 152, 153, 156, 157–159, 167–169, 171, 178, 197, 207, 216, 217, 239(48), 249(42), 251(80, 93, 97)

Mahāprajñā Sūtra, 152, 158, 159, 161, 164, 169, 171, 250(63), 251(95, 96)

Mahāprajñāpāramitā Śāstra, 57, 168

Mahāratnakūta Sūtra, 92, 168

Mahāsāṃghika, 26, 39, 51, 53, 236(70)

Mahāvagga, 77

Mahāvairocana Sūtra, 196

Mahāvastu, 26

Mahāvibhāṣā, 27

Mahāyānasūtrālaṁkāra, 57, 135

Mahāyānasaṃgraha, 135

Mahāyānasaṃgrahabhāṣya, 168

Mahīśāsakas, 51

Mair, Victor H., 11, 230(24)

Maitreya, 36, 82, 129, 195, 203, 204, 208, 213

Maitreyābhisaṃbodhi Sūtra, 168, 203

Maitreyaparipṛcchā, 203

Maitreyaparipṛcchā–dharmāṣṭa, 203

Maitreyaparipṛcchopadeśa, 203

Maitreyavyākaraṇa, 203

Majjhima Nikāya, 102, 237(4), 241(37), 242(3, 5)

Mañjuśrī, 14, 84, 93–97, 99, 100, 217, 242(49)

Mañjuśrī Dharmaratnapiṭaka Dhāraṇi Sūtra, 94, 97

Mañjuśrīparinirvāṇa Sūtra, 93

Marks-Tarlow, Terry, 104, 105, 243(10, 11, 14)

Maspero, Henri, 60, 238(36)

Matthes, Klaus-Dieter, 154

McRae, John R., 147, 148, 167, 174, 235(62), 236(72), 247(1–4), 248(17), 251(101), 255(63)

Mendrasena, 93

Milinda, 49

Milindapañha, 19, 49, 231(4), 237(6)

Moggaliputtatissa, 27

Mo he zhi guan, 167

Mou zi li huo lun, 10

Musterberg, Hugo, 136

N

nagas (*nāga*), 76–80, 86, 99,

100, 195, 240(12)

Nāgārjuna, 79, 163, 195, 196, 207, 250(67), 251(88)

Nāgasena, 19, 49

Nan yue si da chan shi li shi yuan wen, 204

Nattier, Jan, 189, 190, 192, 195, 211, 253(6, 7, 9, 10, 15), 255(47, 48)

Nettipakaraṇa, 101, 103

Nienhouser, William, 139

Nikāya(s), 50, 52, 102, 103, 162, 190, 193, 237(4, 7), 241(35, 37), 242–43(3, 5, 6, 7, 8), 245(12), 253(4, 8)

Northern School and the Formation of Early Chan Buddhism, 147, 235(62)

O

one course *samādhi*, 93

P

Pabhassara Sutta, 50

Pañcapāramitānirdeśa, 181

Pañcaviṃśatisāhasrikā prajñāpāramitā Sūtra, 180, 181

parinirvāṇa, 26, 27, 53, 128, 143, 188, 193, 245(11)

Parivāra, 27

Parker, Joseph, 139, 140, 247(46, 48, 49)

Parthians, 87

Pellegrini and Bjorklund, 106, 120, 243(18, 19)

Platform Sutra of the Sixth Patriarch, 117, 121, 210, 235(65), 239(48)

Poceski, Mario, 33, 35, 234(46)

Prajñā, 94, 144, 149, 173, 240(15), 249(30)

Prajñāpāramitā, 10, 36, 79, 99, 141, 144, 167, 175, 180, 181, 195, 196

Prajñāpāramitā as taught by Mañjuśrī, 93

Pratyutpanna, 37, 129, 133, 143, 195, 245(15)

Priestley, Leonard, 52, 237(10, 15–17)

pudgala, 46, 50, 51, 53, 56, 61, 71

Pudgalavādin, 21, 49, 50, 51, 52, 53, 71, 237(10)

Purāṇas, 93

Pure Land, 12, 15–17, 35–38, 40, 41, 58, 68, 69, 72, 95, 110–115, 121, 125, 126, 131, 132–135, 137, 144, 145, 166, 176, 183, 207, 208, 212–216, 218–

221, 234(50, 52, 53, 57, 58), 235(59), 244, 245(10), 246(22, 24, 27, 35, 38)

Q

Qui yu jing, 164

R

"Random Reflections on the "Sinicization", 222, 227, 256(2)

Record of Buddhist Monasteries in Loyang, 89

Record of the Dharma Jewel Through the Generations, 117

Records of the Masters and Disciples of the Laṅkā (vatāra Sūtra), 116

Rig Veda, 77, 126

Robinson, Richard H., 222

root consciousness, 51

Ru dao an xi, 210

S

Sāgara, 80, 85

Sāgaranāgarājaparipṛcchā Sūtra, 80

Śākyamuni, 17, 25, 26, 27, 40, 46, 48, 54, 77, 78, 89, 92, 97, 99, 101, 103, 108, 128–130, 137, 143, 168, 172, 188, 195–197, 203, 208, 211, 245(11)

Salomon, Richard, 193

Samantabhadra, 93, 94

Samantapāsādikā, 152

Samayabhedoparacanacakra, 27

Saṃdhinirmocana Sūtra, 195, 196

Sāṃmitīyanikāyaśāstra, 52

Sāṃmitīyas, 52

samsara, 46, 49, 58, 67, 71, 111, 112, 118, 124, 150, 197

Saṃyutta Nikāya, 193, 237(7)

Ṣaṇḍagarikas, 52

San fan du lun, 52

San mi di bu lun, 52

Saptaśatikā, 93, 133, 169, 181,

Śāriputra, 85, 168, 196

Sarvāstivāda, 39, 41

Sarvatathāgatatattva-saṃgraha Tantra, 196

Śatasāhasrikā prajñāpāramitā Sūtra, 181

Schwartzman, Helen B., 105, 243(15, 16, 17)

Seng Chao, 222

Shandao, 15, 37, 112–114, 121, 131–136, 144, 145, 207, 208, 212, 235(59)

Shaokang, 37

Sharf, Robert, 7, 10, 229(13), 214(21), 246(37)

Shi mo he yan lun, 167

Shinko Mochizuki, 36, 2234(53)

Shu jing, 29

Si a han mu chao jie, 52

Śikṣānanda, 94, 157, 249(35), 250(64), 251(79, 84)

Sima Qian, 30

Singer and Singer, 105

sinicization, 1, 3, 4, 6–8, 12, 16, 41, 43, 73, 98, 100, 123, 126, 145, 170, 213, 215, 216, 220, 222, 223, 227, 230(15), 256(2)

Sinicizing, 1, 16, 181

Si wei lue yao fa, 204

Six Dynasties, 84, 240(19)

Smith, Richard, 200, 254(27)

Song Dynasty, 9, 31–34, 41, 96, 97, 99, 132, 139, 140, 143, 201, 216, 232(24), 233(39), 240(5), 242(47, 53), 246(28), 254(27)

Spring and Autumn Annals, 29

śrāvaka, 58, 69, 143, 158, 219, 238(32)

Śrīmālādevī, 54–56, 149, 153, 155, 158, 159, 178, 197

Sthaviravāda, 51

storehouse consciousness, 53

Śubhakarasiṃha, 34

Sudhanakumāra, 97

Suhṛllekha, 163, 250(67)

Sui Dynasty, 6, 9, 88, 96, 202, 203, 205, 208, 216, 221

Sukhāvatīvyūhopadeśa, 36,111, 120, 134

śūnyatā, 25, 28, 40, 69, 137, 138, 141, 164, 173, 174, 177, 180, 240(15)

Susthitamati Devaputra Paripṛcchā Sūtra, 93

Sutta Nipāta, 129, 245(13)

Suvikrāntavikrāmi-paripṛcchā prajñāpāramitānirdeśa Sūtra, 181

T

Tai ping jing, 201, 203, 212, 213, 221, 254(29, 33)

Tang (Dynasty), 6, 11, 14, 32–34, 73, 76, 80–91, 94–96, 98–

100, 136, 138, 208, 215–217, 227, 230(23), 233(42), 249(42), 254(26)

Tanluan, 36, 37, 111, 121, 131, 134, 135, 207, 213, 216, 219–221

tathāgatagarbha, 53–56, 71, 72, 153–156, 197, 216, 236(70), 237(19)

Tathāgatagarbha Sūtra, 54, 150, 157

Ten Going and Being Reborn in Amitābha Buddha's Realm Sūtra, 69

Theravāda, 51, 101

three phases, 199–201

Tiantai, 15, 35, 68, 80, 95, 132, 133, 144, 145, 204, 212, 219, 220, 233(40)

Tiantai Zhiyi, 80, 165, 248(17)

Tong dian, 91

Treasure Store Treatise, 7, 229–30(13)

Treaties Elucidating a Multitude of Doubts Regarding the Pure Land, 113, 121

Tridharmakhaṇḍaka, 52

Tripitaka, 25, 79

true self, 47, 57, 68–72, 216, 217

Tshig gsum gnad brdegs pa, 154

Tsukamoto Zenryū, 10, 203, 208, 229(17)

Tuxun, 94

Two Ingresses and Four Courses, 68, 72, 116, 147, 151–156, 158–160, 168, 170–175, 177, 179, 181, 182, 209, 220, 248(10, 11), 249(35, 40), 250(56, 62, 66, 68, 73), 251(77)

U

Udumbarika Sīhanāda Suttanta, 92

Upagupta, 28, 129, 143, 236(69), 245(11)

Upaniṣads, 13, 46, 47, 48. 70, 127, 237(3)

V

Vaipulya sutras, 188

Vairocana, 196

Vajrapāṇi, 196

Vajrasattva, 196

Vajrayāna, 35, 132

Vasubandhu, 20, 21, 23, 36, 37, 49, 71, 97, 111, 120, 134, 135, 162, 168, 185, 207, 231(8), 234(52), 246(34)

Vasumitra, 27

Vātsīputrīyas, 52

Vedas, 79

Vijñaptimātratāsiddhi Śāstra, 163

Vimalakīrti, 97

Vimalakīrtinirdeśa, 7, 92, 94, 197, 230(15)

Vimānavatthu Aṭṭhakathā, 103, 243(9)

Vinayadvāviṃśati-vidyāśāstra, 52

viṣaya samādhi, 167

Visser, Marinus, 76, 239(3), 240(7)

W

Wang Fu, 75

Wang sheng xi fang jing tu rui ying zhuan, 37, 234(55)

Watson, Burton, 29, 229(4), 232(25, 27, 28, 29, 31, 32), 238(33), 239(42, 43, 58), 252(115, 117)

weltanschauung, 4

Woike,B., Mcleod, S. and Geggin, M., 18, 231(3)

Wright, Arthur, 255(43)

Wu liang shou jing you po ti she yuan sheng jie zhu, 110, 111, 121

Wuxiang, 39

Wuzhu, 96, 117

X

Xin tang shu, 91

Xinxing, 205, 206

Xin xin ming, 210

Xiu shang cheng lun, 210

Xu gao seng chuan, 38

Xu gao seng zhuan, 116, 210, 233(38), 234(55)

Xu qing liang zhuan, 95

Xuanzhong Temple, 37

Y

Yanagida Seizan, 32, 233(43), 234(44), 235(62, 66, 67, 68), 239(43), 246(37), 247(2), 249(25), 251(78), 255(60, 61)

Yanshou, 68

Yi Jing, 10, 199

Yogācārabhūmi Śāstra, 161

Yogācāra, 113, 115, 195

Yogācārins, 53

Yuan Dynasty, 76

Yue fu za lu, 91

Z

Zanning, 31

Zhishen, 117

Zhong hua chuan xin di cha-men shi zi cheng xi tu, 68

Zhuan jing xing dao yuan wang sheng jing tu fashi zan, 112, 121

Zhuangzi/Zhuangzi, 9, 10, 11, 14, 58, 62–64, 66, 67, 69–72, 110, 117, 120, 139, 175, 176, 238(33), 239(42, 43, 48, 55, 56, 57), 244(31)

ziyu, 109, 111

Zong jing lu, 68

Zongmi, 68, 69, 72

Zurcher, Erik, 6, 7, 178, 179, 229(5, 6, 7, 10), 252(116), 254(23, 24, 27, 36)

www.ingramcontent.com/pod-product-compliance
Lightning Source LLC
Chambersburg PA
CBHW022001160426
43197CB00007B/225
* 9 7 8 0 9 9 4 9 0 8 8 9 6 *